"The normalization of the abuse and silencing of women inside and outside of the church has been shown for what it is—an affront to the image of God on earth—by movements like #Metoo, #Churchtoo, and #SilenceIs-NotSpiritual. As a result, women's voices are rising and the church finally seems ready to listen. But there is a corner of the church that remains in the dark—muffled; women of color on the evangelical mission field. These missionaries continue the traditions of women of color who led the missions movement throughout the 19th century, but were usurped and replaced by white missionaries at the turn of the 20th century; at the same time that white churches vestries drew red-lines around their communities and devised and implemented systems to ensure white supremacy at home. Over the past two decades, God has been at work in the hidden corners of the evangelical church; raising up evangelical women of color to enter the mission field again—for the sake of the preservation of the faith and the glory of God. These are the voices of those women. Come. Listen. Behold."

> – *Lisa Sharon Harper, President and Founder of Freedom Road, LLC and author of several books, including* The Very Good Gospel: How Everything Wrong can be Made Right

"Voices that have echoed from the margins now burst with telling in *Voices Rising*, resounding with stories of women from diverse walks of life, origin, and color, sharing a common purpose of seeking first the Kingdom of God and His righteousness. Scholars, students, and laypersons alike will be inspired by the narratives of God's faithful daughters who seek to honor him by dedicating their talents and gifts to be a blessing through service. Their stories challenge us to live out our calling more fully in our lives."

> – *Ruth Chung, Professor and Director of the Marriage and Family Therapy Program, University of Southern California, Co-Editor of* Religion and Spirituality in Korean America

"Reading these words reminded me how much we all need to continue listening and learning from the diverse and complex intersections and social locations that women of color bring to the coming of the kingdom of God on earth as it is in heaven. Readers may not be able to relate to every story or every nuance, but isn't that how we interact with scripture? Take your time and wrestle with these stories that take us around the globe, and listen for God's voice."

> – *Kathy Khang, speaker, journalist, activist, and author of* Raise Your Voice, *IVP*

"*Voices Rising* is a gift to the Church from these faithful leaders and ministers. Reading their diverse stories gives broader insight into what God is doing through these sisters in cities around the world, but what I found most powerful was honest descriptions of how they have worked out their callings amidst the diversity of backgrounds as women of color. Their stories also challenged me to reflect and wrestle with my own calling as a Christ-follower in new ways."

— *Sabrina Chan, National Director of Asian American Ministries, InterVarsity Christian Fellowship*

"Reading *Voices Rising* is like sitting down for a cup of coffee with a group of remarkable women from all over the world. As each shares her stories of learning to live true to Jesus' Kingdom and true to her unique identity, I felt inspired, challenged, and grateful. These intimate, poignant stories expand our understanding of who God is using as urban missionaries, and they enable us to learn from their faith."

— *Lindsay Olesberg, InterVarsity's Scripture Engagement Director and author of* Studying Ephesians with the Global Church

"Voices Rising is a remarkable array of stories that intersect racial/ethnic/national identity, gender, faith, and vocation. What makes these tales from the margins so compelling and insightful is their authentic and honest wrestling with the self, culture, and God. Whether you are female or male, a person of color or not, single or married, questioning or embracing God's call to ministry and mission—in these stories you will find allies among those who have been on a journey, often times lonely and confusing, of discovering the transformative power of God's love and grace for self and for others."

– *Michael A. Mata, Director of the Transformational Urban Leadership Program, Azusa Pacific Seminary*

"*Voices Rising* is a powerfully hopeful and redemptive elevation of God's work in and through women of color. Called to be and do life within the urban landscape, they rise and are rising to reveal an everyday orthodoxy that witnesses a prophetic imagination. You will enjoy and be challenged by *Voices Rising*. May you hear the faith, hope, and love of these urban ministers among us."

– *W. Tali Hairston, Senior Advisor for Community Engagement—Seattle Presbytery/Perkins Institute*

"Strong women of deep faith telling powerful stories. That's what you will find in *Voices Rising*. We are past due for a collection of experiences from Christian matriarchs of the twenty-first century. We need their voices to give us courage for the challenge we face and to plant seeds of hope in a world of hardship. In these pages you will encounter the stories of modern-day Desert Mothers. We would do well to heed their wisdom."

> – *Scott Bessenecker, Director of Missions, InterVarsity Christian Fellowship, and author of* The New Friars *and* Living Mission, *IVP*

"For too long the American Church has been content to offer platforms to white men or occasionally white women and to let our theology and practice of ministry be shaped only by that perspective. Yet the crowds who were first drawn to Jesus were primarily those on the outside of such agency! The voices of these women of color are precious gems given to shape the life and future of the American Church. May we heed our sisters' collective wisdom, and in so doing, better understand the heart of God and healthy life and ministry for the Church."

> – *Scott Hall, National Director of Urban Programs at InterVarsity Christian Fellowship/USA*

"The voices of women of color are rising. These are strong and compelling voices, while also humble and gracious. Women of color call the Church and the world to peace, reconciliation, justice, diversity, and hope. They show us the grace, passion, and prophetic wisdom cultivated at the margins of our Church and world. In Voices Rising, women of color offer personal and prophetic stories and insights that can renew the Church, transform the world, and lead to lasting hope."

> – *Graham Hill, Author,* Global Church *and* Healing Our Broken Humanity

VOICES RISING

VOICES RISING

WOMEN OF COLOR FINDING & RESTORING HOPE IN THE CITY

**SHABRAE JACKSON KRIEG &
JANET BALASIRI SINGLETERRY
EDITORS**

SERVANT PARTNERS PRESS

CONTENTS

continued...

CONTENTS, *continued*

FOREWORD

WOMEN ARE AND HAVE always been at the center of mission, compassion, justice, and peacemaking. In the words of pop singer Beyoncé, the Queen B herself, "Girls run the world!" Listening to the stories of those who are most impacted by suffering and injustice will shape how we creatively love those on the margins. Sadly, it's typical to find the same few people giving voice to how we as Christians can love our neighbor. If we want to be equipped to impact the world with the compassion and love of Jesus, we not only need a diversity of voices, we need those who are more socio-economically and racially marginalized to be at the center. This follows what Jesus Himself did in His ministry. It is thrilling to hear the voices of women of color at the center in this book, telling the stories of their communities and the ones they serve alongside in solidarity.

My mother is the woman who taught me to write my own story. She had the courage to move to a new country and re-establish herself. Mi mamá Colombiana is as beautiful as she is compassionate. She taught me that no matter how poor or rich we were, no matter what others said about our community or the people we come from, I should always follow my dreams. She taught me that everyone is valuable to God, and that the more voices are heard, the better we can fully understand His word and the world. Her voice rises!

Migdalia is the woman in my community who has taught me the importance of telling my own story. She is an entrepreneur, a community leader, and a woman of faith. Her beauty salon has been a place of rest and rescue for me in a world of cross-cultural ministry. When I am there surrounded by women from Puerto Rico, Mexico, Honduras, and Ecuador, taking time to take care of themselves, I am reminded that I matter. The intentional atmosphere reminds me that I am loved by God, not for what I do but for who I am. Being around other women of color is a catalyst for me to continue to urge the rest of the world that we have a story, and we can tell it ourselves. The time has come for our voices to be heard, not as a way to appease our egos, but because the Church needs to consider new ways to approach ministry. Our voices rise!

Laquita, my neighbor, has raised two children into young adults on her own, despite the challenges, the statistics, and the insane expectation that one can afford rent on a minimum wage. She worked two and sometimes three jobs to provide for her kids. She fought illness that developed due to the stress of life on African American women. In the decade I've known her, she has come over to drink wine, ugly cry, pray in tongues, eat chocolate, and dream for a new way. At her daughter's high school graduation, we celebrated this next generation of Black women achieving the influence the last generation just could not secure. She is the expert voice I want to hear when my own kids are driving me nuts. Her voice rises!

Rachael grew up in the slums of Kampala, Uganda. God gifted her as an evangelist; her community was transformed by her leadership and that of other youth leaders. She went off to Oxford for training. Today she is one of the apologetic and evangelistic speakers for Ravi Zacarias Ministries in Uganda. She is the expert on the questions like "Is God fair?" and "Why does He allow injustice?" She continues to congregate and lead a youth worship team in her hundred-person church. She is proclaiming and living out the gospel and allowing her voice to rise.

Now more than ever, we need to hear voices rising from women who are working alongside those on the margins, and who come from a context similar to that of the many people we will live with and love. The time has come to focus on the women getting it done. There is a famous saying by Mexican actress Maria Felix, "Soy más cabrona que bonita, y mira que bonita soy," which loosely translated means, "I'm more badass than beautiful, and as you can see I'm very beautiful." Women are the force of nature on the ground who mobilize the masses to show up and speak out. The women in this book not only capture that spirit in their own ministries, but in the stories they tell of the communities they serve. We as a Church are in need of their biblical insight and creative approach to ministry. We can learn from them how to love and live at the intersection of worship, compassion, and justice. From these women, we can learn how sit for tea with the widow, bandage the wounded, and march right to the center of power.

Our *abuelas* (grandmothers) taught us to fast and pray, and to access our identity in Christ, not in the praise of others. They taught us to rely on the resources of the Holy Spirit and not self-sufficiency. They taught us to persevere through suffering, not to run from it. They modeled courage and faith in a manner only an abuela can. Abuelita theology is the set of values, beliefs, and practices passed down to us as we spent time with our grandmothers in the kitchen. It is a spirituality rooted in our communities of origin that informally influences generation after generation on how we both understand who God is and what our role is in the world. In many majority world cultures, our earliest religious education comes from the mothers and grandmothers. Cesar Chavez's mother and grandmother were huge influences in his life. Some say that he was able to develop a new type of non-violent peacemaking because of the strong female role models in his life and their influence over him. Abuelita theology was the bedrock for everyone in the community, not just the women. These voices rising will be a foundation for all in the generations to come, not just the women.

Women of color embody a spirituality of sacrifice, decision-making, and worshipping on the run—with all the noise and chaos of our families and communities in the background. We don't spend much time debating the best approaches to loving God and loving neighbor—we simply neighbor. I know you will find wisdom in the stories of joy, surprise, pain, surrender, and faith that are captured here. May you hear the voices rising.

– *Sandra Maria Van Opstal, July 17, 2018*

A NOTE FROM THE EDITORS

WHEN WE BEGAN to explore the concept for this book, we both felt some hesitancy to lead such a large project. My life and calling have not panned out as I (Janet) had expected. I grew up in a non-Christian, conservative, immigrant family. My parents owned a restaurant where I worked during my entire childhood. My education was intended to lead me on a path toward comfort and prestige. The idea that I would be called to be a full-time minister, and to fundraise my own salary and benefits, was not a notion I had ever considered. This calling has been meandering and surprising at times. When the *Voices Rising* book project began, I hesitated. I do not love doing new things, especially when I don't have a lot of experience. I soon realized that the type of book that Voices Rising would be—a book that spoke directly to women of color, about women of color, and written by women of color, especially women of color seeking to learn and grow in an urban poor ministry context—was not something I had on my bookshelf. A book like this was needed. God began to bring to mind the experiences of women in Servant Partners who I knew were following God's call to learn and live among the urban poor around the world, and their stories needed to be shared. The beauty of giving space for these voices to rise helped to overcome my hesitancy.

Similarly, I (Shabrae) was encouraged by the idea of helping to facilitate new spaces for women of color. As we prepared to take on this new challenge, I recalled a short conversation that I had with Dr. C. Rene Padilla some years ago. I wanted to hear his opinion regarding who were the up and coming new voices of justice emerging in the world. He calmly replied that he believed that there would not be a specific individual or outspoken movement leader in the future, but instead there would be a rising of many around the world who would lead out in big and small ways, calling forth justice and reshaping our world. He emphasized that some may come to be known and others may not, but the response to injustice would be one embraced by many and not focus on just a singular leader. Dr. Padilla may not remember me or our conversation, but that brief encounter has remained with me these past twelve years. In the years since, I have met many along the way—men, women, youth, and children—whom I would identify as agents of change. Their lives and prophetic voices bring good news in their own unique ways. They are responding to the complex challenges in our world, which require a response from a multitude of leaders.

It has been a joy for us to dive deeply into the stories of fellow agents of change, to learn from their experiences, and to share their stories with others through this book. It is our hope that one more voice can be added to the multitude of voices working on behalf of the poor around the world.

In setting out to create this compilation of stories and experiences, there was much to consider. The more contributors we included, the more perspectives would be shared. This sounds great in concept, but it can also mean that though we are all connected through the same organization, the beauty of Servant Partners is that each voice is unique. We all have felt called by God to urban ministry, but the ways in which we live that out varies vastly. We have chosen to allow each author to keep her voice in preferences for her description of community, race, and ministry calling. Within these pages you will find a variety of writing styles, from personal essays to more academic reflections. Additionally, at each author's discretion, some names throughout this book were changed for privacy.

Despite this diversity, a few specific decisions were made regarding capitalization for the sake of consistency. All references to race or any cultural or ethnic groups have been capitalized. As stated earlier, our desire is to provide space for each voice and experience, even when those individual expressions could be in contrast to each other. An example can even be found in our title, "Women of Color," a phrase that is not commonly used outside of the United States or Canada and that may have a different meaning or connotation in other settings. In reality, there does not exist one specific name or title to describe each author, nor this grouping of us, nor is there a phrase that completely or conveniently expresses our individual or collective lived experience.

As editors, we are aware that terminology used throughout the book may be incomplete, in process, and ever changing. We recognize that some terms are seen as social constructs and have no biological grounding, and yet we have given space for the process and conversation to happen even with our always-imperfect words, even while we try to press forward with the best use of words possible. With this in mind, we would like to offer four invitations.

First, if you come across anything that is uncomfortable, we invite you to go deeper and enter into a dialogue with us. This book does not completely represent Servant Partners nor all women of color who have gone into mission. Rather, it is a representation of a group of women who are on their own spiritual journeys and have something to offer to the global Church.

Second, if you are a woman of color, we wrote this book for you. We collected our stories and worked and talked through them and tried to make sense of our experiences for you. Many of us had never read a book like this in which we saw ourselves reflected. We hope you find resonance, connection, inspiration, challenge, and encouragement in these pages.

Third, if you are not a woman, or a woman of color, you are also welcome in this book. Although our primary audience is women of color and we geared some of our editorial decisions to that audience, you are also welcome. We hope you too find something for your journey—a word of life, challenge, encouragement, or invitation.

Finally, the effort to give voice to one's experience, to take pieces of a life and share it with another, is not easy and at times vulnerable. Thus, our final invitation is one towards grace as we enter into each other's stories. We offer a series of stories that uncover and elevate the experience and memories of women of color living into their missions and callings around the world—adding their voices to the masses. We acknowledge that we are here because of the many women who have come before us. We stand on their shoulders as we look to pave the way for the young women who will come after each of us.

INTRODUCTION

THERE ARE NOT MANY women who are written about in the pages of mission history books, nor many women who have authored them. Found even less frequently in the index, table of contents, or bylines of those books are women of color. Although we as women of color are not often represented in "official" mission numbers internationally, there are innumerable women of color who are agents of change working for Christian transformation, and who are ministers of the transforming gospel, serving all over the world in countless contexts and communities.

Yet where are these stories? Who are the women of color who labor for peace and justice, who speak Christ's words of light into a dark and suffering world? And why are our stories so hard to find? Is development and mission work only for those with money and who come from a specific class, race, or country? Certainly not. But when one sees only people of a certain group around the mission board, the decision table, or on stage at the latest ministry or mission conference, then this can support an incomplete perspective that only a certain type of person can be called as a minister of the gospel. Incomplete models create incomplete perspectives, and those incomplete representations of the body of Christ can create obstacles to Jesus rather than opportunities. A more complete representation provides opportunities for as many people as possible to be invited into God's kingdom, into the jubilant celebration of all peoples, nations, languages, and colors described in the biblical model of church (Acts) and surrounding the throne of God (Revelation).

At the time of this writing, to be a woman of color in missions is to be continuously on the outside. We recognize that the struggle for representation continues in many contexts where women are working for full expression and acceptance. We are still living in a world of many firsts—the first Asian American female executive director of a major missions organization[1] to the first successful blockbuster movies with full casts of actors of color[2]. And when thinking about missions, women of color are often some of the last images that are represented in the mainstream, emphasizing the incomplete narrative of who is called and who responds. Yet we too are here to serve, to return to our communities, to go into new communities, to build movements, to preach from the pulpit, and to respond with our voices and our lives.

Voices Rising: Women of Color Finding and Restoring Hope in the City is a compilation of the stories of many women in mission. In these chapters, themes of belonging, identity, calling, loss, privilege, and more emerge, outlining the difficulties in this type of work and challenging the image of missions while calling new voices to help shape the narrative. This group of authors has also journeyed together in embracing their own unique calls in an evangelical environment that does not always see or hear them with clarity or fullness. It traces the discourse of intersectionality, margin, colonialism, and Scripture–aiming to invite and encourage all women to participate in the mission of God within our world and in whatever they may do.

Each story outlines the joy and grace we have found working in the margins of our world. The empirical data used by the United Nations and many other groups employ a variety of colorful words in how to define and describe a slum, a squatter settlement, or an urban neighborhood. But for the authors of this book, these spaces are home. Despite the challenges, we have grown, we have found hope, and we have been taught by those whom we have sought to serve. The communities represented in this book move beyond data and are defined by the people whom we have come to know and by the lessons we have found in this space of margin. This too forms part of the narrative–what we have learned when we have responded to God's call.

God's call to serve the urban poor is a crucial call that many more of us should consider, as we are living in a world where nearly one half of the world's population–more than 3 billion people–live on less than $2.50 a day. A world in which more than 1.3 billion live in extreme poverty–living on less than $1.25 a day. Our world is urbanizing, rapidly.

According to Doug Saunders, a Canadian-British author and journalist, and author of the book, *Arrival City: The Final Migration and Our Next World*, 130 people are migrating from rural to urban areas each minute.[3] Our urban areas are often characterized by difficult housing conditions, which frequently include the following:

insecurity of tenure; lack of basic services; inadequate and sometimes unsafe building structures; overcrowding; and locations on hazardous land. Over one billion people live in such conditions.

The issue of urban poverty is one of the most important issues facing our world in the twenty-first century. And yet it is one of the areas in which fewer number of churches and workers are present. Servant Partners, along with a small group of other organizations named *The New Friars* by Scott Bessenecker[4], were all moved by the Holy Spirit to answer the call into this kind of work. They call their work "incarnational," being moved both by the command to love the poor and by Jesus's own becoming flesh and "moving into the neighborhood" (John 1:14, The Message Version). And people from all over the world have responded to that invitation. As urban poverty is complex, this work has required a holistic response in working towards whole-person and whole-community transformation, engaging physical, spiritual, emotional, mental, social, and communal needs. The combined strategy of discipleship-based faith communities and grassroots community organizing became the tools Servant Partners chose to engage this challenge.

But this is no small task. It is no small mission. It is no small need. So we seek new molds and movements that embrace the diversity of all our voices and our unique expressions of mission to be the hands and feet which move toward the calling of a whole-person, whole-community transformation. The world needs an image of the Christian minister, missionary, and worker that goes beyond what we may have previously seen.

This book is not Urban Ministry or Racial Reconciliation 101. It is a collection of stories, a snapshot into some aspects of our lives, ministries, and callings. You may learn something about urban ministry, poverty, racism, reconciliation, or cultural competency, yet ultimately these are stories from our lived experiences.

Voices Rising is an invitation for the reader to recognize the need for diversity in mission and to see the uniqueness that women of color bring. We strive in these pages to expand the current narrative and discourse by providing space for new voices to arise. We hear their voices, and we hear Christ's voice interwoven. And yet there are still so many new voices to be heard.

Our own stories are still in process, and we invite you to journey with us. We invite you to enter into all the pieces of the stories that we carry. We have let our voices rise within these pages, as a beginning.

---

[1] Megan Briggs, "Tom Lin and Sharon Koh Becoming the Key Executives of Prominent Ministries," May 17, 2016, accessed August 16, 2018, *http://bit.ly/2o52HCR*
[2] Jamil Smith, "The Revolutionary Power of Black Panther" (February 19, 2018), *Time* magazine. See also Suyin Haynes, "Crazy Rich Asians is More than Glitz and Glamour. It's Groundbreaking for People Like Me" (August 10, 2018), *Time* magazine, accessed August 16, 2018, *https://ti.me/2PvP63U*.
[3] Doug Saunders, *Arrival City: The Final Migration and Our Next World* (Toronto: Vintage Canada, 2010).
[4] Scott A. Bessenecker, *The New Friars: The Emerging Movement Serving the World's Poor* (Downers Grove, IL: InterVarsity Press, 2006).

1

BRINGING A DISH TO SHARE WITH THE WORLD
Michelle Kao Nakphong

Michelle Kao Nakphong served with Servant Partners from 2003 to 2015, starting as an intern in Los Angeles and ending as a site leader in Bangkok, Thailand. In Bangkok, she started a bilingual internship for both Thai and American young adults, transitioned an organization from a charity-based approach to one with a sustainable development approach, and organized around land and housing issues. With a desire to affect more broad and systemic change, Michelle is now pursuing a PhD in Community Health Sciences at the UCLA Fielding School of Public Health. Her research explores how economic policies and programs affect health outcomes. Michelle, her husband AJ, and son Pascal like going around the corner for donuts while they figure out what to eat next.

AN ALL-AMERICAN GIRL

I HATED WHEN KIDS at youth group told me I smelled like stir-fry. I hated that at camp, I was called "Kim" three separate times in one summer (because all Asians are named Kim?). I hated that I was teased by the sing-song rhyme,

"Chinese, Japanese, dirty knees, look at these," while classmates pulled their eyes up and down into slanted slits. I hated when kids asked me if I could actually see through my eye slits. Being one of four people of color in my grade, I hated my differences. I learned to cringe at them and was embarrassed by any vestiges of my Chinese culture or ethnicity. I just wanted to be "normal" and tried my best to paint over myself and my life with a glossy coat of all-American.

By high school, I virtually thought of myself as a White person. Not much of my life resembled anything Chinese, besides my face. To keep my "all-American" identity alive, I even asked my mom to wait outside when she needed to come pick me up from school so I wouldn't be embarrassed by her accent and unusual mannerisms. I saw nothing good about being Chinese.

When I arrived at Johns Hopkins University, I encountered more Asians, but still had a difficult time embracing my ethnicity. I was now in Baltimore: a raw, complex city with a fraught racial history. The disparities in class, race, and economics I saw in Baltimore were jarring at a core level. As a young student, I attended classes on a pristine, landscaped, perpetually renovated campus while drugs and blight plagued the community a ten-minute walk away. I was disturbed by the juxtaposition of poverty and my own privilege. How could I make sense of my own identity amidst this dissonance?

At the same time, I had recently become personally acquainted with Jesus the summer before I began college. As a new freshman, this nascent spiritual relationship was cultivated by a deep interest in the Bible and my involvement with InterVarsity Christian Fellowship, a campus ministry. Precisely in this unsettling context, biblical passages about justice, poverty, and healing were coming alive to me.

This compelled me to dive into opportunities to minister and connect with people in the city. I wanted to work with vulnerable populations, know them, and know their stories. I was particularly drawn to an incarnational approach to ministry. Jesus, in His ministry, became flesh and dwelled among us to show us His love up close and personal. Modeled from this aspect of Jesus' life, incarnational ministry emphasizes being present with people in their challenges and their pain. I sought to engage with people and communities in this way and found opportunities to live and get involved in communities in Baltimore, Philadelphia, and Los Angeles.

But my new journey towards justice and God's Kingdom posed a new predicament for my Chinese identity. As a young, resourced, Chinese woman from Michigan, I felt like I couldn't identify with my urban neighbors enough. My neighbors and I did not share the same background, ethnicity, education, or opportunities, and all of my unearned privilege burdened me with a sense of guilt. Guilt for being born into a nice neighborhood. Guilt that my life trajectory was higher education and a professional career. Guilt for being a "model minority." Guilt for having options and opportunities and resources. All of this caused me to feel even more insecure about being Chinese. I looked more like the owners of the liquor stores whose businesses profited from and perpetuated harmful dependencies in the community. I wanted to identify with the people in the neighborhoods where I was beginning to minister and exist as a neighbor, but whether it was Baltimore or later Los Angeles, I had the nagging feeling that I could never identify the way I imagined I should. I cringed at my own identity: it wasn't good enough for urban, incarnational ministry. And yet, that is exactly what I felt called to do.

A BOWL OF SOUP

IN MY MID-TWENTIES, I had a persistent thought: God's work is global. This realization motivated me to look beyond the poverty in the United States and recognize poverty around the world. It was this thought that compelled me to move to Bangkok, Thailand and into an informal community[5] to see what God was doing there and how I could get involved. Even as an Asian American in Asia, I struggled to fit in, exacerbated more by the fact that I also needed to learn the Thai language. It was obvious to neighbors that I was American by my mannerisms, my gait, and my independence. On top of that, my Chinese ethnicity also associated me with the more affluent Chinese merchants and businesspeople in Thailand. Would I ever experience a connection between my identity and my vocation?

One of the first people who caught my attention when I moved into my Bangkok community was May. At eight years old, she was silent and rarely spoke. When I first met her, I mistakenly thought she was a boy because of her short hair. I learned that she never had a chance to grow it out; she caught head lice often and her parents' convenient solution was to shave her head. May's parents were addicted to alcohol, and both passed away within a few years of each other from multiple diseases caused by excessive drinking. As a result of their drinking, May was born with cognitive disabilities and was unable to keep up with kids much younger than her. Her less developed cognitive skills made her an easy and constant target for teasing and bullying. But despite the hostility and neglect she experienced, she was still an incredibly sweet girl with a knack for nurturing. She was the primary caretaker for her baby niece, and though she did not always make the healthiest choices in caretaking (a daily breakfast of soda and candy for a one-year old), she demonstrated incredible patience and care. Some church members and I regularly spent time with May, and she became a regular in church. As a part of our house church, she came out of her shell and became a talkative, sociable, and confident kid. I consider it a tremendous gift to have seen her discover her confident, lovable self.

Part of worship in the house church included sharing a potluck lunch together every week at church. Each person would bring something to share, and we would eat family-style on the floor. Some members brought curries, some were famous for their Thai desserts, while others might bring street food purchased on the way. We loved to eat together and we were always glad to include anyone, especially May. For her, we knew that this was the heartiest meal she would eat all week. The rest of the week, she ate little besides plain rice or snacks neighbors might give her.

One particular Sunday, May received ten baht (about thirty cents) from her parents, which was uncommon. At church that day, she told one of the church members, "I have ten baht. I want to bring something to share for lunch." The church member, knowing how seldom May received an allowance and how little she ate, responded kindly, "Don't worry about it, May. Keep it for yourself. Buy some snacks for yourself later." May became silent and looked disappointed.

When confronted with poverty and need, well-meaning, well-resourced people often reinforce attitudes of helplessness. They see others' needs and their own expertise and resources and think, "You need X? I have X to give you!" They only see apparent needs, like May's need to eat beyond Sunday. But too often, if well-intentioned acts or projects seem like good solutions but are actually driven by outsiders' ideas of what is necessary, they bypass the most critical factor of success: an individual's own self-determination. This kind of model of giving and receiving without thought of the recipient can also reinforce the idea that the resource-poor person or community is impotent. Instead, solutions must hinge on people's own motivation, effort, and resources. Human capacity should not be discounted or underestimated.

Fortunately for May, another member noticed the change in May's countenance and mood and offered, "It's ok, May. If you want to buy something to share, that would be great!" May smiled. She quickly got up, and walking out the door said, "I'll be right back!" She soon returned with a child-sized portion of noodle soup and a huge smile on her face. This was the first time she was able to share something, and she was proudly beaming. That day, like everyone else, she brought something to the table.

For me, May's dish was humbling and healing. The majority of the time, I saw bringing a dish as a chore and a duty. Not an unwelcome duty, but a responsibility nonetheless. May, however, saw bringing a dish as a way to give. The act of giving was her chance to be a part of a community as an equal member. It did not matter that the bowl of noodle soup was small or that it was difficult to share. We all shared and treasured her dish.

That little bowl of noodle soup put this feeling of "not being enough" in perspective. Objectively, May's dish was not actually enough to feed everyone and was an unusual dish to share. It's not easy to scoop spoonfuls of broth and slippery noodles over rice. But three things made her dish spectacular: her few resources, her enthusiasm, and that her contribution was one part of the whole spread.

Similar to the widow's offering (Mark 12, Luke 21), May's offering was proportionally great compared to what she had. It is not an offering to pity nor patronize. We should not think, "Aww, isn't that cute?" Jesus' response to the widow was, "She, out of her poverty, gave everything—all that she had to live on." He saw the dignity of her gift, which was not the value of a mite—that child-sized noodle soup—but the gift of May herself expressed through giving all she had. It was May's heart that was revealed through her dish.

May's enthusiasm to share made her dish outstanding. And it strikes me as wholly different than an attitude of entitlement we may sometimes have as Christians, whenever we treat our relationship with God or others as a spiritual quid pro quo. This is the idea that I will serve or do something for God and expect something back from Him, whether it be happiness, the prevention of suffering, or whatever we might wish for. As a minister, this was an especially deceptive mentality for me. "Lord, I have poured out my career/life/energy for you, why don't I have _____?" For years, I struggled with bitterness over singleness, bubbling up from an underlying belief that I deserved a family in exchange for kindness and care for others. And this entitlement took subtler forms as well. "Why are my prayers for my neighbors not answered?" "If this is my calling, shouldn't it be less difficult? Shouldn't I feel more fulfilled in my work?" "If God wants us to live in harmony with our brothers and sisters, why is my team falling apart?" I expected that my work would result in outcomes I wanted.

The reality is that our lives are not meant to be a ledger with a series of clean transactions with God. This is evident in the lives of those in Scripture who were chosen and called by God, yet faced incredible hardship, encountering things they neither expected nor desired. But nevertheless, whatever outcomes transpired—even if they were disobedient—God displayed His goodness, power, and faithfulness. May did not share her noodles to boost her self-esteem, to show off, to win others' approval, or even to feel more deserving of eating others' dishes. Her eagerness to give and share was simply out the joy of being able to do just that, to give to her friends.

May's dish was also significant because it was one part of the whole meal. Each week, our church delighted in seeing what foods everyone would make or bring. The more variety, the merrier. When two people coincidentally brought the same type of food, we were not shy to express our disappointment. We loved it all—the papaya salad and grilled chicken, the smoky stir-fries from Mae Tuk, the special coconut desserts from Kaew, the curries from the local market—everything. May's contribution added even more flavors to the mix. Why would we tell someone like May not to share? It was *her choice to contribute*, not the soup itself, that brought her fully to the fellowship table.

For me, the idea that the Church and this world need diversity and that each person brings a different flavor was not new. These were truths that I promoted and espoused. Yet, when it came to myself, to embrace and delight in my own differences seemed much more complex. May helped me internalize these truths more deeply. The fact that she possessed this confidence in belonging and equality humbled me. I could theologize about it, but she lived it. Her generosity in sharing not only her resources, but herself, showed me just how much we are revealed though our participation. I saw that my feelings of not being or doing "enough" were what held me back from full partnership, not my culture or ethnicity. May taught me how to give eagerly and directly from my heart.

THE GIFT OF FAILURE

MY OWN FEELINGS of not being or doing enough were gradually exposed to me during my years in Thailand. Experiences like the one with May helped reveal these underlying insecurities that went deeper than ethnicity and cultural identity. But on a deeper level, my inability to be at peace with who I was went back to my belief that my value as a person came through only what I could achieve. I thought that if only I could do enough or transform myself into the ideal identity, whether cultural, social, or ethnic, I would feel fulfilled and connected. That failed to happen in my childhood, failed to happen in my early adulthood, and thankfully, failed to happen as I lived and ministered in the city. Failure is one of God's greatest gifts to me.

God also gave me the gift of failure when I tried to compete with Thai people. When I moved to Thailand, I had a plan. The plan was to be as kind, generous, patient, and morally upright as possible to be a witness. As a Jesus-follower, I wanted to demonstrate how great Jesus is and how good He was at imparting gifts of character and goodness. I decided that I would try my best to share as much as I had. I deliberately bought extra fruit and snacks so that I could give some away. I opened up my house as much as possible to neighbors and kids. I made myself as available as I could be.

The only problem was that my Thai neighbors were so much better at giving and hospitality than I was. Some nights, I would eat three dinners at different neighbors' houses. One time, while chatting with a grandma walking home from her minimum-wage construction job, she handed me her own dinner that she had bought. Neighbors selling food would routinely refuse to take payment or if I insisted, they would give me free extras. My Thai mom, the woman who adopted me as a daughter in Bangkok, regularly dropped off curries, yogurt drinks, mango salads, and many other dishes she had made or bought for me despite struggling financially. Neighbors cooling off under the shade of the tamarind tree in the center of the community brought fruit and papaya salad to share with whomever was around.

It was wonderful. But it was also exceedingly frustrating. I felt so frustrated that people were giving me so much because I wanted to be the one known for giving, inviting, and sharing. When compared with my neighbors, I just could not compete. They could always out-give and out-share me. When I shared fruit, I still bought myself a secret little stash from the market so I wouldn't feel pressured to share it. I wanted to be hospitable and keep an open-door policy like my neighbors, but I also craved privacy. I realized that I wanted to give and share on my own terms, in ways that felt comfortable. More often than not, I chose what worked better for me. It made me feel like a failure as a missionary. The people I was trying to show Jesus' love to were better at showing love than I was. How were they to see Jesus and His love for them if I wasn't able to be more loving than they?

Looking back, I see that my frustration was foolish. My posture and perspective was twisted. I believed that showing a spiritual and moral superiority was the way to minister to people. My stronger character and righteous acts would show people what they were lacking, and at their low point of discouragement, I could introduce Jesus' higher way. It was a self-righteous approach that was actually inconsistent with Jesus' own ministry. On the contrary, Jesus never broadcast nor flaunted His own perfection, but was instead present and accessible to those around Him and offered forgiveness from the Father. I learned that it was not my virtues that would reflect God's love and care for broken people, rather it was precisely my inability to be enough or do enough that could reveal our common need for Jesus. We do not need perfection from others, we need love and acceptance. I thought I was failing to do or be enough. My real failure was being self-centered and missing the heart of the Gospel.

I began to embrace my imperfections and less-than-ideal self. I had tried my hardest to do and be enough, but I learned to recognize that it was not God who required or expected me to be the ideal. It was the demands and ambition that I had placed on myself that drove me to strive for unreachable standards. It was a fundamental shift in perspective to realize that I was not starting from a deficit that I needed to compensate for. Instead, confidence and security were the grounds I stood on. The love of God welcomes me (and all!) into His presence and drives out any fear or insecurity.

Such love had implications for my identity. Doubts about my ethnicity and culture were rendered irrelevant. I did not need to fight against myself or try to negate who I was: a woman, Chinese, American, educated, etc. I could accept who I was in fullness. Likewise, I was not defined by my actions, my work, or my success. This alternative view of myself and my place of belonging provided a different impetus for life and ministry. Instead of a motivation of duty, a feeling that I ought to give in a manner befitting of an ideal "caring Christian," my new attitude birthed a way of participating in ministry that came from security, love, and affection. I could finally embrace the beauty of my being enough in who I was, along with the various areas of "not enough" in what I was able to do and instead see God's intervention in and around me.

A HOUSE FOR JIN

THIS WAS A LESSON that God continued to teach. A good friend of mine from church, Jin, began sharing her concerns about her parents' home in her village. In the Sisaket province, a fourteen-hour train ride away, her family's wooden stilt house was falling apart from termite infestation and the roof had nearly rusted away. Her elderly parents and nephew lived there, but urgently needed an alternative solution before the house fell completely apart. A few steps on the staircase had already broken while family members walked up; falling through the elevated floor meant certain injury. Jin raised this as a prayer request every week at church for several months, asking the church to pray for her family and their home.

As a church, we were happy to pray for Jin's family. Jin's sister was also a part of our church, and we knew many of their other family members. Some of us had even been to her house upcountry. But as we prayed, we began to wonder how God might answer our prayers. We also started asking questions: "What's the condition of the house?" "How much of the house is livable or salvageable?" "Are there options for them in their village or with relatives?" And eventually, most critically, "What can we, the church, do?"

Because the house was in such a state of disrepair, Jin thought that the best option might be to tear down the existing house and build a temporary house on their neighboring relative's land while the family got together the resources to rebuild a permanent home. Soon, people began offering help. "If you need any tools, you can borrow mine." "If you need a pair of extra hands, I'm willing to go and help where I can." "I have experience in construction; let me know what I can do." Eventually, we had a hodgepodge of offers: a couple construction workers, two cooks, a handful of unskilled teenagers and adults (like myself), some borrowed tools, a donated power saw, and some financial gifts. But we still wondered, "Do we have enough people? Do we have enough skills?"

With our motley crew, we planned a trip to go back to Jin's village, but because of limited time away from work, we would only have four days to finish the whole project—demolishing the old house and building a new temporary house using salvageable materials and buying whatever else was needed. On top of the time constraint, our trip was planned during flood season. If it rained, it would be impossible to build. We received news that it had been raining nonstop for weeks at Jin's village, and they were experiencing flash flooding. We would barely have enough time, even if the rain held off. Finances were also a concern. With only a few tools and our total bankroll being a few hundred dollars in gifts to build a whole house, we feared for the worst. "Do we have enough resources to build a house, get us there and back, and feed everyone?" From all angles—manpower, skills, time, and resources—it seemed we simply did not have enough.

But when we prayed, we felt that God was encouraging us to take on this project, despite the numerous (and increasing) limitations. And in the time leading up to the project, the situation only seemed to get more bleak. Up until the day we arrived, rain had been pouring daily. Jin's relatives and neighbors kept asking her, "Why are you planning on building during flood season?" It seemed a foolish decision. On top of everything else, a week and a half before the trip, Jin's mother was hospitalized, in critical condition, for a serious infection. We had no idea how long she would need to stay in the hospital. Jin and her siblings took turns staying with their mom at the hospital that was two hours away. With prayer as her and our foundation, Jin confidently told us, "I'm not worried about anything. I believe it's God's will to make this possible." In faith, knowing that we had absolutely no way to control the weather or Jin's mother's health, our team of twenty-two set off for Jin's village.

Getting to Jin's village was a feat. We took the free overnight train to her province's main city, bumping along on benches, kept awake by the frequent stops and vendors hawking snacks. At four in the morning, we hired two pick-up trucks to drive us another hour to the village. Exhausted, we napped briefly before starting work. When we woke up, it was dry, and we could work! We immediately began to take the house apart to salvage as much wood as possible. Once we began working, many people from around the village were curious and came to offer a hand. Many were construction workers; one man was even an electrician. Our crew leader could give direction in everything except for electrical wiring. God was fitting a puzzle together with our team and all the volunteers. By the end of the first day, the house was entirely dismantled.

That night after dinner with our local friends, our cook, Pai, who is from a nearby province, took out a water jug and made a humble announcement to the group. She said, "I'm not anyone special, and I don't usually like singing in front of people, but I have a song on my heart that I want to share." She began drumming on the water jug and sang songs about Jesus' grace in the local northeastern Isaan style with heartfelt conviction. These were the songs that she sang while cleaning as a housekeeper or doing chores at home, songs dear and familiar to her. It was beautiful to see Pai, normally a reserved woman, who self-consciously covers her smile with her hand to hide her teeth, share with such assuredness and confidence. As soon as our local friends heard the familiar melodies and Pai's strong voice, people began dancing and clapping along. More neighbors wandered over and came to listen. Some began asking others in the group about God: "Who is Jesus?" and "Can He help me?" People shared about difficulties in their lives, and we had the opportunity to pray for many people. In sharing the Gospel, Pai was more than enough.

Without one single drop of rain, the next three days of constructing the new house went quickly, as everyone worked from dawn to dusk. The cooks woke even earlier at 4 a.m. to go to market and prepare food. Everyone pitched in to do dishes, move belongings, and tidy up. Everyone put in their best effort, and together we were able to finish the building in only three days. The house was complete with electricity and an outdoor, covered kitchen area. We were exhausted and grateful.

In Jin's culture, every new home must be christened with a housewarming party before the family can move in, and this house was no different. It was expected that Jin's family would invite the entire village—around a hundred people—over to dine the night we finished the home. Jin had also recently graduated from college, which was a significant milestone in her life. As an adolescent, Jin quit school in sixth grade to work in a factory to help out her family. While working as a teenager and young adult, she supported herself, sent money home, and earned both her high school and college degrees on her own. Her college degree was the fruit of her hard work and determination, an achievement she wanted to share with her family. She had even brought along her cap and gown to wear to simultaneously celebrate her graduation along with the housewarming. But Jin's mother's sickness meant the party needed to be scaled back to a smaller, more solemn affair. The cooks planned accordingly and bought just enough produce to feed the team and close relatives.

As we were finishing up final touches on the last day, installing window shutters, lights, and cleaning up, preparing for the modest housewarming, we received a call from Jin's brother. He had great news: their mother's health was stable and the doctors were discharging her from the hospital! She arrived home in the afternoon, just in time to move into the new house and join the housewarming party. We were all overjoyed and stunned by God's sweetness to their family. This was sure cause to celebrate! In an instant, a full-blown housewarming party was back on and we busied ourselves with preparations.

Jin and her siblings went around the village inviting the elders, relatives, friends—everyone.

Now, we only had one problem. We had food to serve about fifty people but were now expecting well over a hundred. We contemplated the idea of going to the market, but we had neither a car nor the time to make the two-hour round trip. Our team decided to scour the village on foot, searching for whatever raw ingredients or ready-made food we could buy. Meanwhile, Pai collected whatever leftover curries we had and tried to infuse new life into them with gathered herbs and vegetables. But by the evening, even after all our efforts, when we assessed what we had we were still nervous—there did not seem to be enough. As a team, we decided that we would eat last, to make sure guests had enough, and we were prepared not to eat if we ran out of food. While guests were arriving, we said a quick prayer asking God to provide enough food and started serving. Soon enough, people filled the house and sat outside, encircling the house on straw mats, eating family-style. We could barely serve food quickly enough. People began murmuring while they waited to be served. We gave each other nervous looks as we tried to accommodate everyone and distribute the food appropriately.

At the peak of attendance, Jin's sister Pawn pulled Jin and me aside. "We ran out of food!" she anxiously whispered. "We still haven't served everyone. What should we do now?" Our worst fear was now reality. Knowing we had no other options, the three of us prayed, "God, we know that we don't have enough food. But we know that you are able to provide, and we ask that you would provide like you did with the miracle of the five loaves and two fish. Amen." As soon as we opened our eyes, a guest walked through the door carrying an armful of grilled chicken. Pawn saw her and immediately started laughing. We knew God would answer our prayers, but to see Him answer them immediately was sensational.

Every guest ate and was full. The celebration that night was electrifying: a new and sturdy home, a healthy mother, and the celebration of Jin's hard-earned graduation. God's grace was so apparent. Once all the guests left, the team finally had a chance to sit down with all of Jin's family to eat. We gathered all the leftovers, hoping there would be enough for us. To our amusement, there was exactly enough.

While we ate and told stories of the night, Pai shared with us that guests had commented to her, "This food is so good! I've never had curries like this before. Can you give me the recipe?" Pai glowed as she recounted trying to hold back laughter, knowing that these unique leftover-curry blends could never be recreated. Pawn continued to gush over their reconstructed house, saying, "I love this house! It's so beautiful!" But Jin's response was perhaps the most poignant: "I love this house. This is the house built by the faith and unity of our friends." We all marveled over God's outstanding work during the trip, exceeding all our expectations.

The experience of the house project taught us all about God's incredible ability. He showed us that despite the lack of resources, lack of power, physical limitations, and even personal insecurity, that He always has more than enough. He provided for all that we needed and then some.

Through it, I was impressed by God's special intention to include us as participants. Could He have provided a house for Jin's family via some other means? Absolutely. He could have had a rich person donate a large sum of money and hire professional builders or even make a house appear out of thin air. But something would have been lost. Through the process of involving us, He developed our sense of unity as a community of believers. We learned to appreciate each other's abilities and the joy of collaboration. We learned to trust even with everything stacked against us. We learned that with God's leading and provision, we were more than able to achieve any goal before us.

And just like any good program, the fruit borne from the experience extended beyond the project. The elements that were developed—faith, unity, and the ability to achieve—ultimately inspired an active hope in us. For people who are immobilized by marginalization, despair, or insecurity, this type of hope is key to empowerment. In my experience, I have come to believe that possessing an active hope is the greatest indicator of an individual or community's potential success. These three aspects allow this hope to take root and grow. Faith combats fatalism and cynicism; it is choosing to believe that God is at work and that the current reality can be positively changed. The experience of a unified community provides a backdrop of support, grounding people in love and belonging. And finally, the ability to achieve, being the most personal, instills trust that the individual or community is indeed capable and sufficient to act and accomplish goals.

For Jin, this temporary house led to a permanent one. The permanent house was eventually built by her own family with the help of a low-interest loan from our foundation's housing program.[6] They built it section by section, using what they could afford, and over time she paid back the full amount of the loan. In the end, it was their family's achievement, and it was right for them to acquire the means, and follow it through to completion. The experience of the temporary house project showed her that building a house was possible, that she could take initiative, and that it was possible for their family to finish it. Our partnership with them in the temporary house building was a small step in the longer journey of their family's empowerment, an event which helped inspire faith and hope through the love of a community.

For me personally, the project also had a profound impact. It solidified a deep knowledge that God is enough. He is enough to lead, to provide, and to both inspire and fulfill hope. In the grand scheme, personally not being or having enough did not seem to matter anymore. In light of His completeness, whatever I am is enough. I could be content in my shortcomings because God's obvious supernatural work was bigger than any doubt of mine. I also no longer felt the need to prove myself. My efforts and my work lost an angsty edge. Instead, my identity and work could be based on the understanding that God will guide and support us in accomplishing our efforts of love. God invests in me and in my work so that I can achieve His purposes. To this day, when I struggle with doubt in myself or God or I find myself worrying, I remind myself of our experience with Jin's house. That house became a monument of faith for me.

WITH GOD, WE ARE ENOUGH

IN THE BROADER SCOPE of ministry and work with poor people and communities, it is imperative that we bring this same philosophy of development to our work on the ground. People need to discover and know that they are enough. The community or individual being developed must be at the helm of their own development. They must know that their motivation and initiative—their active hope—is enough. Once people take charge of their own development and actively seek it, the outcomes are amazing. I have seen this firsthand working with informal communities struggling with land issues, for example. Several informal communities I worked with who faced impending demolition had the ability to organize themselves and implement a solution. One community negotiated a long-term lease with the landowner and established a rent-fee collection process to collectively cover the land rent. Another community situated on a polluted canal was awarded full land rights from the government because they kept their section of the canal cleaner than any other section.

Unfortunately, not all communities and individuals are driving their own development. People may not be confident in their ability to lead, may not believe their efforts will be effective, and may believe they deserve the lot they have received in life. A mentality of poverty can often cause people to believe, "I don't have anything. I can't do anything. I need someone else to do it for me." In Thailand, as with any society, cultural and social beliefs can even reinforce each of these false ideas. As a collectivist society, only a few are encouraged to lead while the rest are expected to support with loyalty. With over 93 percent of the Thai population practicing Buddhism, the Buddhist concept of karma and reincarnation also teaches that one should accept one's fate in life since it is determined by one's deeds, either in this current life or a previous one. Unfortunately, I have also witnessed communities unable to organize themselves and individuals who do not act because of this acceptance of their lot in life. It is difficult to watch people choose inaction or destructive paths. Friends have died from uncurbed alcohol and drug use, communities have been demolished while residents make no plans, churches have dissolved, and businesses have faltered or stagnated. My heart grieves for them and their lost potential.

Implicit in every attempt at success is the possibility of failure. Without the potential of failure, success is meaningless. Would attaining an educational degree be as significant if it did not take focused effort to pass tests, gain competencies, and earn grades? Would you be ecstatic if you already knew that the person you asked on a date would certainly say yes? This possibility for failure, rejection, and disappointment makes every endeavor suspenseful and risky.

Practically, then, what can we do to encourage active hope and empowerment? How do we build up faith, unity, and the ability to achieve for individuals and communities who do not believe in their own potential? I have found that inviting people into small projects that simultaneously address these three aspects can sow seeds of confidence that can grow into accomplishment. Development agencies, mission organizations, community organizers, and mentors can do the same to fit the needs and settings of the people they are working with.

As a mentor, I worked toward developing those three areas (empowering faith, developing a spirit of unity, and allowing a participant's own accomplishment to point the way) in our internship program in Bangkok. One small application is illustrated in the pre-internship fundraising experience. Before beginning the internship, interns needed to fundraise for their internship costs. They needed to build a supportive community, overcome fears, and achieve basic goals through planning and effort. Similarly, in community organizing, the organizer aims to first encourage the community by identifying a small, winnable action. Then the onus of development is placed on the community so that it must gather, organize itself, and act together. The experience of producing results from planned actions builds momentum for larger issues they will address in the future.[7]

From a development agency perspective, where the agency has significant resources, the initial empowering project can invite the community to organize and motivate itself. One example is from an organization I worked for in Thailand. They termed projects like this, "Quick Hits." A Quick Hit describes a basic process that engages the community in a simple project where it is easy to succeed, usually choosing a basic infrastructure or health-related program. If the community was struggling with access to transportation, the organization would propose a deal with the community. If people in the community felt they needed new or improved roads, the organization would offer all the materials and training, but the community had to physically build the road, in our case, with a simple road design using concrete to form bricks that fit together in a jigsaw pattern. Volunteers were taught how to make bricks, level the ground, and construct the road. The road was contingent upon the collective effort of the community. Usually the community was motivated by the incentive of free and improved access, so people were eager to volunteer. And if it fell into disrepair in the future, the community had already gained the skills to repair it themselves using minimal resources. Generally, a road would be finished quickly within a week, and the community was energized by the unity unleashed from the project, a sense of trust that the organization and community would follow through, and a sense of achievement from completing it themselves.

Though these are only a few examples of how empowerment can work, there are countless ways we can encourage people to use what they have toward solving problems. Realistically, this same process applies to each of us. We should be compelled to exercise faith in our God who can provide, to work together with others in unity, and to work toward achieving our goals with the hope that drives us to keep living, working, learning, and loving, even in the midst of any possible failure.

Sometimes, my fear of failure or inadequacy reappears. I still get nervous when I embark on unfamiliar projects, work in new fields, or step into the unknown. My old questions, "Will I be enough?" and "Can I do enough?" re-emerge in different forms: Am I giving my son, my husband, my work, my service, and God enough? Am I already behind in my career in research and academia? Am I doing this working-mom thing right? Now that I feel confident in my Chinese heritage, am I passing on enough Chinese language and culture to my son? But each time I hesitate to engage or hold back from taking a new risk, I remember Jin's house. I remember our team. I remember how we always, somehow, had enough. And I remember May. I remember her bowl of noodle soup. I remember the joy in awkwardly sharing her slippery noodles. And I bring my own dish to the table.

I pray that the eyes of your heart may be enlightened in order that you may know the hope to which He has called you, the riches of His glorious inheritance in His holy people, and His incomparably great power for us who believe. (Ephesians 1:18-19, NIV)

---

5 An informal community is a community where houses have been constructed on land where the residents have no legal claim or where housing does not comply with regulations.

6 The Thai Peace Foundation, while Servant Partners was affiliated, initiated and managed a program to loan money to low-income families to help them afford their own homes.

7 Robert C. Linthicum, *Transforming Power: Biblical Strategies for Making a Difference in Your Community* (Downers Grove, IL: IVP Books, 2003).

2

ESCAPING AND RETURNING TO
SAL SI PUEDES
Annabel Mendoza Leyva

Annabel M. Leyva is a native of Northern California and long-time resident of east San Jose where she currently lives with her husband Natanael and their two children, Emily, 13, and Nathanael, 11. She began her journey as an urban minister in 1998 through her work at the non-profit Mayfair Improvement Initiative. She earned her Master of Arts in Theology degree from Fuller Theological Seminary in 2015 and has worked as an academic advisor, program manager, recruiter, teacher assistant, and research assistant for the seminary. Since 2014, Annabel has been working with Servant Partners in the Mayfair neighborhood of the San Jose site, first as a contract employee and volunteer, and now as staff. Currently, she is a board member for San Jose Bridge Communities and continues to work serving the urban communities of Santa Clara County. Annabel enjoys stories, music, and writing.

I LIVE IN A NEIGHBORHOOD in San Jose, California, known officially as Mayfair. But since the 1960s, it's been nicknamed *Sal Si Puedes*, or "Escape If You Can." Mayfair's claim to fame is that Cesar E. Chavez, the founder of the United Farm Workers, moved here with his family in the 1930s, when he was a child. He and his wife went on to raise their own family here in the 1940s.[8]

No doubt, Chavez was aware of the nickname of our San Jose neighborhood, but that didn't stop him from the work he did from here, starting at Our Lady of Guadalupe Church, and continuing on throughout California, fighting for the rights of farm workers and farming communities.[9] He could have escaped Sal Si Puedes, but he stayed. Thinking about Cesar E. Chavez and the impressive work he did humbles me. Though I may not be Chavez, I love this community and I hope I can do even a small amount of the good work he did.

When I started college working toward my undergraduate degree in the 1990s, I wanted to help my community by running a center where immigrant families could learn English and mainstream cultural expectations, search for employment, and utilize childcare and counseling services. With this goal in mind, I focused my studies on classes that would help me do that. But I wanted to be a commuter servant. I wanted to serve my community specifically, but not live there. I wanted to move out and drive in every day to work. I'm ashamed to admit it now, but it's true. Though I was burdened to help, I absolutely wanted to escape this place. I did not want it to be my home. I thought I would grow up and work to help people in the neighborhood where I grew up. I just wanted to get out of Sal Si Puedes while I still could.

EARLY FAMILY LIFE: HOW I ARRIVED AT MAYFAIR

MY FATHER JESÚS immigrated from Michoacán, Mexico in 1966 in search of work to help his family who was struggling financially, as my grandfather was ill. He was only eighteen years old. After two years of suffering homelessness, hunger, inhumane treatment by immigration officers and employers, he was able to legalize his stay and help his family. My mother Reynalda came to the United States on a tourist visa from Mexicali, Baja California in 1965 when she was seventeen. While in California, her aunt helped her change her visa to a student visa so that she could stay and study.

In 1972, my parents met at a dance hall called "The Starlight" in San Jose. It was my mother's birthday, and my father was only there as the designated driver, so he planned to just stay in the car. His plan failed, though, when his brother and cousins pressured him to come inside. My father says that when he walked in, "the first person I saw was your mother. My eyes could not see anyone else. I asked her to dance and I stayed with her the rest of the evening."[10] After that, my father made a thirty-five-mile drive to visit my mother every Sunday so he could walk her home after church. My dad succeeded in his pursuit. My parents married in 1973 at Our Lady of Guadalupe Catholic Church in San Jose, and they moved around for few years before settling in Mayfair in 1979.

The neighborhood was surrounded by farms and had many Mexican shops, schools, and Spanish-language churches. These were all the essentials that a young Mexican family needed to live well, and my parents decided to settle down here. We would later find out from long-time neighbors and city employees that our new neighborhood had a nickname in San Jose: *Sal Si Puedes*. Escape If You Can.

LIVING IN THE *BARRIO*

MY EARLIEST MEMORIES of living in the Mayfair neighborhood were pleasant. My sister and I, just a year apart in age, each had our own bedroom and a backyard in which to play and run. Our church was nearby, and we had everything we needed. But everything was changing—first in our household, then in the neighborhood.

My anxiety started early. I remember going to kindergarten and having to speak English only. And at home, we were not allowed to speak English. It was confusing remembering which language to speak; I felt tense trying to figure it out, trying to remember. At the same time, my mother had an accident at work that was bad enough that she couldn't return to work, so our finances were strained. My father worked as a gardener, and he was gone long hours and returned home very tired.

Beside the stress from work making for an anxious home, my father became angry because my mother had begun deepening in her relationship with God and then converted to Pentecostalism without his permission; he felt betrayed because he was committed to the Catholic religion.[11] On one occasion, my father said to me, "Annabel, dile a tu mamá que deje de hacer lo que me está haciendo." *(Annabel, tell your mother to stop doing what she is doing to me.)* I had no idea what he meant, but I remember

46

thinking that my poor father was being treated badly by my mother, so obediently, I went to tell her.

But his anger quickly became much worse than that. About a month after my mother had converted, two weeks after she was baptized, when I was six, my father beat my mother so badly he nearly killed her. There had been other instances of domestic violence but nothing as bad as that evening. But he was so distraught by what he had done that he prayed and asked God for forgiveness. He struggled all night and had visions from God. He saw himself alongside others and they were all in a place of perdition. Jesus told him that he needed to repent and accept Him for salvation. He then saw himself in the woods and on a rock and alone. He called on Jesus, and he saw a bright figure of a man in white robes appearing to him with outstretched hands, telling my father to come to Him.

The next day, a Monday, he went to work, but he could not work because he kept seeing Jesus still calling him with outstretched hands. So he went to our neighbor, who had been taking my sister and me to church, (a man, incidentally, whom my father had threatened to kill, showing him a gun, if he did not stop taking us to church). My dad asked this neighbor's forgiveness and asked our neighbor to baptize him. They sat together for two full days in Bible studies, and then my father converted and got baptized, and things changed for the better from that point on, though there was a different kind of stress.

A year after my parent's conversions, by the time I was seven, my parents started to give shelter to people. We took people into our home to live—family and other people we had met through church friends— who were undocumented and needed a safe place to live while they figured out how to manage in this new country. There were people living in our garage and in my sister's bedroom. Then my cousins (three boys and one girl) came to live with us. We were a full house! Having so many playmates was fun, but we could not avoid the fighting between the children, the noise, and all the tensions that came with having so many people in one house. A few years after that, my father would become a deacon in our church and then an ordained minister, and so our family was in some ways under a microscope for good behavior.

The stress and chaos within my home life was hard, but it did not compare to what was happening on my street. I remember going to church for mid-week service and seeing the street behind us surrounded by police cars. Officers were wearing vests and pointing guns at a neighbor's house. Violence and noise were becoming constant. Our house was near a major freeway, so we were used to the humming of the cars that traveled along the freeway all day long. But I could never get used to the frequent yelling of the youth who gathered to fight after school across the street from our house, under the freeway's pedestrian overpass.

Every week, there were teenagers from the middle school. Either a group of kids would chase some unfortunate kid who was being bullied, or groups of opposing gangs would gather into one spot there to "war." Police and ambulance sirens would wail on a constant basis because there were so many problems in the middle school in the eighties and nineties. Our neighborhood was infused with gangs and drugs, and our local schools' test scores were the lowest in the city.

In 1999, our local school, Cesar Chavez Elementary, had an API score of 425, with a state-wide rank of 1%; our local middle school, Lee Mathson Middle School, had an API score of 448, with a state-wide rank of 1%.[12] It was difficult to complete homework at home. We grew up hearing helicopters circling our street, loud music blasting from our neighbors' houses, and cars rattling our windows with the bass on their stereos. When we were standing, we could feel the beat on the soles of our feet. Trying to be a serious student in Mayfair was not easy.

In the late eighties, my older sister started high school, and I would soon follow. Independence High School was the size of a community college and did not do well by academic standards. The large size made it difficult for my sister to make friends and connect with teachers, which led to her feeling isolated. She transferred to the smaller Overfelt High School where she knew a couple of kids, but at that school one of her teachers, a religious zealot, pressured her to confess her sins every Friday. My parents decided to make the financial sacrifice of sending my sister and me to a small Christian school in our neighborhood. My mother worked hard providing childcare for some neighbor children in order to help pay for our schooling.

My brother faced even more issues than my sister and I did. He was five years younger than us, so he never had a sibling to watch out for him at school. He faced bullying because we were so poor. My mom bought us plastic shoes from Payless and she made him wear turtleneck shirts, thinking they were good for him because they kept him warm. The dreaded turtlenecks and Payless shoes were favorite jokes of many kids, and my brother usually found himself isolated and without friends. My brother remembers, realizing, "I knew that I needed to be like the kids who got into trouble if I was going to get any respect."[13] So by the time my brother was in sixth grade, he had joined a gang.

The middle school my brother attended was the worst performing school in San Jose. The levels of violence were so high that there were police officers stationed at the school. One day we learned that my brother's principal was selling drugs out of his trunk on school grounds.[14] He was arrested at the school, in the parking lot. This was the beginning of the ghetto entering our home in a way that was much more real than any of us could have imagined. My brother was constantly getting into trouble by breaking school windows, joy riding, and fighting. He managed to finish middle school, only thanks to my mother's constant intervention.

As one might imagine, high school didn't get easier for my brother. We had police coming to the house looking for him. He would not come home for long periods of time. My mother would cry and pray for him because she was afraid that he would be murdered while on the streets. I would get up and pray with my mother, and I would wait for him to return, looking out of my bedroom window. I would go to school tired from long, worrisome nights.

When he was home, he would fight with my parents, or smoke or do drugs in his room with his friends. To help my brother find a way out of this trouble, my parents took out a loan against the escrow of their house and sent my brother to a school in Texas—a military academy. My brother later told us how he was yelled at and insulted there, called a "spik"[15] because he initially did not allow anyone to tell him what to do. He fought back, but he was alone. He had no one there to turn to, so he often cried to himself. But my brother made a decision to prove that he was more than that and chose to rise above the insults. After the grueling summer of boot camp, my parents and I went to see him graduate, and we saw something different in my brother—a very disciplined soldier on his way to something new.

As the middle child, I watched both of my siblings' challenges, but I had issues of my own. When I was eight, my parents were on a trip and left the three of us with our maternal grandmother, and everyone was enjoying themselves except me. I was crying inconsolably. I wanted my parents, and I was afraid I would not see them again. My grandmother held me in her arms and comforted me. I generally wanted to be near my parents and please them. I was so afraid to disappoint them, and I feared that disappointing them would result in their not loving me. Fear was my constant companion. As I grew, I entrenched myself in education and used my studies as both my escape and a way to please my parents.

When I was beginning my university studies, I had to decide what I would study, what I would do with my life. What was my purpose? I wanted to pursue a theology degree at a Bible college, but in my Christian tradition, women did not lead or preach where men were present. My father had converted to Pentecostalism a month after the horrific domestic violence episode we witnessed, and he went from being an angry man to a loving husband. He even began teaching and leading others to a new life in Christ. My father was so committed that he studied and became an ordained minister. I had seen God's power transform his life. However, when my father began as a minister, all eyes were on our family, especially when my brother and sister had so much trouble in school. Because of my Christian tradition, I wouldn't have much freedom as a woman to lead, and because I knew that life in ministry was difficult, I assumed a theology degree would not benefit me in any way. So I eventually talked myself out of Bible college.

Instead, I decided in favor of a career in social services to help Latino families like my own deal with the emotional and social problems we all faced every day. I decided to pursue a degree in sociology with a focus on family and a minor in religious studies from San Jose State University. For the moment, moving away from my neighborhood was not an option because I was too afraid to leave my parents. But I certainly did not want the children I would one day have to live the way I had. Eventually, I *would* leave. I would get out. I would find a better place to raise my children.

The desire not to return to Mayfair was only increased by a message I internalized at some point—I have no idea when—that I was not good enough to be used by God because of my background. Because I was a woman. Because I was Hispanic. Because I was from Mayfair. The truth was far from that, but God would need to take my heart on a long journey through the wilderness before I could hold onto that truth and live it out. In reality, my heritage, including my culture and where I am from, is a gift that can allow me to see and understand my world in a unique way. Because I am from what some might consider the margins of my society, I can understand how the good news of Jesus is particularly and powerfully given for those on the margins, and even the particular culture that infuses the margins of Mayfair.

In his work, *Walk with the People: Latino Ministry in the United States*, Juan F. Martinez quotes Latino church leaders Oscar and Karla Garcia as they consider God's gift of culture: "God works untiringly to reconcile and renovate the cultural spaces that destroy and oppress God's creation. The culture in which we were born is a divine gift, and an acquired culture is an opportunity to enrich and develop ourselves without rejecting what we inherited."[16]

Another author, Justo Gonzalez, argues that "marginality, poverty, mestizaje[17] and alienness contribute to the Hispanic understanding of the Scriptures and insights to issues unseen by others."[18] Because of my life experience, I am able to understand God's saving grace in a special way. All of the suffering that I've endured can be used by God as a part of the bigger picture of redemption that, in my anxiety to escape, I kept failing to see. It was difficult for me to see my heritage as a gift because I was listening to the message from the larger society that called me to leave my location. And not just to leave, but to escape. I grew up watching television shows and movies that portrayed neighborhoods like mine as frightening and terrible places where bad people live and suburban locations as the ideal places to call home.

In his book, *Where the Cross Meets the Street*, Noel Castellanos contends that "Jesus approached ministry from the margins where he found himself as a Galilean living in poverty together with the people in whose midst he ministered."[19] In Luke 10:1-9 (CEB), Jesus instructed the seventy he sent in pairs to partake of life and serve those who accept them into their communities. Castellanos asks questions that are very compelling for a person such as myself who wished to flee the ghetto rather than stand in solidarity and incarnate from within. Castellanos asks, "Can you imagine if God had taken a safer and less costly approach to bringing about salvation? Can you imagine Jesus commuting to Nazareth from heaven every day instead of being fully present in the everyday situations of his family and neighbors?"[20] But when I was twenty-two, I wasn't ready for this part of Jesus' call to follow Him in the way that He served others, by being fully present with those I wanted to serve.

ESCAPING THE BARRIO: MINISTERING FROM A DISTANCE

AT TWENTY-TWO, I had three goals for my future: not to be or marry a minister, to have a non-ministerial job helping families in need in Mayfair, and to get out of Mayfair. I wanted to be like one of the many outside people (Asian, White, and Latino) who helped at the schools and in the afterschool programs in Mayfair. They cared about people in Mayfair, but at the end of the day, they could go home and not deal with all the problems of living here. I thought working in Mayfair but not living there was a fantastic compromise. I could come during the day, help people through my job, and then at 5:00 p.m., I could drive out of Mayfair—to a big house in a nice neighborhood where my kids would be safe and have the best opportunities for their education.

I feared that if I stayed in Mayfair, my kids would go through the same things I and my family did, and I did not (and do not) want my kids to go through the same things I did. I did not (and still do not) see anything wrong with this way of thinking because I was thinking about the well-being of my future children. The hurt I had grown up with, the pressure of growing up in a ministerial family, the issues of poverty, the educational discrimination, and the neighborhood violence had taken its toll on me.

I still believe that it is good to want a better life, and I'm happy for anyone who is called by God in that direction. What I did not see was that God had called me in a different direction, to see that Mayfair has nuggets of wealth that need to be found and restored. We, the people from our neighborhood, can make a difference for our neighborhood. While many escape, some of us who are called to stay have the opportunity to make a huge difference from within. I did not see this before. I thought I had to become "better" (smarter, richer, more "American") to bring answers.

Throughout my childhood, I had moments when I saw the hand of God working miracles and wonders in my family, and yet I chose to hold on to the difficulties of being a child of a church leader in the ghetto. I wanted to do good and serve people in need, but I also wanted to do things on my own terms. As a lay-person. As a commuter.

I found myself like Jonah.[21] I was running away from what God had for me. I was trying to escape...and even my neighborhood's nickname suggested that I should! I felt a great desire to serve people, but I wanted to be the one who was going to decide how to do that. So I got on a "boat" and planned to escape the *barrio* and only come in when I wanted to. But like Jonah, a large fish swallowed me and spat me out back in the neighborhood. Only, unlike Jonah, this had to happen to me more than once.

I met my husband Natanael in 1995 at our church. We married two years later. We did not have the financial means to move out on our own, so we stayed with my parents for a little while until we were able to save enough to move out and rent a tiny room in south San Jose. But we ended up moving back to a studio room attached to my parents' garage, since it was roomier and we wanted to save money to purchase a home of our own. During the time that we were living in my parents' studio, I began working for a non-profit grassroots organization in the Mayfair neighborhood, Mayfair Initiative (now SOMOS Mayfair). This part of my future was coming together. At Mayfair Initiative, I learned how to express my ideas, organize, plan, collaborate with other organizations, and advocate for people in my community. We only needed to move out, and my plan would be complete.

Finally, two years later, my husband and I bought a house an hour and a half away in Stockton. This was perfect because I could come and go as I liked! It was the housing boom of 2001, and thousands of people were buying houses in faraway cities and commuting to work in San Jose. We had to wake up before 4:00 a.m. just to be at work by 8:00 a.m. Four hours of traffic, one way. So, we stayed in Mayfair with my parents during the week and went to Stockton during the weekend. It's almost comical how Mayfair—or God—kept spitting us back up on its shores. But I was very stubborn, worse than Jonah. I did not want to be in Mayfair, but it seemed I had no choice. Maybe the reason I couldn't escape was because God was the one who was calling me. Maybe I was going to have to let Him call the shots. Maybe I could let Stockton be the last time I learned this lesson.

DYING TO MYSELF AND EMBRACING GOD'S WILL

LIVING ACCORDING to God's will is more than simply praying for God's will. Living in God's will means dying to yourself and giving up whatever keeps you from hearing and following the will of God. In my case, dying to myself meant to die to my control, to let go of trying to direct my own path, and to ask God which way He was calling me to go. Without praying, my husband and I had decided to move to Stockton, and there were consequences associated with that move. The stress of our commute was so intense that we suffered infertility after two miscarriages. I became depressed, my husband was stressed, and we were not doing well in our marriage. We had to sell our house before things got any worse.

Once again, we made my parents' home in Mayfair our home, but soon after we returned to Mayfair, my husband left, needing time to himself to think things through. My depression led to anxiety and panic attacks. I clung to my husband, wanting him to be everything for me. As I clung tighter to him, my husband was also suffering our childlessness and wanted to isolate. During that time when my husband had left me, I had an encounter with God. I felt stripped of everything. I had no children, no home of my own, no husband, *and* I was back home with my parents in Mayfair, the place I had wanted to leave since my youth. *Sal Si Puedes*. But, no, I couldn't escape.

I cried out to God in desperation every day for over a month. I was not able to sleep or eat. I had no energy left in me. My mother and a group of women joined me in fasting and prayer. They interceded for me and we prayed that God's will would be done in my life. Before this, I do not remember ever praying for discernment to understand what God was doing in my life or in the life of my community. I had been so afraid of God's will because I wasn't too sure I'd like God's will. I wasn't too sure God's will would be the same as mine. (It's not.) This makes it hard to pray the Lord's Prayer, welcoming "His will to be done."

During this time, I was finally willing to try God's will, and surrender my own. Soon, life began to return to me, body and soul. I found myself enjoying being a part of the choir, a ministry I'd enjoyed as a girl but had since lost touch with. I started to sense my purpose once again. I began to feel a part of Mayfair again, like I belonged here. Like I needed to be in Mayfair to serve Mayfair the way God wanted me to. And I began to realize that maybe being in Mayfair was what I needed too.

Nine months after my husband left, we reconciled. It was as if the nine months were a gestational period. We'd both had time to heal and I had been nurtured by God—a new relationship with God was developing, resulting in a new life with Him. As we reconciled and moved back in together, things were still hard, but in a different way. We were both raw and tender and we had to learn to live life together, we had to learn how to fight for our marriage, and we had to learn to trust God first. It was overwhelming, but it was also beautiful. We soon moved into our own apartment in a prosperous part of the South Bay.

During the year that we lived there, I was finally living the life I had always desired. I would drive into Mayfair for work and return to our home in Sunnyvale. At the same time, God was healing my heart from my miscarriages and from my broken relationship with my husband. We were learning to be a couple who trusted God. And as we did, God granted us a third pregnancy, and this time we would not miscarry.

I went into labor the week that our one-year lease was up. When I left the hospital two days after giving birth to our daughter Emily, the three of us returned to Mayfair. We were starting a new life as a family and a fresh relationship with God. We needed support as we started this new journey, but things were different for me this time. We moved in with my parents—again—but this time with a baby and with open hearts. We were overjoyed at the birth of our daughter. We were also overjoyed knowing that we would be surrounded by family and friends we loved and who loved us as we learned to be parents, that we would be surrounded by a whole community we identified with. I began to see more than people with needs and what I could do to help them. I saw *my people.* I heard *my language.* I smelled *my food.* I was home.

Not only did I give birth to my daughter, but a new openness for urban ministry in Mayfair was birthed in me as well. The way I had seen people before, as a bundle of needs, and myself simply as a filler of those needs, had robbed us all of our humanity. I had resisted opening my heart and my mind to the very community in which God had placed me. I had the intentions of helping, but helping from a distance is different from helping from within. Being back within my community, this time with purpose and peace from God, helped me see that the distance wasn't just due to my commute but the way that I kept people at a distance emotionally. My new, more vulnerable openness to my community was necessary for my work in urban ministry to be effective.

Alan J. Roxburgh states that joining God in the neighborhood "calls us away from ecclesiocentrism and church questions, and toward a whole set of disruptive questions about what God is up to and how we can join Him. It calls us into the risky space of discerning where God is at work rather than depending on our own assessments of needs, which conveniently leave us in control of agendas and relationships."[22] This change in my attitude toward my community was not a small shift, although it may have been imperceptible to anyone who didn't know my heart. It was a massive shift that would change everything about me and about how I would engage. Now I didn't want to escape. I didn't want to be somewhere else. I was ready to be here, to live in Mayfair—for anyone God called me to serve, and to also receive with open arms whatever God had for me.

✳

I see my family and my experience as a parallel modern-day story, not only to Jonah, but to the people of Israel walking in circles with Moses around the Promised Land. The people of Israel complained and were not able to understand what God was doing for them, and so they circled the Promised Land instead of walking right into it. The older generation even had to die off—the younger generation were the ones who entered.

In my immediate family, some could see the kingdom of God before others, and these began to walk by faith. They began to be Jesus' hands and feet for the people they were called to reach. My brother, for example, who had so many struggles as a child and teen, was able to make a complete turnaround when he opened his heart to God at nineteen and finally could see God leading his life toward a calling beyond his expectations. After my brother made the commitment to follow Jesus, he started discerning God's call for him to reach people on the margins where he had been. When he was only twenty-five, he founded an international faith-based nonprofit, Jordan International Aid, to care for countries stricken by natural disasters, which he still leads. Today he is also the senior pastor of The Gathering, a church reaching people who do not know of God's saving grace. Who would have thought that a boy who was bullied for his plastic shoes and turtlenecks, a boy who turned to gangs, would become a leader for the kingdom of God? But the gospel of Matthew does say it will happen this way, if we "desire first and foremost God's kingdom and God's righteousness, and all these things will be given to you as well" (Matthew 6:33, CEB).

Not everyone in my family has had such a quick response to God's leading. Some of us—including myself—have had to take a few more trips around the desert. I have wondered why I have had such a hard time trusting in what God is doing in my life and in the life of my community. Was it because I am a woman and I have been taught to be dependent on others? Was it because I have been taught that as a woman my role is to support and not lead? Was it because I have always doubted myself and been afraid to fail? Was it because I have felt the need to please to be considered acceptable? Was I too caught up trying to survive in the *barrio* that I couldn't see what God was doing here? When I try to make sense of my long journey towards obedience, these are the questions that play over and over in my head.

More than frustrating, all the questions were at points debilitating, not allowing me to see what God was doing in me nor in my neighborhood, because through all that questioning I wanted to control my future and understand my past—instead of just joining Him in the present. But I was asking all the wrong questions, questions stemming from fear and control: things that had to die within me. If I was to do God's will in my life and follow God's leading, my life would need to be guided by different questions, as Roxburgh suggests, "questions about God's actions in our neighborhoods and how to join with God in these places."[23]

THE URBAN MINISTER, REDEFINED

I HAD UNDERSTOOD ministry as a task you have at church when you are ordained, and when you hold a credential from the denomination. I had never been taught what ministry was outside of a Sunday worship service. I had considered the work I was doing in my community as only a job, even though it was a blessing to me and others. I had somehow missed the fact that I was already an urban minister! But with my heart newly opened to living in my community, only ministering through a job, even in Mayfair, still just didn't feel like enough, nor did it now feel like the right approach. I wanted to talk to my neighbors and really get to know them.

In 2013, a few years after my decision to choose to live in Mayfair, I met Andy Singleterry at Fuller Theological Seminary's Menlo Park campus while taking an Ethics Class. Andy shared that he and his wife Janet were ministering in downtown San Jose where they also lived. They were tutoring children, working with youth, providing resources to mothers in the local elementary school, and telling them about Jesus. My ears were ringing and joy filled my heart because someone understood this new dream I'd had...and they were doing it right next door, in my own community!

Andy and Janet walked with me as I discerned God's calling for my life, and slowly I began to serve my community in ways that I had not done before. I began to use the skills God had equipped me with for my community in new ways. I saw the needs of my community and understood them because I was a child of the community and I was raising my children in that community. I spoke the verbal and cultural language which allowed me to make connections with people. I had knowledge of the churches and organizations that were present to support us, and I knew how to approach them. I was connected to people who could help make an impact for my people.

Andy had a desire to establish a non-profit organization that would focus on assisting people living in poverty by helping them become aware of the systems that oppress them, in order to give them tools to reach their goals and live more stable lives. My longing had been to walk with my neighbors by sharing resources and information that could help them thrive in our community through a faith-based organization. Our visions aligned. God led us to begin a new urban non-profit ministry organization together. Andy, Janet, and I met regularly and we prayerfully took steps to bring our dreams to life. San Jose Bridge Communities was born, an organization that allows us to help our neighbors attain resources and form cross-class relationships to build the bridges they need to walk forward into their future, by reaching the goals they set for themselves.

My husband and I began to teach our neighbors about the systems that hold people in poverty and the resources available to them, and to link them to mentors and form community-building opportunities so they can get out of poverty. We would also pray for any needs that were shared, and we regularly broke bread together with our neighbors. Those who wished to continue working toward life goals after graduation from our program joined together on a monthly basis to continue in the journey of wholistic growth, with our board comprised of local residents supporting these participants.

Recently, my husband and I hosted a class based on the book *Getting Ahead in a Just-Gettin'-By World*, for community members to learn about the systems that keep people in poverty and to learn ways to get out of poverty. A couple who had been participating in our class opened up to my husband and me about their marital issues. Because we had faced conflict in our own marriage, and as a child of a conflicted marriage, we were able to connect in a more personal way with them. We were able to understand the stress of being an immigrant family with financial worries living in a city where life is difficult. They were open to us praying with them, and they reached out to us as particular needs for support arose.

Before, my inclination to escape would have driven me away from my neighbors instead of bringing me closer to them. Because I was nearby, we were able to walk with them as they grew through their challenges. We got to learn together and experience both frustrations and happiness together with our neighbors. This is more than I could ever have asked for.

Beyond helping to lead San Jose Bridge Communities, I also have a daytime job in which I serve the urban community of San Jose and Santa Clara County. I am tasked with visiting the homes of families with young children. While in their homes, I listen to their concerns, assess their needs, and connect them to resources that can help resolve or alleviate some of their worries. While I am not at liberty to preach Jesus with words, I am able to be Jesus in action.

I wear several hats: wife, mother, daughter, church leader, mentor, neighbor, servant, board member, and employee. Some of these hats overlap in the work that I do day-to-day. For example, as a wife and mother, I work as a church leader with my children and husband, leading the junior high school group of my local church. As a servant and employee, I serve the needs of my community while earning a living. Lastly, as a daughter, board member, and neighbor, I listen to the needs of my community and work towards meeting those needs. God has blessed me with being bi-vocational. God has blessed me by calling me to Mayfair. My ministry is within the church body and outside the church body. I am coming to understand that I need to be where the people are, to listen and to bring any shalom, any wholeness and peace I can. This is what Jesus did, and it is what I work towards every day.

8 *Mercury News*, "Lofgren Leads Call to Designate Cesar Chavez Site in San Jose as Historic," June 28, 2013, *https://bayareane.ws/2L9hpGN* (accessed April 23, 2017).

9 *Mercury News*, "Cesar Chavez Meeting Hall in San Jose Closer to National Historic Landmark," November 13, 2014, *https://bayareane.ws/2uLAWSQ* (accessed April 23, 2017).

10 Jesus Mendoza, interview by author, San Jose, CA, April 27, 2017.

11 My father had family members who were members of the clergy, and being a devout Catholic was not just a religious identity, but also a cultural identity, something that is shared by family and defended. Converting to a Protestant denomination, and in this case a Pentecostal denomination, meant a betrayal to the religion, culture, and family. This was grounds for allowing divorce by the Catholic Church.

12 California Department of Education, "1999 Academic Performance Index (API) Report," April 24, 2000, *http://bit.ly/2zUZgHG* (accessed January 23, 2018).

13 Jesus Mendoza, Jr, interview by author, San Jose, May 29, 2017.

14 *LA Times*, "School Principal's Drug Arrest Creates Shock and Anger," December 4, 1992, *https://lat.ms/2uH43Yr* (accessed March 27, 2018).

15 The term "spik" is slang for a Latino or Latina person.

16 Juan Francisco Martínez, *Walk with the People: Latino Ministry in the United States* (Nashville: Abingdon Press, 2008), 60.

17 *Mestizaje* is a term that refers to the mixing of Mesoamerican and Spanish ancestry and cultures.

18 Justo L. Gonzalez, *Santa Biblia: The Bible through Hispanic Eyes* (Nashville: Abingdon Press, 1996), 103.

19 Noel Castellanos, *Where the Cross Meets the Street: What Happens to the Neighborhood When God Is at the Center* (Downers Grove, IL: InterVarsity Press, 2015), 79-81.

20 Castellanos, *Where the Cross Meets the Street*, 82.

21 In the Bible, Jonah was a prophet who was given a message from God to deliver to the city of Nineveh, God's enemies. He was to tell them to turn from their evil ways of oppression and corruption or else they would be destroyed by God. Jonah boarded a boat traveling in the opposite direction because he did not want to deliver the message. He was swallowed by a huge fish and spat out on the shore near Nineveh. He eventually completed his mission and the King of Nineveh, along with the people, repented and were saved.

22 Alan J. Roxburgh, *Joining God, Remaking Church, Changing the World: The New Shape of the Church in Our Time* (New York: Morehouse Publishing, 2015), 40.

23 Roxburgh, *Joining God*, 45.

3

DEBORAH'S SONG
Jennifer Chou Blue

Jennifer Chou Blue lives and ministers in South Los Angeles with Servant Partners, currently as one of the pastors at Church of the Redeemer. She and her husband Kevin are grateful to minister together at church and at home with their three children. As a Chinese American woman who grew up in the deep South and who now lives in a mostly Latin-American and African-American community, she has spent most of her life in a cross-cultural setting. Jennifer is grateful to be part of the multi-racial and multi-cultural family of God. She started her work as a minister with InterVarsity Christian Fellowship, serving on staff for twelve years at various campuses in California and with the Los Angeles Urban Project. She has been with Church of the Redeemer since 2003 and with Servant Partners since 2010.

IN OUR CHURCH, people don't come because we have a worship team of professional musicians, which is common especially in the entertainment industry capital of Los Angeles. People don't come because the preacher always preaches in the style they prefer. People come because they sense God's love. They come because they are surprised to see so many people of different races and cultures together as a church. And in such a multi-racial group, they are shocked to see the love of God in our midst.

The first time Verna, one of the moms from my oldest son's school, walked into our Sunday worship service, she said under her breath, "Oh no, this is trouble." She was talking about all the Latinos and Asians and White people and Black people mixing together. She said to her husband, "This is not going to work. All this mixing of people, this is not going to work!" Verna knew that in our neighborhood, people got shot for being in the wrong part of the city. So much of the gang violence in our city is race related. People generally keep to their own kind. So as a good Central American immigrant, she dutifully kept to her own people.

But as God started to draw Verna closer to Him and into deeper friendships in our church with people who were not just Guatemalan, she started to see the beauty of what God was up to. Verna has become one of our bridge-builders who is able to connect with all the different types of people who are part of our community. Our fellowship is not without conflict and misunderstandings. But with the love and grace of God, and a value for reconciling those conflicts and misunderstandings, it works. For newcomers who come to worship on Sundays, or to one of our neighborhood Bible studies, or to any other church gathering, what most often stands out to them is the clear love of God drawing people from such different walks of life together. This is the church God has called me to lead within.

Every Christian is given the invitation to walk and lead in spiritual authority as a follower of Jesus. But it is an invitation that is not often heard by Christian women. And for a number of reasons, it may be difficult to respond when the invitation is heard. Over the years, God has been clear in inviting me to take up the spiritual authority he's given me, to really lead and minister to others. He has spoken to me powerfully particularly through one woman, the biblical character Deborah, time and time again throughout my journey. Deborah's leadership story begins in Judges 4:4-5:

> Now Deborah, a prophet, the wife of Lappidoth, was leading Israel at that time. She held court under the Palm of Deborah between Ramah and Bethel in the hill country of Ephraim, and the Israelites went up to her to have their disputes decided. (ESV)

God first called me into leadership in high school when I first became a Christian and somehow ended up as our new youth group president. In college, God continued to call me to step out in faith and leadership, from leading evangelistic Bible studies for my non-Christian friends, to teaching the Bible to fellow Christians growing in their Christian faith. When I graduated from college, God called me to pursue vocational ministry with InterVarsity Christian Fellowship (IVCF).

CALLED TO GO WITHOUT PARTIALITY

ONE OF MY MOST formative experiences during those early years of full-time ministry was during an IVCF staff gathering where we were visioning for our campus and discerning how God was calling us to focus for the next five years. We were torn between the values of evangelism and racial reconciliation. We deeply believed in both values, along with several others, but we believed that we could only focus on one. Then our staff leader, Susan, led us in studying Acts 10.

These chapters tell the story of Peter, a Jew who was a disciple of Jesus, and Cornelius, a Roman Gentile. Through a supernatural vision from God, an interaction with Cornelius, and the work of the Holy Spirit, Peter gains an understanding of God's heart for all peoples, for all nations. In his declaration in verse 34, after seeing the Holy Spirit fall on Cornelius and all his friends and close relatives, Peter exclaims, "I truly understand that God shows no partiality, but in every nation anyone who fears him and does what is right is acceptable to him." (NRSV) His words were full of awe and emotion. God blew up Peter's preconceived notions of whom the gospel was for. As our staff team studied these chapters, the verse that stood out to me the most was when Cornelius's men asked Peter to come to their master's house. The Holy Spirit said to Peter in verses 19-20, "Look, three men are searching for you. Now get up, go down, and go with them without hesitation; for I have sent them." (NRSV)

The word for "hesitation" in the Greek is *diakrino*. It means to separate from, to withdraw from, to discriminate, to be partial. The pause or "hesitation" comes out of a doubt or judgment of partiality; it comes from discrimination. One could translate verse 20 as reading, "Now get up, go down, and go with them without partiality."

I remember teaching at one of our weekly large group gatherings at the time—one that was predominantly Asian American. I said, "Imagine if Peter and the early Christians only shared about Jesus with people who were like them, with people who were Jews. Who here would know Jesus?" Not one student rose a hand. We didn't have a single Jewish believer present. We were all non-Jews, Gentiles, foreigners to the gospel. If missionaries never went to China, Korea, and Taiwan, some of us who were present would have never known Jesus.

That verse, "Get up, and go, without hesitation," became our rallying cry as a staff team, and it was our catch phrase for our vision directive: Go—without partiality, without prejudice. When we were wrestling between choosing evangelism or racial reconciliation as a vision directive, the Holy Spirit led us to where those two overlap—cross-cultural evangelism. We knew that sharing the gospel cross-culturally was not the same as racial reconciliation. A focus on racial reconciliation would entail addressing our own racism and working against the ways racism is built into the very fabric and systems of our world. But it was a place of overlap. And it was what the Holy Spirit told us to focus on.

That study in Acts 10 solidified my core conviction that the gospel is inherently cross-cultural, and that I was called to minister cross-culturally. So I did. I spent my summers staffing the Los Angeles Urban Project, a six-week intensive for college students to live and serve in an under-resourced urban community. I gave myself to teaching and preaching the often-overlooked passages in the scripture that describes God's preferential concern for the weak, the vulnerable, the poor, and the way race and culture intersect these issues in American society. I sensed God leading me to cross-cultural, urban ministry. It was when I was in those settings that I felt a unique sense of life and the Holy Spirit's confirmation.

Later on, God brought along a man who had centered his life upon these same convictions. Though any stranger would look at us and immediately see our differences, we were strikingly similar when it came to these core convictions. Within a few years of that pivotal study in Acts 10, I had moved to South Los Angeles, was called into a cross-cultural marriage, and joined the planting team for a cross-class, cross-cultural, parish-model church focused on sharing the all-surpassing love of Jesus and the transforming power of the gospel in our local community.

CALLED TO BE A BRIDGE

THESE DAYS, I am often reminded of how being a bridge person ministering cross-culturally can be uncomfortable yet powerful. During my son Samuel's first two years at our neighborhood school in South Los Angeles, I was the only Asian parent. Now there is another Asian mom there, also from our church, who is also stepping out to love cross-culturally in the name of Jesus. But for a while, I was the only one in a sea of Latino and Black parents. And people noticed. Other parents from the school would often remember me from the briefest of encounters because I was the only Asian-American. But God can use that, if we choose to reflect His light. When I choose to extend friendship and kindness, it stands out to people. I have found that people often aren't expecting kindness from a stranger even of their same race, much less kindness from a stranger of a different race. The gospel and the love of God seem to shine more clearly when poured out across these cultural divides, against the grain of ethnocentrism and prejudice that the enemy has our nation trapped in.

On the last day of Samuel's kindergarten year, we threw a celebration party for his class at our house. Quite a few classmates and families came over—even their beloved teacher jumped in the inflatable bounce-house jumper. As I chatted with Ricky, a man covered with tattoos, the dad of a good friend of Samuel's, he shared earnestly, "I've been watching you and your husband. To see if you are real. There aren't many good people in this world. But I've been watching you. And you guys seem like you really are good people. I could use some good people in my life."

We stood out to him, as an Asian-American and African-American cross-cultural couple. But that standing out gave an opportunity for the even greater thing to stand out: the life and love of Jesus in us. After Ricky shared that comment with both of us, we were able to talk with him about God and how our relationship with God is a huge part of our lives and our parenting. Growing up fatherless, he told us how he deeply wanted to be a father to his own daughters. He opened up about running away from home when he was sixteen and how he had not seen either of his parents since. We talked about how God loves us and heals us even as we parent.

Ricky and his wife Karla haven't had an easy road. The following year, Ricky struggled with severe depression and even attempted suicide. When I heard what had happened from Karla after school one day, I offered to take care of her daughters so that she could go to the mental health facility where Ricky was being treated, since she had no one to watch her kids and had only been able to have brief phone conversations with him. When I offered, she hesitated at first, but then she agreed, saying she knew Ricky trusted us, and that he didn't trust many people. We were able to give her a gift from our church benevolence fund to help make rent, with no strings attached, as our church has a practice of setting aside money to help with urgent needs inside and outside of our church.

As the weeks went by, Ricky started to tell Karla that being in the mental health facility may have been the best thing that could have happened, because it gave him access to the therapy and help that he didn't even know he needed, but now felt so helped by. She was overjoyed. Once he was able to come home, they moved away to live with her aunt so they could have some time to get back on their feet.

Now, don't get me wrong. I am not saying that simply being a minority in a cross-cultural context will automatically open doors for outreach. But what I have found to be true is that as you give yourself in love and friendship, your actions will stand out all the more. Our brothers and sisters in urban poor communities rarely talk about people from other ethnic and cultural backgrounds treating them with kindness and love. But when they do, they take note. In 1 Peter 4:8, we learn that love covers a multitude of sins. I have also experienced first-hand that love builds a beautiful bridge over a multitude of ethnic, cultural, and economic barriers. And these barriers are not insignificant.

As I've reflected on the historical context of racism and systemic injustice in the United States, I've come to more deeply understand the unique way that I can be a bridge person as an Asian American. Like many sisters and brothers of color, I have experienced the backhand of partiality and discrimination. I have tasted the sting of being called Ching-Chong while walking through the hallway in high school. I have known what it's like to be one of only two Asians in my entire elementary school in Stone Mountain, Georgia, and to feel different and unknown. I remember my family enjoying a day at the park that bears our town's name, only to discover that a KKK rally was assembling. I remember my parents loading my brother and I as quickly as they could into the car to get out. I remember walking home from school and seeing my older brother being surrounded by a group of kids calling him all kinds of racist names.

But even as a person of color I have tasted privilege. Even though many parents of Asian Americans struggled with low-wage jobs, my parents were given the gift of higher education in this country. My brother and I had the opportunity for success and wealth through the doors opened by a good education. Those of us whose

parents were resourced with education when they immigrated to this country know what privilege, money, and
resources provide.

CALLED INTO THE BATTLE FOR EDUCATIONAL JUSTICE

THE EARLIEST MEMBERS of our Christian community
up through our whole community at present have been
convicted that God would have us share our privilege
and the resource of education. Education opens doors
for work and stable income, which then provides a stable enough home environment for a child to learn and
grow. It is hard to focus on school when you don't have
enough food to eat or a stable home to live in. There
is a child in my son's class who is several grade levels
behind. His family has been evicted from their home
multiple times in the past two years alone. A parent's
capacity to provide a stable home environment in terms
of meeting basic needs is closely connected with his or
her own education level, and a child's education level
is correlated to his or her parents' education level. It's a
vicious cycle. In our current economic system, we have
no protections against long-term entrenched poverty.

Even education is becoming more and more a privilege
of the wealthy. In February 2015, a study done by the Pell
Institute showed that in the previous forty-five years, our
education system has become more and more unjust.[24]
They found that children from wealthy families were
eight times more likely to graduate from college than
children from poor families. We should be ashamed of
ourselves as a country, that we are letting this happen

to so many children. Especially as believers, we should work toward God's protective direction given in scripture. If we were living in the time of Judges and we brought this case to Deborah, she would have ruled that this was injustice and against the Lord's commands.

In 2017, at the local elementary school that our church rents for our Sunday worship services, 91% of the students qualified for free or reduced lunches. Only 13% of fifth graders tested proficient in English Language Arts, and only 5% tested proficient in Math—five percent![25] This is a student population of entrenched poverty. We aren't given eyes to see, ears to hear, and the resources we have just to stand idly by as our neighborhood children get sucked into gangs, homelessness, and dead-end jobs. But what can we do?

We can do whatever we are able. Our church members began tutoring neighborhood kids in their living rooms. Then they eventually started Redeemer Community Partnership, which has built a small but thriving tutoring program called Adventures Ahead that helps children make great gains in math and reading. With limited staff and funding, we are only able to serve thirty to forty children. And in the larger scheme of all the problems in our school district, these kinds of improvements seem small. But the impact on each individual child who has been able to catch up to grade level is not insignificant. The message they internalize is that they are able to learn and improve, that they are smart, and that with hard word and help, they are able to do what they set their minds to! The pay-off is huge in their own lives and within their families.

This emphasis on education has been a very important part of what God has called us to as a church community. Over the years, we have had to wrestle with the privilege of education and our own desires and expectations for our own children. If we were to place education as our highest value, there would be no way any of us would put our children in local area schools. They are so poor in comparison to schools in other wealthier neighborhoods.[26] Yet the Lord has called us to live here, to minister here, and yes, even to send our children to the schools here, and support the educational system serving students in the city in the best way we can.

My husband and I decided to send our oldest son, Joshua, to a charter middle school that started only a few years ago. It is an intervention model of fourth through eighth grade where the kids make the social transition to a new school in fourth grade before the awkward middle school years. It also is structured to give kids focused time to "catch up" if needed in fourth and fifth grades so that by sixth grade the children can be performing at or above grade level, ready for the rigors of middle school. It is built with the goal to close the rich-poor achievement gap. Last year at Joshua's fifth grade culmination ceremony, half of his class was honored for improving in math by two grade levels or more during that year. The joy and pride in the auditorium from the children and all the families was palpable, as all of my son's classmates and their parents now set their sights on higher education and a college degree.

Many of us who have moved into these communities to be part of working for justice and sharing the privilege that was given to us have had to wrestle with a number of idolatries. We would not have followed the Lord's call to this kind of ministry if we had not laid those idols of personal success, wealth, privilege, and prestige at the altar years ago. But having children and having to grapple with educational choices has been new ground for deeper discipleship and repentance. Do I trust the Lord to help my child get "enough" of a good education through the local schools? I don't need my child to get "the best" education that is perfectly catered to him—or do I? Will my child "miss out" on opportunities for her life because of the choices I am making—or am I thinking about her future with the old idols on the throne?

In some places in our country and around the world, the local schools are so dangerous that they may be a non-option. Wisdom from the Lord may dictate an alternative option. I understand that every context has its unique challenges. But are we willing to ask ourselves the hard questions and be honest about our own idolatry of education as parents? If we aren't willing to be honest, then we are simply fooling ourselves.

CALLED AS A WOMAN, A MOTHER, A LEADER

AFTER HAVING MY second son, Samuel, I thought I was done with having kids. I was grateful for two healthy boys. But I was exhausted—and declared that my childbearing shop was closed. Little did I know what the Lord had in store for me. Right around Samuel's second birthday, I was praying with the spiritual director I was seeing at the time. Very clearly, I heard God speak to me:

"I will give you a daughter for your healing." I immediately brushed it off. I thought to myself, "That can't be the Lord. He knows I'm done with having kids. I can barely manage life with the two kids I have!" I decided to tuck it away and leave it alone.

Two months passed, and I was praying at home, reflecting on a recent Advent sermon at our church. The sermon had been about all the ways God communicated with His people about the coming of His son, Jesus. He sent angels. He spoke in dreams. So I told the Lord, "Ok, Lord, is there anything you want to say to me? I want to be open." I couldn't find a pen on my desk, so I opened up the center drawer. To my shock, there were the two positive pregnancy test sticks from when I was pregnant with my boys. I quickly shut the drawer. I knew what the Lord was saying. I just wasn't sure I wanted to hear it.

I decided to ask some friends to pray with me about adding another child to our family, and I dawdled in scheduling it. A few months passed before that prayer time happened. But when it did, the Lord spoke powerfully through Judges 5:7 (ESV): "The villagers ceased in Israel; they ceased to be until I arose; I, Deborah, arose as a mother in Israel." When the friend who heard that scripture shared it with me, I felt that sense of conviction and confirmation you get when you know something is for you. God was calling me to follow Deborah's example and to rise up. To rise up to the call to have another child, and then to rise up to the challenges ahead of me.

Yet, I was filled with fear and anxiety. How could I manage a third child and be in full-time ministry? How would I have anything to pour out to my neighbors if I was barely keeping myself afloat as a mother? But the Lord was speaking to me, loud and clear: *I have called you to be a mother. Ministry and motherhood are not opposed to each other.* I prayed to release my fears to the Lord, and then I felt God reminding me of that earlier prayer time months ago, and the promise from God: *I will give you a daughter for your healing.* I talked with my husband about my sense from God, and after he took a month to pray about it, we decided to ask God for another child.

Within a few months, I was pregnant. A few people who had been praying for us and for our church shared with us about dreams they had, even before they knew I was pregnant. The dreams were of our home expanding, and even of a girl full of spunk and assertiveness. But that pregnancy miscarried. I had suffered a miscarriage a few years prior to this, but this second one felt even more painful and surreal because of the whole process of working through the process of wanting this third child. After that miscarriage, I reread the email from one of our intercessors. I sensed that the Lord was confirming He would indeed give us a daughter. Within one month, we were pregnant again, and that pregnancy carried to full term. Sure enough, the baby was a girl. I had a clear sense that we were to name her Deborah. Every time I would call her name, she would remind me of who the Lord had also called me to be.

God's continual call to me to step into leadership continued. I sought to minister with no partiality, and with confidence in who Jesus had made me to be. As I was transitioning from an associate pastor role to a co-pastor role in our church, a significant increase in authority and responsibility, God brought me back to the story of Deborah. He also began to do a work of healing in me, to free me from wounds I had received as a woman in leadership.

One day during that season, I was at a time of prayer ministry training, and the guest minister began teaching about the hatred of women and the hatred of men, misogyny and misandry. After speaking, he led us into a time of prayer ministry. God brought to mind two painful incidents when I had been criticized in my leadership simply because I was a woman. I had never thought of those two incidents as misogyny, but as God brought them to mind during the prayer time I was overcome by a sense of burden and grief. I started to weep. The minister walked over to pray for me, and prayed for the Lord to remove the spirit of misogyny and the effects of those two experiences in my soul. I felt an immediate lightening and release.

After that training and prayer time, the Lord brought to mind the measure of authority and leadership Deborah walked in as a woman in her time, when women were rarely if ever in positions of authority. Not only does Deborah hold court, but she also leads the nation forth in battle. She receives and gives a direction from the Lord to Barak, the commander of Israel's army, to go and defeat Sisera, the harsh commander of the Canaanites. When Barak does not accept her direction, she pronounces judgement on Barak. God then uses Deborah and another woman, Jael, to deliver Israel from their twenty years of suffering at the hands of Sisera, and the honor goes to them instead. Judges 5 (ESV) preserves Deborah's song of praise for us, and verse 7 summarizes Deborah's story for me:

> The villagers ceased in Israel;
> they ceased to be until I arose;
> I, Deborah, arose as a mother in Israel.

She was a leader whose song is recorded in scripture, at a time when a woman's sole worth and value was measured by the kind of man she was married to and the number of children she bore him. In a time when a daughter was not even deemed worthy of an inheritance, Deborah was leader, judge, and military victor. And in that culture of entrenched misogyny, Deborah arose a mother, a matriarch of Israel. A protector of Israel. A prophet of Israel. God would not abandon her, and God would not abandon me, even in the most intense battles. Through Deborah's story, God has taught me that being a mother, being a leader, and trying to follow in Deborah's footsteps has also meant standing up against the forces of evil that exploit and destroy life. Being a mother means protecting life in a community. In my life, it has meant going to battle against our community's Sisera.

CALLED INTO THE BATTLE FOR ENVIRONMENTAL JUSTICE

FROM JUNE 2, 2013 to August 1, 2014, 24,000 pounds of acid were pumped horizontally into the ground under our homes. The labels on the truck gave us a hint of the poisons being used: Hazardous Material label 3264 for "corrosive liquid, acid" and 1789 for either hydrochloric acid or muriatic acid. The Jefferson Boulevard drill site holds thirty active oil wells just ten feet away from an apartment complex, the shortest distance from drilling site to residential homes in all of Los Angeles County. Apartment residents tell us that even with their windows closed they can smell the idling truck exhaust. The mature trees on the block have begun to die. Our tutoring program is two blocks down the street.

When the executive director of Redeemer Community Partnership, Richard, met with that company's Director of Environmental Health and Safety and Government Affairs, that director mistook the tall Anglo man across the table as an ally—a fellow Anglo man of power and privilege who understood how the world works. So the director leaned in and said to Richard, "We aren't talking about the Ritz Carlton at Laguna Niguel, now, are we?" The 2016 median household income in Laguna Niguel was close to $100,000. In our neighborhood, it was $29,606. What a chilling window into the mindset and soul of these oil companies—it's fine to poison people in poor communities to make billions.

After that rude encounter, Richard decided that he would do everything in his power to demand that the lives of people in our neighborhood be counted equally as precious and valuable as the people who live in Laguna Niguel. Richard stepped up, and he took up God's call to fight against the environmental racism and injustice at the Jefferson drill site. God soon brought the perfect lead community organizer, who would become Richard's right-hand woman—Niki, who had just moved into our neighborhood to be part of the two-year Servant Partners internship team in South Los Angeles. She had just finished her master's degree in public health, and she had sensed God calling her to use her privilege and expertise to fight for under-resourced communities.

Niki led the charge with our neighbors— putting together flyers and pamphlets in Spanish and English, and explaining the dangers of these toxic chemicals and all the immediate and long-term side effects. She went door to door, to every residence along all the blocks surrounding the drill site, asking if they knew what was happening behind the concrete walls. Niki listened to their accounts of the fumes, the loud sounds during the day and in the night, and the diesel trucks filled with chemicals that were idling for hours in front of their homes. She heard the neighbors share about their children getting chronic nosebleeds and asthma, headaches, lingering respiratory illnesses, and she heard about more severe situations of numerous residents living on the same block of the drill site who were battling cancer, some of them dying. The injustice became more and more apparent with each resident's story.

In the process of researching city files for our case against the Jefferson drill site, our lawyers found blatant bias in how the city regulated and limited oil drilling in wealthier communities, while leaving drilling sites unchecked in poorer communities like ours. The effect is that Black and Latino residents have been, and continue to be, disproportionately exposed to the toxic chemicals that cause respiratory diseases, cancer, and other health problems.[27] A federal civil rights lawsuit was filed against the City of Los Angeles; the lawsuit, of course, was settled quietly.

But as we continued to fight, we saw the Lord of hosts defend and protect our community. The City of Los Angeles finally issued a determination in October of 2017, requiring that the Jefferson drill site be given all of the protections that drill sites in wealthier parts of Los Angeles had been granted twenty years ago: fully enclosed oil rigs in permanent structures instead of open-air oil rigs, electric oil rigs instead of diesel rigs, twenty-four-hour air quality monitoring instead of no air quality monitoring, and an up-to-date emergency fire extinguishing system instead of no emergency fire system. But just three months later, in January of 2018, that drill site had quietly changed hands to a new company, which had immediately filed for an appeal.

This company insisted that the protections were unreasonable and financially infeasible and that the City had no authority to issue such requirements. But after the public comments portion of the hearing, the Planning Commission rejected the oil company's appeal and reaffirmed the City's determination in our favor. As I watched the five commissioners, one by one, make comments and vote in our community's favor, I was so moved by God's faithfulness to us. Though we are relatively powerless in the world's terms, God has helped us to break the power of the unrestrained greed of the oil industry. We are praying that the Jefferson drill site will simply be closed. And we are praying that God will use the power of legal precedent to encourage other efforts to bring justice against drill sites in communities like ours.

In the midst of this battle, God has grown me in my willingness to use my voice and my story at rallies, with reporters, and in public hearings. Part-way through the battle, as I was reading more closely about the chemicals being used, I saw that some of the chemicals are endocrine disrupters. Endocrine disrupters are known to harm the reproductive health of both women and men, and worse yet, the harm can be passed down to future generations. Studies have shown that they can harm semen quality, menstrual health, and fertility; they can even lead to miscarriages, stillbirths, preterm birth with low birth weight, and birth defects.[28]

I was preparing for my public comments at an upcoming hearing, and it dawned on me that perhaps my own two miscarriages could have been caused by the chemicals at the Jefferson drill site. I also realized that between four of my friends and myself, who all lived within a half-mile of the drill site, we had suffered eleven miscarriages. The question started to haunt me—what if all of our babies had been lost because of all the endocrine disrupters that were pumped into the ground? We had also learned that the oil company had started spraying a chemical deodorizer as residents started calling more often to report chemical smells. The deodorizer ingredient list included nonylphenol ethoxylate, yet again another endocrine disrupter. As if it wasn't bad enough that they were pumping these chemicals into the ground, they were spraying them into the air as well.

God gave me some new words to speak at that next hearing. I felt stirred to talk about my own miscarriages and my friends' miscarriages and the dangers of endocrine disrupters in the chemicals used in oil and gas operations. At that hearing, there was only one city official sitting there, the Zoning Administrator, whose job is to make sure land use laws protect the health and safety of residents in Los Angeles. During this meeting, I looked him in the eye and called on him to do what was right, to do what was just. When I saw the same Zoning Administrator at yet another hearing a year later, when the new oil company had appealed the City's determination, he spoke powerfully and built the case for why the Jefferson drill site was dangerous and needed more stringent protections. I felt so proud of this man's willingness to stand up for what is true and just in the face of the oil company's threats to sue the City. I would have never thought that God would use my miscarriages, my most painful points in motherhood, to fight for justice in our community.

THE LORD'S CALL TO EACH OF US

IN OUR TIMES, we need more Deborahs. We need more Joshuas and Samuels too—godly men who will follow the Lord, who will help their generation walk into the promises of God—but we certainly need more Deborahs. We need women who will lead in the ways that the Lord has called and anointed them to lead. Our enemy may not be named Sisera, but he is no less evil and oppressive. He works to attack the people of God and the work of God in all kinds of ways, through the selfishness of individuals, the greed of oil companies, and the evil of misogyny that diminishes and beats down women. Our enemy is perpetuating all spiritual strongholds that are opposed to Jesus and the kingdom of God coming on earth as it is in heaven. But God has given us authority over all this evil. Let us take up our authority—men and women of God—and fight by prayer and daily courage for the advancement God's kingdom of justice, kindness, and mercy.

For any woman who is struggling with the question—can I be a mother and a minister? The answer is a resounding yes. The specifics of how exactly will look different depending on the specifics of your life, but in any situation you may be in, with young children, many children, old children, or spiritual children, I pray that you would lead how God has called you to lead. I pray that you would hear the Lord's call to you. I pray that you would rise up as a leader in the city where you live—that you would be a prophetess, a judge, a ruler, and, like Deborah, a mother in whatever way the Lord calls you to be one.

---

[24] Erik Sherman, "Wealthy Kids 8 Times More Likely to Graduate College than Poor," *Forbes Magazine*, February 25, 2015.

[25] Anna Park, "School Choice Guide: Expo Park," *https://www.redeemercp.org/*. The school where we meet is the third lowest-performing elementary school in our area. See page 2.

[26] Even though California shifted the way school districts are funded in the late 1970s, from a heavily locally funded model to a more heavily state-funded model, there is still a huge gap between school quality and student achievement in under-resourced communities and wealthier communities. See "Who Pays: Where California's Public School Funds Come From," *https://ed100.org/lessons/whopays*.

[27] The *New York Times* wrote a compelling piece on this lawsuit. *New York Times*, "The Danger of Urban Oil Drilling," November 28, 2015, *https://nyti.ms/2mtX2FF*.

[28] Webb et al., "Developmental and reproductive effects of chemicals associated with unconventional oil and gas operations," *Reviews on Environmental Health* 29 (4) (2014): 307-318.

4

UNTIL THE DARKNESS BECOMES LIGHT
Robyn Barron

Robyn Barron is an African American woman originally from southern California. She moved to the Silicon Valley in 2002 to attend the University of California at Santa Cruz where she graduated with a degree in biochemistry and molecular biology. In 2010, she interned with Servant Partners in Oakland, California. Robyn lived in Oakland for four years before returning to San Jose in 2015. Currently, Robyn works in children's and women's ministries both with the Servant Partners church plant, Shalom Iglesia, and with her church of twelve years, The River Church Community. A major part of her calling has been as a bi-vocational minister, and as such Robyn has spent the past ten years working in Environmental Health & Safety as a research coordinator. In addition, she has recently completed her Masters of Public Health at San Jose State University and is planning to focus on the health of women of color and their children. Robyn has a desire to see God's holistic healing in the lives of women and children of color from disinvested communities.

I REMEMBER VERY LITTLE about my dad, but I do remember this: he and I snuggling on his bed on Saturday mornings, watching *Popeye the Sailor Man*. I looked forward to these Saturdays, just the two of us. My siblings from my mother's previous marriage had little to no desire to play with a toddler, and that was fair enough; my sister and brother were four and eleven years older than me, respectively. As an adult, I can express now what was only felt then—it meant a lot to me that anyone wanted to enter into my world and spend time with me. Then and now, I'm so glad it was him.

My dad was very tall and I was very short. Because I was always looking up at him, if I close my eyes, I can still see his long skinny legs. He always wore dress pants and thin, shiny shoes that had a slight point. It's true that he had old-fashioned sentiments about dressing respectfully, and he was also just plain old to have a toddler. In my memories, my dad smells like something I can only describe as moth balls and soap, but my mom says that he smelled like cigarettes. She is probably right, because he smoked all the time. When I was born in 1981, the world was just waking up to the health hazards of cigarettes. Family legend has it that though I don't remember his cigarette smell now, as a child I was well aware. So much so that one day I wouldn't give my dad a hug because he smelled, I said at the time, "tinky." My mom says it really hurt his feelings, and the next day he stopped smoking cold turkey. But it was too late. Less than a year after he quit smoking, we found out he had lung cancer.

And less than a year after his diagnosis, when I was three and a half, my dad died and my little heart was crushed. There were so many people who I didn't know at my dad's funeral and I resented their presence. Every time someone came by to pay their condolences to me and my family, I would turn away. Instead, I played with my cousins. At my father's funeral, I found a single yellow wildflower growing in a field of multi-colored wildflowers. While everyone else was grieving, I was captivated by this yellow flower. It was the only one. It was lonely. That yellow flower held a secret about being different and lonely, a secret about sadness that only I knew. My siblings adored him though he was not their biological father. And my dad had a developmentally disabled adult daughter from another marriage, Rose, who was mostly unaware he had lived or died. Everyone there that day had lost someone they cared about: a friend, a brother, a stepdad, a husband. That day, it felt to me, that my grief was different from everyone else's, because it was only me who had lost my father as a small child.

※

Death is like the acquaintance whom you never want to have visit your home—the one who always stays too long. Though unwelcomed, death came and it stayed. It did not leave us after the funeral. No, death swept through our house, taking my father and the emotional stability of my family. It never seemed to leave. My dad's death changed our whole family, but it was my mom who changed the most. I can still see the look on her face after the funeral. It was as if all of the life had been sucked out of her, leaving an empty shell. As an adult, I can only imagine her level of pain and devastation. As a child, I knew only my own: even though I had only physically lost one parent that day, I had emotionally lost them both.

When my father died, my mom became a single parent—something she never intended to be—times three. She threw herself into work so that she could keep a roof over our heads. She was exhausted from working full time, from being the only parent, and from her grief. She went from a nurturing mom to someone who was distant and bitter. She was angry at God for taking away her husband. But God wasn't there. We were, and usually we were in the way or doing something—whatever it was at the time—wrong.

Mom worked at the post office, which was her first job, the place where she met my father, and the job she held until she retired. She had worked there before dad died but only part time; now she needed extra hours to make ends meet. We had always had an adult at home before. The reality of her very full-time job meant that mom was either not around or she was always tired, which resulted in what felt like her being angry all the time. When my mom wasn't working, she was at home in front of the TV, trying to recover from a life and a job that sucked the life out of her and the grief and anger that seemed to know no end. She went to work every day with the sole purpose of paying the rent and utilities, feeding and clothing us. Despite her hard work, we lived paycheck to paycheck and more often than not, a few bills didn't get paid.

※

We lived in Inglewood, California, which is known to the larger world mostly by way of rap lyrics. At the time, Inglewood had a very high percentage of African Americans and a significant percentage of the population living in poverty: homeless, on welfare, and those who had jobs but were still living paycheck to paycheck, like my family. I grew up thinking that being Black and poor was a pairing like salt and pepper: they just went together. Seeing prostitutes, public drunkenness, homelessness, and death were also normal. Growing up in Inglewood taught me a lot about death, actually. I lived next to a cemetery where there was frequently a funeral for a young person killed by some form of violence. My childhood in Inglewood, though, is my own. Inglewood is bigger than my experiences; it's wider than I could have perceived then or now. It has beauty and ugliness, like any other place. While I remember it as a place full of poverty and its markers, it is not only that—even if it was that to me, in that season. All I am trying to say, is that if you only know Inglewood from reading this, you don't know Inglewood.

Growing up, God was real to me but not tangible. My family attended Sunday morning church, Bible study, prayer meetings, and so on. I could list the chapters of the New Testament, but I am not sure I had the capacity at that time to think about things like "a relationship with God." Up until the sixth grade my family attended First AME (African Methodist Episcopal Church) in South Los Angeles. As a child in the early nineties, it seemed that if you were Black and lived anywhere near Los Angeles, First AME is where you went to church. It is also the church where my parents were married and my father's funeral was held. Although the term "megachurch" hadn't yet become popular—with three packed services on Sunday mornings, it was definitely a megachurch, full of Black people. Our Black megachurch wasn't the only place in our lives full of Black people; everyone in my neighborhood was Black. Everyone I interacted with, every day, was

Black. I was Black, my family was Black, the mailman was Black, the librarian was Black, and all my teachers were Black. I'm sure there were other people who weren't Black, but honestly, I don't remember them. When we saw White people, it was usually the police or child protective services or a representative of some other kind of institution that created fear. White people were outsiders in my neighborhood, and to a large degree, not welcome in our homes. But in elementary school, I would decide to throw caution to the wind and befriend the one White girl in my class because I felt badly for her and I knew what it was to be lonely and I knew what it was to be made to feel different.

One day, when I was eight years old, I was on the bus with my sister, coming home. She rang the bell for the bus driver to stop. My sister got off first, and as I made my way down the steps and out the door, the doors slammed shut in my face, hitting my forehead. I turned to the bus driver, a White man, in confusion thinking maybe he hadn't seen that I was trying to get off the bus. The look on his face, though, wasn't one of confusion. He was amused. In that moment, I did what most Black people do with their first experience with racism: I blamed myself and thought that I had done something wrong, something he found funny. As he opened the doors for me to get off, I stepped back down the steps again. And as I was about to step out, he closed the doors in my face again, and again I hit my head. I finally realized he was doing it on purpose and felt stupid for not understanding sooner. Thankfully, the people on the bus weren't having it and told him to let me off, which he did. But that day I understood that to people outside of my neighborhood, I was different, and that my kind of different was not good.

You would think that I would have been prepared for such an interaction after the countless stories I had heard from my mom about her experiences with racism. Growing up during the Jim Crow era, racism for my mom was more than just a poor interaction with a bus driver. My mom would recount stories to me about growing up in Texas and how she had to walk on the opposite side of the street as White people. And she told me about lynchings. Sometimes I would hear her stories and think, "Man, I'm so glad that we don't have to go through that," as if her experience of racism was somehow a distant past. But she would always respond to my thoughts with a statement like, "Just because racism doesn't look the same as it did for me, doesn't mean it isn't there."

✳

After my brother went away to college, things continued to change, and not for the better. Death still hadn't left us. My brother used to walk us to and from school, and he was there with us afterwards. Sure, we were latchkey kids, but we had my brother. Probably no comfort to him, but it was to my sister and me. After he left, Mom would pick us up from school on her break and take us back to work with her. Every once in a while she'd bring us inside to help her organize things. Mostly, she would have us sit in the car until she got off work, telling us, "Sit on the horn if you get into trouble," as if the car horn would save us from danger. But I wasn't scared of any danger outside the car; what most frightened me was the loneliness. When she didn't pick us up, she either had a friend pick us up or we took the bus and then walked home.

Memories of my childhood feel like they were on a "wash, rinse, repeat" cycle. Same circumstances. Same arguments. Same problems. Different day. Our arguments mainly centered upon making Mom late or household chores. My mom was always running late, and my sister and I didn't help that. I don't have kids, but I have friends with kids and I know how hard it can be to get out the door with kids in tow. As a single person I often take for granted how easy life is to get up and go on my own timing. Mom didn't have that luxury. And she did not have time for us to be little kids.

My sister and I were expected to take care of ourselves. Only we really didn't want to. So when we took the bus and were home alone after school, one of us would call Mom when we got home. Actually, we would call her about three or four times every afternoon about nothing and everything. What was there to eat in the fridge? Could we go to the store? What time was she coming home? And of course, incessant calls about which sibling was getting on the other's nerves.

My mom started every day frustrated that she couldn't get to work on time, and she ended every day frustrated both from work and the approximately one million phone calls she got from us while we waited for her to come home. When she finally did come home, she was angry at us and at the world. Sometimes my sister and I would greet my mom at the door, not to welcome her home as much as because we were hungry and wanted her to make us something to eat.

The first time my mom called me worthless was because she had asked me to wash the dishes and I didn't do it. I was mad that my brother was gone and my older sister wasn't helping me. My sister and I were expected to keep the house clean like my brother did, but he was a lot older than us. I was nine years old and I mostly only wanted to play games and watch TV, like many of my friends were doing. So on that day, I stood in front of the sink, looking at dishes piled taller than me, and I thought about how unfair it was that I had to clean them all by myself. So I decided I wasn't going to clean them anymore, ever, no matter the consequences. My mom's first recourse was to threaten with a whooping if I didn't go wash the dishes. When she saw that I was not afraid of getting a whooping, then she did something far more effective. She used words that cut so deep I am still hurt recalling them today. She gave me a new name. Worthless.

I'm sure in some ways she regrets using those words to describe her frustration. But in that moment, she meant what she said. I was not helping her and she was frustrated after working all day and coming home to a dirty house. The truth is, she did need support and neither my sister nor I was being supportive. But that's not what she said. What she said was that if I didn't manage the household chores then I had no worth to her. It hurt. And it would happen again, and again. My faults were always clearly and sharply pointed out, my value regularly clarified as little to nothing.

As children we are taught that annoying little chant, "Sticks and stones may break my bones, but words can never hurt me." But that is a lie. Words do hurt. Only there were no outward signs, no broken bones or bruises. The heart is hidden and its wounds are secrets buried deep inside us, shaping our thoughts without our realizing it. My dad had been taken, and I had no value to my mother. I began to view the world and God with suspicion; neither could be trusted. But it wouldn't be for many years—until I went to college—that I would start to see the "broken bones" in my heart and mind.

It wouldn't be until nearly the end of a long adult process to heal those broken bones that I would understand that sometimes, my mom may have thought she was trying to help me. Sometimes my mom's impatience with me was a lashing out for all that I couldn't or didn't do for her. But sometimes there was something more complex going on.

In my family, we would always joke around with each other when someone was being overly sensitive by saying, "She's tender-headed." This is a turn of phrase probably every Black woman in the world can understand. When you get your hair plaited, it is pulled tightly in order to make beautiful, long-lasting braids. It hurts, but that is not unusual. If you wince, the hairdresser won't say, "I'm sorry," but rather, "Oh, you must be tender-headed." Like braids, my mom knew life was going to hurt, all the time. Even more than toughening me up for the general hurt of the world, African American families typically have to have very frank conversations about racism. Being from Inglewood, being Black, I was raised on the stories of racist encounters my family had experienced in the South and in California. And I had encounters of my own. We also had to talk about the police. "The talk" about how to engage with the police was short but clear in my family: "Don't run and don't fight them, even if they mistreat you." Sometimes I think my mom was preparing me for something more important than my tender feelings.

In *Between the World and Me*, Ta-Nehisi Coates explores this complicated space between preparation and abuse in his own family: "Later, I would hear it in Dad's voice—'Either I can beat him (meaning me), or the police.' Maybe that saved me. Maybe it didn't. All I know is, the violence rose from the fear like smoke from a fire, and I cannot say whether that violence, even administered in fear and love, sounded the alarm or choked us at the exit."

My relationship with my mother, her words to me and actions towards me, cut me deeply. Whether intended or not, I experienced it as abuse, not physical like Coates describes but verbal. The verbal abuse from my mother served as a warning about this world, a preparation, and at the same time it was the wounding I would need decades to heal from. My mom's experience of life was that it was cruel. Racism. Death of spouses. Single parenthood. Because I now understand that she felt she needed to prepare me for that cruel world, and because I know now, as an adult, that she did the best she could, I don't begrudge her for it.

❈

In 1991 things started to go from bad to worse. The change around the household from my brother's absence, was more than just chores and school pick-ups and drop offs. For five years before he left for college, we'd been living in survival mode, trying to recover from my father's death. My brother was the glue that held our family together. Without him around things began to spiral out of control. The years of living in survival mode, which had protected us from our deepest pain, had left each of us with our own emotional wall, which each of us would try, and largely fail, to bring down in our own ways.

I was ten years old and my sister was fourteen. Our grades started to slip. My sister started showing up drunk at school. My mom didn't know she had started drinking, and I certainly wasn't going to tell her. My mom wasn't picking us up as much anymore since my sister was in high school, so we'd go from school to her friend's house—where I would watch her smoke weed and drink beer with her friends. I didn't mind it at first. It was cool being around older kids who treated me like one of them, especially because I was in that phase of life where every part of me was growing and awkward, and I didn't feel like I belonged anywhere. But then one of the guys asked me if I wanted to have sex with him. What had felt like a game of hanging out with the big kids quickly shifted into focus: this was grown up stuff, and I was scared. My sister saw my panic and told him to go away. The next day I told my sister I didn't want to go there anymore. She said I was overreacting. We walked home separately, and our relationship was never the same. My sister had found a coping mechanism to deal with our shared trauma: alcohol and sex. She was older than me, and because of it, in some ways, her trauma was deeper.

From there I took a very different path in order to cope. I focused on the one thing I did have control over, which was school. By the time I was eleven, I had my whole life planned out: go to Spelman College, become a doctor, and then I thought I'd go ahead and cure AIDS. My plan wasn't just a way to eventually get far from home and make serious money, it also gave me something to think about, something to do, instead of feel. I realize now that I believed my plan would protect me.

At the age of twelve, I was sexually assaulted by an eighteen year old. I had heard about rape and imagined it as something that strangers did to women in dark alleys, not something that could happen in your own house by an acquaintance. I assumed it was always taken by force, not as something that would feel coercive and confusing between a young adult and a child. My sister brought a couple of guys over to our house to party with while mom was still at work. She was making out with one of them and the other, I guess, wanted some too. He kissed me, and I kissed him back. Things progressed rapidly. And I was curious about sex. But I wasn't ready for this. I didn't know what to do, so I froze. I didn't do anything. I just laid there. I said nothing, not even "no" or "stop." I finally heard the word "no" as if it came from someone else, even though it had been me. He froze and then, even though I was much smaller, I pushed him off of me. I ran and hid in the bathroom until my sister came and got me and made them leave. We told my mother and she said, "You just need to keep from showing men your vagina." My mother and sister never talked about that day, until ten years later when my sister admitted that she blamed herself for my being assaulted.

※

In high school, although there was plenty to distract me, I did not take my eyes off the prize. My sister had a baby when I was a freshman. My mom remarried and converted to Islam when I was a sophomore. I was too emotionally connected to my grandmother and my late father, who were Christians, so I did not convert and was not pressured to. I did celebrate holidays with them and attend prayer at the mosque, and I am used to hearing the "Allahu Akbar" call to prayer at 6 a.m.

Two people and a lot more change had been added to the household, but for better or worse my roles mostly stayed the same. I got into a public high school in Long Beach to which either my step-dad drove me or I took a hour and a half bus ride to every morning. I kept my head down and in my books or in school activities. The only other thing I did besides study and housework was to be a kind of second mother to my niece. And somehow, during my senior year of high school, everything seemed to be going according to plan. I had been accepted to Spelman College, as I had been planning for seven years. I graduated from high school. I knew the classes I needed to take to prepare me for medical school. I was ready.

But, all that planning and hard work aside, by the end of my first year at Spelman, I began to notice little holes in my life plan. The first was that there was no answer to the question of how I was going to pay for an out-of-state education with a single-parent income. No counselor in high school nor at Spelman sat down with me to discuss financing my education and the costs of going to a private, out-of-state school. I had been able to pay for that first year using money from a settlement (I'd been hit by a car and injured when I was four), which had been held in a trust for me until I was eighteen. But there was nothing left for the subsequent years, and Spelman didn't offer me much in loans.

The second hole was that I actually missed home. When I thought about going to college, it was more of a how-far-away-from-home-can-I-get kind of thought. I wanted to escape the poverty of my youth and the pain of home. Spelman was a great choice, far away from all of that, and as an HBCU (Historic Black College or University) there were still a lot of Black people, which I was used to and around whom I felt most comfortable. But I didn't know how much I would miss the very things and people I wanted to escape from. As much as I wanted to run away from home, I was not emotionally prepared to live away from everything and everyone I had ever known.

So I moved back to California at the end of my freshman year, spent a year at a community college, and then transferred to the University of California at Santa Cruz (UCSC) during my junior year. I chose UCSC because Stacey, my best friend from high school, was going there. That, and home was only a six-hour drive away. There was enough distance from the people and things that felt hard, but it was close enough that I could visit when I felt homesick. UCSC, I would soon realize, is probably the most culturally isolating place a Black woman from Inglewood could go. I went from a large city full of Black people to an all-Black college to what seemed to be a forest full of White people. I'm being serious about the forest; the buildings are hidden among the redwood trees. I felt like I was in exile. But in this place of exile, I would come to realize that for years I had been so busy trying to protect myself from painful experiences that I had built a wall right between me and God.

✳

I joined InterVarsity Christian Fellowship (IVCF) at UCSC because Stacey, the high school friend who had introduced me to UCSC, had gotten involved with them somehow. She was always more involved in church than I had been in high school, and she wanted to be with Christians. I had gotten to know some of her InterVarsity friends before, when I had visited her during prior years, and they were pretty fun. Culturally I felt out of place, and I wasn't yet sure how much time I wanted my spiritual life to take up. But I kept coming around. I stayed. I stayed because they had started to feel like family. They didn't look anything like me, and it was hard having to regularly be someone else's first real experience of having a Black friend. But, I guess the way I see it, in every family there is at least a little dysfunction. I knew that the people in InterVarsity were not just my friends but people I could trust. Trust was big for me—I was fearful about feeling isolated in the woods with what I perceived to be a bunch of hippies who may or may not violate my personal boundaries by touching my hair or giving me hugs.

I also think I stayed because I am that person who stays when no one else will. I have this deep sense of loyalty to people who have gained my trust, regardless of whether or not that loyalty and that staying is good for me. And I stayed because I was hopeful that things would change. When I say "things," I mean things for people like me in the fellowship. When I transferred to

UCSC, there was a huge push in InterVarsity to talk about race and care for students of color. We even started an outreach called "Exhale" that was meant to provide space for Black students in particular to come to Jesus with all of the baggage they were carrying and share one another's burdens, but without having to attend Christian functions where they were the only Black person. It was a way to provide a little respite from the cultural isolation and to connect with God in a way that was more familiar. There was a deep need for someone like me to stay in InterVarsity, and I just so happened to be able to stay. I think in some ways I stayed for those who couldn't stay. And I did understand why they might not be able to stay. I was new and excited about InterVarsity, and there were supportive, loving people willing to care and love students of color, and that helped. And graciously, God used my willingness not only to be a part of this change in the fellowship, but also to begin to show me that wall I had built up around my heart, and then to slowly dismantle it, to bring me healing.

The result of changing universities, of being sent off "into exile" in this city that was so different from what I was used to was that I felt raw and vulnerable and exposed. There is something awful about that. But in my case, it was also productive. When you are in exile, the things that feel familiar aren't there anymore to comfort you. You look for what to cling to and school was no longer enough. It is only in exile where you start to see the ways you have relied on other things instead of God. And so I turned to God in a new way. Not in a "go to church" way, but in a way of trying to know and be known by God. And by people. And even though being in my Christian fellowship was uncomfortable in many ways, the fact that we were openly and actively talking—about race and our families and our pain—gave me space to finally admit that I had, perhaps, a little bit of that.

✳

I remember the first time I heard the phrase "incarnational ministry." I had just transferred to UCSC and was at a large group meeting where someone was preaching. Incarnational ministry. It was a very odd term, really. When it was explained to me, I basically heard it as, "They want me to spend time with people in their own space," which seemed to me not to need a special term like incarnational ministry. Coming from a culture that is very relational and communal, I felt like incarnational ministry was just some fancy term White people needed in order to be normal and just hang out.

Fast forward to the next year. I was a Bible study leader and I was going to move off campus. It was cheaper than living on campus, and money was always scarce. I sat down with the staff member who was overseeing the ministry and told him I needed to move off campus. Because of the incarnational ministry approach, he said that in order to continue to be a leader I had to live on campus, alongside the people we wanted to reach out to. I was annoyed. Being a leader meant I had to sacrifice something that would have been not only more convenient for me, but more financially responsible. From that moment on, I began to question this whole concept of incarnational ministry because it was rubbing up against my sense of what I felt relationships should be, which is more natural and convenient.

To this day, I feel mixed. Being with people in their space is what Jesus did, and people are comfortable engaging on campus. I get that. The call for me to stay on campus was also an important leadership lesson. It is nearly impossible to truly lead and minister without any kind of sacrifice. I learned early on: to love well is costly. But because campus living is so much more expensive, it puts students of poorer backgrounds (mostly, but not only, students of color) in a difficult position: either accrue more debt or leave leadership.

Most of the student leaders came from a different cultural background than I did; they were learning to identify with "the rich young ruler" in Mark 10. Let me tell you about him in my own words:

The Rich Young Ruler comes up to Jesus and asks how he can inherit eternal life. Jesus replies with the two most important commandments and the young guy is basically like "cool, been doing that since kindergarten." And then Jesus was like "oh, but one more thing," and He tells him to go and sell everything he has, give it to the poor, and then he can be a part of Jesus's crew. The Rich Young Ruler walks away so distraught he wants to tear out his bowels. He felt he'd done everything right to follow God's commandments. But when he was asked to give his whole life over to the commandments and to sell everything he had, only having and loving one master ("love the Lord your God...") and to give everything to the poor ("and love your neighbor as yourself") and then, to follow Him, the Rich Young Ruler went away sad. The end.

The Rich Young Ruler was a regular in the preaching topics for InterVarsity and other social justice-minded evangelical communities. And with good reason, the love of money is a problem. It is a big problem. It is a problem for White students and Asian students and Black students and Latino students—it is a problem for everyone. And yet, this passage is spoken to one with privilege and power who is asked to give it away—both to give up a false idol of status and station and to love the poor.

Students who are not coming from positions of power really need a more fitting and useful type of teaching or vision. I wish I had received teaching that addressed questions like: When I do finally have resources, what do I do with those? How do I get out of debt and make wise financial decisions? How do I know when to sacrifice and when to invest in my financial stability? Financial stability was so lacking for me and so many people like me. What if we were taught how to be stable while not loving money, how to be generous without regularly overdrawing our accounts? I hope "The Rich Young Ruler" story is preached and preached with conviction until every last one of us no longer needs to hear it. But the passage about money that really moves me is the rich man and Lazarus from Luke 16:19-31.

I first heard it during a summer mission with the Los Angeles Urban Project. I'd heard Kevin Blue preach before, but this sermon was by far the most memorable—like my mouth dropped open and stayed open, from beginning to end. Let me just tell you the story in my own words:

There was a really rich guy who had everything: designer clothes, real jewelry, a Mercedes Benz, and a nice gated house to keep away any unwelcome visitors. Well, this very poor man, Lazarus, sat in front of his gate every day. He was dirty, probably diseased, and covered with sores that local street dogs would lick. He would dream of the rich man's leftovers, the stuff he threw away or put in his compost bin. Eventually Lazarus died and angels carried him to Abraham's side. Abraham is the spiritual father of the Jewish people, so he welcomed Lazarus home to heaven. The rich man also died, had a nice burial. But he doesn't end up by Abraham's side but in Hades—hell. The rich man looks up into the heavens from his torment and sees Abraham and Lazarus. He is in so much agony he asks Abraham to have Lazarus just dip his finger in water and send him down to give him some relief. But Abraham had to inform that rich man that no one crosses between the worlds. And remind him that he had every good thing while he was alive. As for Lazarus, he suffered and the rich man didn't do one single thing to help him. So now, he's with Abraham.

Interestingly, the rich man didn't go to hell because he was rich, but rather because he ignored Lazarus's cries for help. Likewise, the rich man would now be ignored in his crying out for help. To ignore the poor comes with clear consequences, and Jesus cares about the poor—this passage is a call to address poverty. It's both challenging and invitational. It says that addressing poverty is what it means to be a Christ follower. It's not warm and fuzzy, but it is real talk.

The Los Angeles Urban Project (LAUP) is a six-week internship for college students to explore what it could look like to do incarnational ministry among the urban poor. I participated in LAUP in 2004, just before my last year of college. It was my first missions experience outside of campus. It was also the first time I noticed I was living in "survival mode."

At our ministry site, we often heard gunshots, which triggered most of my teammates. Which is a reasonable reaction. Gunshots are scary. But I wasn't scared. It felt normal to me, and it took a lot more to rattle me. Near the end of the internship, my teammates and I were on our way to a meeting when we drove by a Black man who had seemingly just been shot. There were no paramedics or police around, but there were lots of people on their phones making calls. We wanted to stop and help, yet there was nothing we could really do; we would have been in the way. The man may have lived, but from what I saw, he was either already dead or on his way. And that did it. That rattled me: watching a Black man bleeding out on the streets of Los Angeles.

Yet I was numb. I didn't want to be numb, and I was disturbed by my reaction. I wanted to be normal and have a normal reaction to this scene. Crying for instance. But my well-honed survival mode skills had protected me from feeling pain for years, and it protected me from this too. I wanted to care, but my mind wouldn't let me. At some point in life I learned to survive by never again feeling helpless. When there wasn't any food in the house, I would scrounge around for a can of tuna. When my student loans weren't enough, I got a job tutoring other students in calculus. I always kept moving, and I never again felt helpless. If anything made me feel helpless, I chose not to care about those things.

Of course my teammates wanted to process with me about the man and the blood, but I couldn't find the words to express how I was feeling. I think my lack of reaction was pretty uncomfortable for them. They were all Asian American, and I just didn't have the energy to interpret for them what was going on for me. The last two weeks of that summer internship were probably the hardest for me because I was fighting with myself to go ahead and actually feel the brokenness I was experiencing—my own and the city's. The voice of never again somehow didn't make sense to me anymore. I wanted to feel, to care.

When you walk in numbness, you close yourself off from feeling not just your own pain but also the pain of others. When you mourn you are saying, "I care." Caring about something makes you feel things that may or may not be in your control. When I saw that man bleeding out on the street, I felt so helpless. I felt vulnerable. I knew I needed God to help me sort it all out, but I couldn't imagine letting go control of the floodgate of feelings I had kept closed to help me survive. So God gave me a word from the beatitudes to carry with me from then on: "Blessed are those who mourn, for they will be comforted" (Matthew 5:4, ESV).

❖

My last year at UCSC was the most transformational. It was the year I got my driver's license (even though I'd never had a car to drive, it seemed like an important thing to have at my age). I was beginning to stretch myself. Beginning to change the narrative of how I viewed God and life. That year was also the year I first went to Urbana, a huge missions conference that InterVarsity Christian Fellowship puts on every three years.

The world of missions was so strange to me. Growing up, my church taught that missions was giving food out to the homeless—not getting a passport and traveling the world, Bible in hand. I think in some way, by choosing to attend Urbana, I was hoping that I would find a sense of belonging. I was trying to merge my ethnic identity as a Black woman with this very White and Asian Christian world I had found myself in. This missional life that was being discussed, which caused people with fairly educated backgrounds to leave everything behind and go. But what could I leave behind when I felt like I had very little to begin with? To me, they had found a sense of purpose and belonging in life that I had not. I wanted to find out how to get where they were. I wanted to find that piece that I seemed to be missing.

So even though I had no money to go, and even though I really had no interest in "missions," I had one reason to go to Urbana: all my friends were going. To ensure I wouldn't be totally uncomfortable, I made a deal with the other Black students in my region that we'd all go together. Safety in numbers. And the staff workers and others in our fellowship raised enough money for anyone to go who wanted to go. So I joined the 20,000 other people there learning about faith, about mission, about Jesus.

There are only two moments at Urbana that I remember in crisp detail. Both spoke to my racial and Christian identities, in different ways, and both really affected me. There was a session on Black people in missions. I needed to know that being missional did not mean I needed to be White. That I belonged in this world of being incarnational and that I could bring myself as God made me. I was pretty excited to go and learn about how to bring these parts of myself together. But what I remember most is being in a room full of Black people and singing, "I Love You Lord." There was no projector, no lyrics handout; everyone knew the words. None of the other workshop sessions I went to involved singing, but then again none of the sessions I went to involved a room full of Black people. I closed my eyes and stopped singing, so that I could hear everyone else singing together. The zeal of my college faith with the cultural connection of the AME church of my youth were present all at once. A little bit of heaven.

The other session that affected me deeply was in the main hall, with the whole group of Urbana attendees. A young White woman who had been praying for the conference got on stage and called us to submit to God's direction in our lives. She said, "There is a throne, and you need to get off it and let the King of Glory reign." Those were the words that would forever change my course in life. Not just in that my heart was shifted towards being incarnational. But also that part of the wall between God and me began to crumble. For many years, I had been the one in charge of my life. My ability to control my feelings and my future were my only protection. I was the one on the throne. I'd had to be, but now I could see that it might be time to ask what it would be like for God to have control and reign in my life.

I didn't know it then, but I had been living a life where I thought I told God what I wanted to do in life and I expected Him to just fall in line. I felt like I was being self-sufficient and ambitious by making my own plans. I was surviving. The lie I was believing was that God didn't want me to be successful and that I needed to make my own success. God's word says that He desires to give His children good gifts, and that He withholds nothing from us (Matthew 7:11). Even though I wanted to believe that God wanted to give me good gifts, it was really hard to believe that truth because everything around me growing up had felt so different from that. Through the media, encounters with White people, growing up in Inglewood, and even from various teachers, I had learned that because I was Black, I had very little power. Letting go of the little I felt I had control over was an extremely painful prospect.

It was painful for me to hear this woman—this White woman—call out my self-reliance and offer me a rightful perspective. She was calling out everyone, but it felt like she was speaking directly to me. I can see now that over the preceding years, while "in exile" at UCSC where I'd realized I had this wall between God and me, that God had been slowly tilling the soil of my heart for this word. I said yes to Jesus sitting on the throne of my life that day, and instead of pursuing my own plans, I started to ask God what His plan was.

As the wall between God and me began to crumble, things in my life started becoming clearer. One of the things that I started to see was that I didn't know what it meant to trust a loving heavenly Father when I still felt abandoned by my earthly father. This realization did not lead to resolution; I would wrestle with it for a long time. The first step to asking God about His plan was to let go of my own plan, so I could listen for His call on my life. My plan since I was a little girl, as I've shared, was to be a doctor. And there is nothing wrong with being a doctor. In fact, I think we need more doctors of color. But in the unravelling after that word at Urbana, I realized that for me, being a doctor wasn't a passion; it wasn't about healing the sick. It was about control. A future of medical school and practicing medicine weren't bad, but it had a grip on me that didn't feel right. I had to let it go. I opened my hands. It was terrifying.

As a result, my mom stopped talking to me for a year. In her eyes, I was throwing away the future she had worked day and night for me to achieve. Yes, I was paying for college myself (on loans), but she had—during a season of great agony—kept a roof over my head, clothes on my back, and food in my mouth. She had sacrificed so much for me. This was how she loved me, even if all of these things exhausted her to the point she couldn't love me in the way my tender heart wanted. My mom was angry that all her hard work and all my hard work seemed to be coming to nothing. I also think she felt a little betrayed. All this striving wasn't just so that I'd be successful; it was so that I would have a way out of Inglewood. Out of poverty. All the striving wasn't just so that she could be proud of me; it wasn't just for a "better future"; it was, as she saw it, for any future. In her eyes, I had squandered the gift of her hard work. Things would stay broken between us for a while. And the way I left UCSC didn't help.

Although I had surrendered to a complete life change, it was clear that there was something deeper God wanted to do, which at the time I couldn't figure out. I asked God for a word of knowledge, and I simply heard the word, "healing." This was not the word I wanted. It was not a word

I understood. I was so frustrated with God and with my life. I was so confused about the future. I was so messed up and jumbled up that I didn't have the energy to finish my exit requirement for my biochemistry major. So, I just left. After years of hard work and heartache, I didn't even have my actual degree as proof.

⁜

I didn't go very far. An hour away. San Jose. I told myself that I would come here, find a job and just work, while I figured out what "healing" meant. I started therapy to help me figure out what this deeper work was that God wanted to do in me. The first time I showed up for a counseling session I sat down and told my therapist that I was going to get all of my healing done in a year, because I wasn't trying to spend hella money just to sit and talk to someone. Hmm. Well, five years later I was still in therapy, but at least I had made peace with the process. I also added a class at my church on healing and found a spiritual director. Basically, I used every tool available to me to help unpack the baggage I had been carrying with me.

I felt a lot of shame about where I was in life. I didn't have any significant accomplishments, I wasn't happy with my career (mostly because I just had a "job," not a career per se), and most of my ministry experiences hadn't been life-changing. I wasn't sure where God was leading me either. Past, present, and future all felt bleak.

The more I asked God what He wanted me to do with my life, the more it seemed He asked me what I wanted to do. I hated it. I hate the question, "What do you want?" whether it is about what I wanted for dinner or about what I wanted to do with my life. It was just too much work to push against a voice inside my head that said, "Your needs and desires don't matter." It was a lot of work to find and hear the voice in me that wanted to say, "I need this" or "I want this." Day after day, year after year, God was saying to me, "You are important and you can do whatever you want to do and be whomever you want to be." Like proud parents who encourage their children to dream big, God wanted me to choose who I wanted to be. This was as terrifying to me as when I gave my prior plans for medical school into His hands.

I was so afraid of choosing the wrong thing. I was so afraid of failing. I was paralyzed with fear. I prayed, and my friends prayed for me; God began tearing down the lies. God opened opportunities for me to take risks and do something that brought me out of my paralysis. God uses our brokenness to teach us how to walk with Him. That is not to say that brokenness left unchecked is helpful, but that you can and will be used by God even as you struggle to find healing. Going to UCSC, then LAUP, then Urbana had been risks that helped me start this healing journey. But there was still more.

I took the risk of dealing with the complication of finishing the exit requirement for my degree. I took the risk to begin asking myself if I wanted to go to medical school or to school to be a physician's assistant or a nurse or some other kind of medical professional. I let myself revisit it, not as a way out or to prove my worth or to escape, but as a passion, as a vocation. I continued to be prayed into new risks, ministry risks, and these continued to open me: I went to Malawi with my church, I went to India, and I did a bi-vocational urban internship in Oakland with Servant Partners. God was making me stronger with each risk I took. I took a risk to move back to San Jose to be a part of a Spanish-speaking church plant with Servant Partners when my Spanish was at a kindergarten level. It has been a lot of risk and change and wall-breaking and tearing down of lies. But it has all been important.

Each risk with God helped break the lie that my life had no value and helped me see where God was calling me—little by little, year by year. I used to think I needed to wait until Jesus healed me to figure out my next steps, as if there would be a big event—a double rainbow or something—as I kept taking risks with God and community. But the double rainbow never came. Instead, God called me into healing while being a servant to others whose needs were greater than my own. Then one day, I was out walking with my spiritual director, which is my favorite way to process life. I told her that I felt like something had shifted for me, and that it had shifted without me being aware of it. I said I was maybe starting to feel..."healed." She smiled. Then she said, "We often can't see healing coming or perceive it while it's happening; it's usually something we notice in the rear-view mirror." And that has been pretty much my experience.

My story isn't a happily ever after story. But rather, a faith over fear type of story. It was not an overnight process nor a year-long process. It has been a fifteen-year process. Step by step, God walked/ran/sat with me in my darkness because even the dark is as light to Him. God pursued me into my darkness and sat with me until I was ready to come out. And here I am.

Three years ago, I decided to apply to a Master of Public Health program. I was tired of feeling like nothing was being done about the gun violence in our San Jose neighborhood, and gun violence is a public health issue. I got into the program and dove into all kinds of research about public health in disinvested communities. After about a year of my program, I came across data about the maternal mortality rate for Black mothers and I was disturbed. It was then that I decided not to stop when I finish my master's degree, but to go ahead and apply for a PhD program in public health. It's a clear path; it's a big degree. But it feels different from my previous ambition for medical school. These degrees are not something I want just to give me a ticket out of a place I don't want to be, and they are not for proof that my life has value—that I am not worthless. Instead, I am motivated to make a difference about things I really care about.

Unpacking the lies lodged in my heart from a broken world is hard. The alternative, carrying their weight, is far worse. For me, though difficult, it has been a strengthening process for my soul and it has clarified my purpose. My purpose isn't to get out and stay out of poverty. And I don't have anything to be afraid of. I don't need to fear that my life has no value. I don't need to fear that the burden of poverty is too great. This time the purpose is between God and me. And on my clearest day, I truly believe in this purpose and that He has good things for me.

5

EMMANUEL, GOD WITH US
Teresa Ku-Borden

Teresa began her post-college journey as an intern with Servant Partners in South Los Angeles, and has been affiliated with Servant Partners for the past 13 years. She has been involved with New Life Community Church in Lincoln Heights, a Servant Partners site, since its inception. She received her M.D. in 2010 and currently works as a family physician, living and working in the vibrant community of East Los Angeles in California. One of her passions is taking care of expectant mothers, delivering their babies and helping them transition into motherhood, something her own motherhood journey has enriched. She enjoys experiencing and creating mixed media art, trying new vegetarian recipes, napping with her babies, and on most days, learning how to stay present and peace-filled as a working mother of two.

THE WEEK I BECAME a mother was the most beautiful and terrifying week of my life. On my son's second day of life, my husband and I were told that he was jaundiced—which can be quite normal and temporary. However, we learned that it was a rare form of jaundice, possibly caused by a congenital defect of the liver. We stayed in the hospital for a week of monitoring, blood tests in the morning and afternoon, and a nuclear scan, where a radioactive solution was injected into my son's tiny veins to see if bile would flow correctly, from his liver into his small bowel.

One early morning while my son was still hospitalized, just days after I had given birth, he was getting his blood drawn. The phlebotomist squeezed his heel so the drops of blood would fill the collection tube. I was shaken as I watched his tiny arms flail. Muffled by the clear incubator walls, his screams shattered my heart. My tears fell onto the thick plastic incubator—thud, thud—like heavy droplets of rain falling on a windshield. All I wanted to do was hold him and take away all of his pain.

❋

Seven years before having a child, my husband Ryan and I lived in a small, mostly Latino community in Lincoln Heights, just a few miles northwest of East Los Angeles. This was a far cry from the wealthy suburban neighborhoods where my husband and I had grown up; he was from Orange County, and I was raised in the San Francisco Bay Area. Neither of us would have thought that we would make East Los Angeles our home while we were college students. But during various scripture studies led by our college Christian fellowships, and especially during an urban ministry project in Los Angeles, our visions and plans for our lives began to shift. We were inspired by ministers and followers of Jesus who relocated from more comfortable middle- and upper-middle class communities into neighborhoods of poverty, to live in solidarity with people who were different from them. We had the same hope and intention. I joined the Servant Partners internship in South Los Angeles—a two-year domestic immersion experience designed for young adults who wanted to explore full-time ministry in an urban setting. Ryan and I began dating, and after my internship we became part of a church-planting team in Lincoln Heights. Ryan started the high school ministry, and I started the path to becoming a physician.

When I moved to Lincoln Heights, I was in medical school, doing my clinical rotations at the general hospital that was just over a mile from where I lived. I learned the technical and scientific aspects of being a doctor in medical school; it also introduced me to the power behind the white coat. I remember the first time I set foot into the large, gleaming cement tower of LA County-USC Medical Center, a bulwark in the geographic and emotional architecture of Northeast Los Angeles. It was bustling with people from all walks of life: patients and families from the local community, hospital staff dressed in uniform, teams of doctors in their long white coats all waiting for the same elevators. After taking care of patients who had the rarest of diseases and the most brutal of injuries, I understood why many doctors and researchers were drawn to this place—there was so much to learn and see. During this time, I also witnessed how the medical community saw and treated the local community. While the medical care was usually excellent and up to exacting standards, and many of the physicians genuinely wanted to help this underserved community, I couldn't help but notice the cultural misunderstandings, the language barriers, and the emotional distance created by decades of education and training.

I was one of very few medical students who resided in the neighborhood surrounding the hospital. I got to know my neighbors, practiced my Spanish, and helped out with the youth ministry while I studied medicine. I felt that I was putting into practice what I learned in my urban internship. Ryan was coaching a local high school basketball team, and he had gotten to know some teen-age neighbors as well. He invited these boys over to his apartment for a weekly time of dinner and Bible study, and I would sometimes cook for them. But that group never really grew in the way we had hoped.

Then an opportunity arose to take some of the high school football players to a camp in Arizona, and we saw it as a chance to invest in the youth who were part of the football team. After going together to one player's home to ask his mother for permission to take her son on a road trip, we felt our own naïveté as she questioned us, "Who are you? And why should I trust you to take my son to another state?" My White boyfriend was going to drive three teenagers he barely knew to Arizona to play a sport he had never played. While they had a good time at the camp, these young men didn't stick around.

A few years later, after Ryan and I were married, the head pastor of our church plant became the JV football coach, and some of his players started coming to the youth group, and they brought their group of friends. We got to know these students as they began attending the youth group regularly, and we tried to invest in them in the best way we knew how.

We became this peculiar couple, clearly not from the local community, who took our new friends out to Thai food and frozen yogurt. We would chat about family, school, friends, boyfriends, and girlfriends. Our youth opened their hearts and their lives to us, and trusted us with some of their deepest wounds and darkest secrets. We cried and prayed with them, and we shared our own stories of pain. We invited them into relationships with Jesus, and did our best to nurture any spiritual hunger we encountered. Soon many from this group of teenagers began to give their lives to Jesus, and became leaders among their peers. We felt a sense of purpose, as twenty-something newlyweds, who were seeking to live out what we understood of God's calling on our lives. We experienced this "sweet spot" in ministry, where our passions and efforts seemed to perfectly align with the needs of those we were ministering to. But my medical training would soon require that we move.

Just a few months prior to moving, we took these high school students on a church retreat. After years of students who came and went, there was finally a consistent group who trusted us enough to spend a weekend with us in the mountains, studying about Jesus's life and teachings together. Some of them even invited their friends. On the two-hour drive, I learned even more about their lives, their friends and family, their dreams and aspirations. From the drive up, to acting out the scenes from the Scripture passages we were studying, to the night when many of our new friends gave their lives to Jesus, the weekend was filled with newfound faith and hope. We extended the invitation for anyone to follow Jesus who wanted to, and I witnessed many genuine decisions to allow Jesus into their hearts and lives. It was an honor to pray with some of them, all of us shedding tears, a mix of grief and joy and great hope for the future. It was as if the Lord was finally hearing our prayers after years of failed ministry and uninterested people. These were new disciples of Jesus, only fifteen and sixteen years old, ready to live out the kingdom, inviting their families, significant others, and friends from school to join them on their journey in following Jesus.

A leadership training team for youth had formed and my husband was meeting with these youth regularly for Scripture study, intercessory prayer, discussions about character development, and inner healing prayer. It was a beautiful picture of mutual trust, a hunger in them to learn and grow, and an eagerness in us to invest and teach.

Just one month after this group had formed, I graduated from medical school. We were reluctant to leave for my upcoming medical residency, as we were finally beginning to experience the first fruits of a beautiful ministry—it was difficult for us to say goodbye to this group of hungry and humble students. But Ryan and I had also dreamed of serving overseas, and a residency I'd been accepted into fifty miles north of Los Angeles was the best place to receive the kind of training and skills I would need to practice medicine internationally. So we packed up to move to this sprawling beach town.

It was during my residency that I learned not just the practice of medicine, but what it means to be a physician. I had decided to go into family medicine, a specialty where I could be on the front lines and learn how to treat every type of patient who walked through the door: young, old, rich, poor, male, female, pregnant, breastfeeding, ones with chronic illness, others with an acute injury, the dying, and the newly birthed. I discovered my capabilities and my limitations, the art of when to treat and when I needed to consult the expertise of a specialist. I worked at a county hospital and clinic, where most of my patients had government-subsidized insurance (Medicaid), and the Lord solidified my passion, calling, and purpose as a physician—to provide the best care to the patients who needed it the most.

After four years of residency and my fellowship, we discerned with close friends about where to go next. We felt called to eventually return to our community in East Los Angeles before going overseas. While I was finishing residency, my husband had been working on a master's degree in business, and there were some opportunities to work in this community to start local businesses. We would also have the opportunity to begin raising a family: I was now pregnant, and we decided to remain for the time being where I had done my residency. Then we would move back to East LA after the baby was born. We planned to pick up where we had left off five years earlier, to live and raise our child in this community that we loved, until a path to serve overseas opened. Jesus had walked with me in my journey thus far, through the difficult and joy-filled times in ministry and in my development as a physician, and I looked forward to the next chapter of my life with hopeful anticipation.

I look back now on those well-thought-out, idyllic plans, and I smile wistfully to myself. I had based all those plans and decisions on my ideals and assumptions—that our son would be healthy, that we would take him along to do ministry with us, that the community we left would receive us and continue to feel like family, that we would invest in the same relationships we had five years prior—and that our lives would continue to have the same sense of calling, purpose, and fulfillment.

❉

But our son was not healthy. And it was not a normal case of jaundice. As a physician, I knew the medical world well, but now I was on the other side of it, as a parent of a very ill child. I knew the medical lingo, all the worst complications, and even most of the doctors, who were once my teachers. But any power I had from knowing the disease process, navigating the system of hospitals, and moving with ease up the hierarchy of medicine was suddenly stripped away. I was not in control anymore. I was at the mercy of the healthcare team trying to take care of my son. I was suddenly a stranger in this world I had once lived in and breathed and loved.

I couldn't heal this baby I desperately loved. As a new mother, I was learning my baby's cries and facial expressions, trying different breastfeeding positions, and doing loads of laundry for spit-up and poop accidents. At the same time, I was also crying on the phone with our doctor, anxiously waiting for results, shielding myself from the worst-case scenarios that I knew so well. The first six weeks of my son's life were filled with doctor visits, twice-weekly blood draws, two nuclear scans, a liver biopsy, and finally, a major life-saving surgery. Where was Jesus, the one who had walked with us through the trials of ministry and residency? The difficulties of getting the youth group to grow, and even the twenty-four-hour shifts in the intensive care unit caring for dying patients, paled in comparison to the heartbreak we were experiencing.

Adam was just five weeks old when I handed his little nine-pound body to the anesthesiologist, surrendering my firstborn to the surgeon who would spend just under nine hours dissecting scar tissue off of the tiny veins and arteries of his liver to save his life. He was diagnosed with biliary atresia, a congenital defect of the liver, born with a non-functioning, withered common bile duct. Without this important conduit, bile remained trapped in his liver, causing inflammation and scarring. The life-saving surgery, called the Kasai procedure, would create an artificial bile duct to drain the caustic bile out of his liver. Although the surgery would save his life, the disease was progressive. The bile was draining, but we were told this disease would continue to spread, obliterating the smaller bile ducts in his liver.

Even after the surgery, we were consumed with more appointments and blood draws, and a continued uncertainty remained. We didn't know what complications my son would endure from the surgery he'd just had. We were told that 75 percent of the children who had a successful Kasai would need a liver transplant by age twenty-one. To us, those were pretty miserable odds. We had no idea what our lives would like look like having a child with significant health needs. We didn't know how long he would remain healthy before his liver would fail and he would need a transplant. We were encouraged to live normal lives—but how could we? We straddled two worlds, one foot still trying to grasp the reality that our son was still sick, and the other foot pulling us forward, to get us to move on. We also needed income and health insurance as my pregnancy leave was coming to an end, so when he was nine weeks old, I went back to work.

In the middle of the night after my second day back, Adam woke up with a high fever, and we went to the emergency room for the first time in his life. It turned out to be only a virus, but we were told by doctors that this could be our new normal, with hospital visits and blood draws for even the slightest fever. The part of the intestine that was draining bile out of his liver also allowed gut bacteria to ascend into the liver, so he was always at risk for liver infections—a complication of the surgery. Just like every other parent I knew, the first few months of caring for an infant were a rollercoaster of exhaustion and emotion. And while we were on this roller coaster, we were also juggling our baby's severe illness and all of the tasks and complications associated with it.

There is no way to convey the depth of anguish and fear and exhaustion we felt alongside the joy of knowing and holding our baby. We experienced the grace of God through a smooth surgery and recovery, but we were also plagued by fear of the next infection or complication. Although we were consumed with our son's needs, we wanted to be people of our word, and honor what we had heard in prayer, to somehow continue to be a part of our East LA community, and a part of our little but growing neighborhood church. We decided to continue in what we had set out to do before our son's diagnosis.

We moved back when our son was four months old—a few months later than planned, because his liver had become infected. Ryan, with his business degree, hoped to help people in our neighborhood start their own businesses. I would work part-time as a family physician at a local hospital and clinic. And we would both try to figure out what it meant to be parents of a medically fragile child.

⌗

When we returned to our community, and the small urban church we had helped to start, we were warmly welcomed back. Yet people were busy, relationships had changed, and we soon realized that we couldn't pick up where we had left off. We were strangers in a familiar place, uncomfortable in the place we had thought of as home. We quickly realized we had no capacity to do any ministry, to serve in the ways we had before and wanted to do now.

We ourselves needed significant support and help to create some sort of stability as new parents of this medically fragile child, who was hospitalized nine times in the first eighteen months life. He would be in the hospital for a liver infection one week, any basic routine completely disrupted, and we would be back in the emergency room a few days after we were discharged. We had never felt more isolated and alone. We were paralyzed by the trauma of having a very sick child, and we were exhausted. Was the Lord forgetting how hard I worked, how healthy I tried to be during my pregnancy? Had he forgotten how faithful my husband and I had been to the ministry? The sacrifices we'd made? The ideals and assumptions I had about following Jesus as a naive twenty-five-year-old had completely broken down.

Slowly, a small group of people from our church started gathering around us in support. These were a mix of friends whom we had led in the youth group and were now young adults at our church, as well as friends who had relocated to do ministry in the community. They prayed with us, texted us, cooked meals for us, visited us in the hospital, and came over to spend time with us. Instead of ministering, we were now the ones being ministered to. When we had no energy to even think about ministry in our community, the community came to us. And as we began to open up about our suffering in this season, our friends—especially the youth we had invested in—began to open up about theirs. These young people had experienced more than their fair share of suffering, and when we shared our story with them, they had the capacity to connect with us in ours.

We listened to their pain, this time from a different place than we had ten years prior. They also shared from a place more honest and raw. They not only shared stories of trauma from childhood and of anger about the inequalities in their education and upbringing, but they also began to share their frustration and bitterness toward Ryan and me, when we had mentored them as teenagers. To be entrusted with their honest reflections about that time in ministry was a privilege and a devastation. Even as it was painful to hear, especially in this difficult season, we knew it was a sacred gift to be invited into these depths.

Our friends felt that we had operated out of a project mentality, rather than from a genuine desire to get to know them as people, as though we were using their community and doing ministry there to feel better about ourselves. Some of them shared that they were asked to be vulnerable, sharing their entire lives and brokenness with those of us who were leaders, before they were ready. Others felt that the kind of leadership that was modeled to them did not culturally resonate. Some local leaders felt that they were not trusted with the responsibility of leading others because of past or current failures, and they felt that they were treated differently from those who had relocated into the community. It became clear to us that even as we had earnestly tried to serve our young adult friends, there had been times when we had also hurt them deeply.

Despite our best intentions, we learned from our friends that the power dynamics within the church, between those of us who had relocated into the community and those from the local community, mirrored some of the damaging power dynamics in the broader political, social, and economic arenas in this very resource-poor neighborhood where we lived. While many in our church from the local community did not express these same concerns, Ryan and I felt led to deeply engage with what our young friends were telling us. If the pain of our son's condition and prognosis was real to us, their pain was just as sharply felt. We needed to take responsibility for how our leadership failures hurt them. We needed to reflect on ministry itself, continuing the process of learning how to serve in ways that were helpful and not hurtful.

Instead of holding onto our earlier roles as mentors—which we simply could not have done because our lack of capacity—we had to surrender to this season and to accept the needs and limitations that arose from our own pain, especially to be able to engage rightly with the pain of others. We learned early on that we could not walk this journey of chronic illness alone. We invited friends and acquaintances, any who would come, into our suffering, to pray for us when we didn't have anything left in us to pray, to hope for us when our son kept being hospitalized, to cry out to God when we felt abandoned by Him. There were those who didn't know how to respond and they kept their distance. There were those who would tell us, "Everything will be okay," or "God has a reason for this," which didn't comfort us. We learned that many of our friends didn't know how to engage or be present with us during this season, and that easy answers were often ways to cope with deep suffering or pain.

Even though our friends in the neighborhood community hadn't experienced the same pain of a desperately sick child, they knew suffering, they knew injustice, and they knew the trauma of having the unexpected and undeserved happen to them—over and over again. They knew that catch-phrases didn't comfort. They were not afraid of our suffering, because they had experienced it themselves.

Just by being there, their knowing presence and commitment to prayer brought us comfort and connection. In baring our messy, chaotic lives to our friends, we were invited into a deeper, more complex window into their hearts. Although our pain was rooted in different sources, when all was said and done, it was still pain that was deep and raw and unfair and unjust. Somehow, in a divine way, out of this pain arose a kindred connection, and an unexpected solidarity between us.

Among those in the humanitarian field, there is an oft-quoted saying by Lilia Watson, an indigenous Australian artist and activist: "If you have come here to help me, you are wasting your time. But if you have come because your liberation is bound up with mine, then let us work together." I felt that I was beginning to experience the beauty and truth of this statement. It turned my definition of ministry upside down. Ministry was not about helping people or praying with platitudes; rather, serving others in the name of Jesus required a deeper and more difficult work of mutual respect and transformation.

I cannot help but wonder if many of the young friends we had mentored also felt betrayed and abandoned, as we had felt when we found out our newborn son was sick. Some expressed that they'd rather not interact with us while they processed their pain and their experience under our leadership, however formal or informal our roles had been.

Our own mentors had taught us to reconcile and clear things up before the conflict spiraled into something bigger and messier. If there was something bothering us or if we were holding a grudge against someone, we were encouraged to initiate a conversation in which we would apologize and ask for forgiveness if necessary. This was helpful most of the time, and probably saved many tears and outbursts that would have been disproportionate to the actual conflict. However, pain that fractures the core of our identities, arising from circumstances completely out of our control, cannot be processed quickly, or healed in a single conversation or prayer time. In a similar way, pain that results from layers of systemic injustice also needs time and space. It sometimes needs to take place away from those we once trusted.

I have learned that the journey of chronic illness is much like the journey in the fight for justice, shalom, and honest relationships across cultures and socioeconomic classes. The road is long and difficult. On the hardest days, I feel like Peter and John in Mark 10, crying out to Jesus, in desperation, "We have left everything to follow you!" They had nowhere else to go, no one else to follow.

Similarly, I often feel like I have no choice but to stay in the fight—I haven't traveled this far only to give up. When my child is sick and in pain from being poked and prodded in the emergency room, I have no choice but to hold him tightly, tell him, "Mama is here," and listen to his screams and cries. When there is conflict or misunderstanding with the few friends who have chosen to stay around and be present with me during my suffering, I am willing to stay in it, to wait, and try to have the difficult conversations, because these friends have sat with me in my pain. Sometimes I make blundering mistakes and react out of emotion and desperation. Other times I relish the deep work that God is doing in me and in my friendships. In both journeys, there are obstacles and setbacks, small victories and defeats, times when hopes are high, and moments that draw us back into despair.

Our friends had trusted us enough to share their own stories of pain. When we listened to them, we felt a mixture of emotions. The way we learned how to do ministry seemed to have backfired, causing more pain and distrust. I began to question my role and calling in this ministry context. Had all of our "hard work" been for nothing?

Did we even belong here? How could God have been in all of this?

I began to wonder if engaging in this kind of cross-cultural, cross-class ministry was worth the cost—the inner turmoil, the questions, the collision and intersection of my identities as mother, physician, and Chinese-American woman, causing more chaos and inconvenience than I had expected. I also wondered if it is even possible to empower those who are marginalized, when one comes from a place of power and privilege, and do it in an authentic, loving, and non-patronizing manner. Some days, to be honest, I still feel like I am only a gentrifier—we are able to rent a home that other families from the community could live in. Other days, I feel trapped in my own world, and isolated from the local community. Some days I feel ashamed for not doing enough. Other days—in what I have tried to do—I feel both responsible and culpable for not realizing how my privilege could affect those I minister to.

This dynamic, between those with power and those without, has always felt nuanced to me. Being a Chinese-American woman, born in the United States to immigrants, but immigrants who had completed graduate degrees and raised my brother and me in a comfortable suburban neighborhood, I felt even more conflicted. I grew up with many of the same privileges as my husband, who is White. I went to schools that prepared me to do well in a four-year university. I was taught by teachers who expected excellence and believed in me. The question was not whether I would go to college, but what graduate degree I would get. This education was my invitation into a place of privilege—about 97 percent of the students at my high school were consistently admitted to four-year universities. When I am in need financially, I can always turn to my parents for help. There are public places where I can frequent where I am not looked upon with suspicion. In most contexts, I don't have to think too much about what I wear or how I talk.

However, unlike my husband, while I am afforded privileges due to my upbringing and education, I am still stereotyped, misunderstood, passed up for leadership positions, and at times, made to feel invisible. I am either told, "Oh, I just think of you as White because ... you speak English so well, or you come from wealth and have completed a graduate degree, or <insert other reason to overlook my ethnicity and culture because I am in your privileged space>." Sometimes I get the icy opposite: "You don't belong here, go back to your country," or I'm asked the infamous question that many Asian-Americans have heard ad nauseum, "Where are you from?...No, where are you really from?"

Perhaps in most cases I'm not overtly silenced, but I am continually aware of unspoken systems in place that undermine my merit, words, and ideas. I have been written off in the past because I have been told I am quiet, hard-working, not one to make waves, and respectful of authority. While these are not negative character traits, I was made to feel like they were. I have also been made to feel that I did not fit the mold of leadership, and even if I did hold a leadership position, some people still did not see me as a leader. I have been embarrassed when I didn't understand a certain vernacular, colloquialisms, and idioms thrown around in a White-dominant workplace, having to explain that English was not my first language. Well-meaning individuals sometimes try to show off their few words in Korean or Japanese, not realizing that I don't speak either of these languages. I have felt the ugly stares of walking into a mono-ethnic, mono-gendered space where I clearly do not belong. I have even hated myself—or more specifically, my ethnic identity, my gender—because of these experiences and others. But what is even more horrifying than the actual experiences themselves, was my decades-long belief that they were all caused by something inherently wrong with me.

When I listened to my friends share about how they had been hurt and misunderstood by us as their leaders, I felt both empathetic to their suffering and marginalization, as well as responsible for causing their pain. This internal conflict, along with working as a physician and being a mother of a child who needed me to be present through unforeseen illnesses, made me question everything in my ministry plan. If I am not a leader in the church, and those whom I've led in the past have been hurt by me, then what is my role here? Is there even a place for me in this community, as a highly educated Chinese-American woman, and mother of a medically fragile child?

I would love to be part of a thriving, multi-ethnic, multi-class church in our urban context, where we discuss race, class, and power openly, and still love each deeply. And I would love to play a part in bringing about complete and holistic transformation of our neighborhood in East Los Angeles, where people are empowered to become physically, emotionally, relationally, and financially healthy.

Yet there are only so many hours in a day: to be a good physician to my patients, to spend quality time with my family, to attempt to maintain a livable household while spending free afternoons in traffic taking Adam to see the liver specialist or get a blood draw. Many days, I feel paralyzed and emotionless as I just go through the motions of my own life. Building relationships or engaging in complexities of already-existing friendships often becomes secondary to survival. But I've also found these relationships often become the grace that allows me to do more than survive.

✻

I remember when my housemate, who grew up in a neighborhood like ours, invited me to take a walk with her to a local grocery store. I took my son in the baby carrier, and as we walked together, I realized that since moving back into the neighborhood, I had been afraid to walk around by myself. I didn't want people to stare at me, to label me as a gentrifier, an outsider, or someone with privilege. I did not want to feel like I didn't belong. And although it is difficult for me to admit, deep down, from a more instinctual place, I was afraid for my son's safety and I did not want him to experience his otherness at such an early age, even though choosing to keep him protected was itself an exercise in privilege. We were probably a peculiar sight to people, a Mexican American woman walking side-by-side with a Chinese American woman with a baby strapped to her chest, and we received more than a couple stares. Walking together, we talked about why I hadn't gone out alone in the neighborhood since moving back. She listened to my fears, with compassion and without judgment, and in doing so, I felt welcomed into her world and also free to be myself. I began to see the neighborhood anew through her eyes. This is the power of the cross, the power of the gospel in my life: the way I see myself is not only transformed and healed, but so is the way I see the world around me. By acknowledging pain and suffering and fear, and inviting Jesus to walk with me in that dark valley, I am able to see God and His kingdom even more clearly.

I've realized that what has brought me the most hope, the most joy in this chaotic season of heartache and grief, is not some abstract idea of transformation. It is the gift of relationship and connection that I've received as I've sought to be part of God's kingdom here in East LA, even in all of my weakness. It is the friendships that are sometimes messy and painful, but simultaneously meaningful and liberating, especially with those whose experiences and lives have been so different than mine. The joy of reconciliation. The sharing of sufferings. The safety of real human connection makes it worth all the complexity and chaos connection brings.

Understanding the suffering of my friends under unjust systems, experiencing the discomfort of cross-cultural and cross-class friendships, and dealing with all the pain that it brings up for all of us, is necessary for my own transformation and discipleship. Seeing the world through my friends' eyes frees me from the bubble of false comfort and security created by my privilege. When I acknowledge my own shortcomings and blind spots, I become a better friend and listener. I feel liberated to be my authentic self. I am able to see more clearly the beauty, strength, and courage of the people in my community.

Instead of seeing dilapidated storefronts with hand-painted signs, I see the ingenuity and determination of a small business thriving against the wave of gentrification. Instead of having pity on a single mother of three unexpectedly pregnant with her fourth baby, I am in awe of her strength and resolve to love and give life to another child, whether or not the father stays by her side. When I complain about how the air conditioner is broken at work, I remember the street vendors just outside my clinic window, who go to the same corner day in and day out, no matter how hot or how cold it is outside, as the breadwinners for their families.

✤

After six months of no hospital visits—a virtual miracle for our family—our son was hospitalized once again. This was his twelfth admission to the hospital in two years. Our hearts broke; we thought he was doing better. For over a year, we had been driving twenty miles every Saturday to receive prayer for physical healing, hoping that Jesus was making Adam's liver new again, so that he would never need a transplant. One night in the hospital, after we were told the results of his most recent ultrasound, the reality of my son's condition settled in me. Not only did the ultrasound jarringly remind us of his fragile health, but it showed us that his liver disease was worsening. I sobbed into the pillow as I held my two-year-old, sleeping peacefully in my arms. I felt betrayed and abandoned by God.

Much like the two travelers on the road to Emmaus in Luke 24:13-35, we too had our expectations and hopes of what Jesus could do in our lives and ministry. We dreamt of producing and witnessing the fruit of our hard work and perseverance. This Jesus, who had performed miracles and overturned the tables of the status quo, who preached freedom for the captives and sight for the blind, was the one who would redeem Israel from its oppressors. He would be the one who would transform our urban communities. He would be the one to heal my son. He would make everything better. And we would cheer him on from the sidelines. Little did we know how disappointed and devastated we would be.

This Jesus, the one in whom they put their hope—was killed. They thought He had left them to face their world and their problems alone. The lives they dreamt of living, walking alongside Jesus, would no longer be realized. Their hopes were crushed. And the weight of their disappointment and grief were like a shroud covering their eyes, keeping them from recognizing Him. Where was Jesus in their disappointment? Just like the early followers, we also questioned, Where was Jesus in our darkest moments?

This mystery companion on the road to Emmaus engaged with the travelers in their pain and disappointment. He asked them questions, listened to their answers, and was not afraid to be corrective. Their hearts burned while He was with them, but they did not know it until He performed the very gesture that caused their grief in the first place—the breaking of the bread, the breaking of His body. In this beautiful yet devastating act, their eyes were opened. It wasn't until then that they realized He had been with them the whole time they were on the road.

In the hospital room that night, my muffled cries into the pillow turned into a deeper grief over an incomplete, fragmented understanding of the living God. For two and half years, I had longed for God to be Healer, to fix my son's liver, so Adam wouldn't have to suffer anymore, and so we wouldn't have to endure the disruption and chaos in our lives. I wanted complete healing, a sense of normalcy, and freedom from the uncertainty of my son's health. But he wasn't healed; he was getting worse. God, as Healer, wasn't able to comfort me. I needed God to be more than a Healer. I needed Him to be with me in my pain, to be present in all things, to be Emmanuel, God with me. Then, somehow, through my tears, I realized Emmanuel, God with us, IS the gospel—the fullness of the living God.

✤

In my twenties, I found it much easier to trust in formulaic stories with happy endings and pithy verses from scripture than to hear the raw and honest tales of the difficulties and failures of ministry. How many testimonies have I heard about some missionary giving up the comforts of life, or undergoing some kind of suffering, whether or not it was the result of her choice, and then experiencing complete relief and a fruitful ministry? Or another giving up a large percentage of his income to the church, and the Lord blessing him with an abundance of money or the potential of financial growth and stability because of that very decision?

But not all stories end this way. Many go to the mission field, with aspirations and dreams of changing the world or serving those on the margins, only to come back earlier than expected because of personal reasons, team difficulties, and unforeseen circumstances. No one wants to hear about the "failed" attempts at ministry, unreconciled differences among teammates, or the emotional and mental exhaustion from living in a foreign place. Some of us may be drawn to the accounts of the very dangerous situations that could cost one's own health or even life, but not if these stories end poorly. Some of these stories are unknown because they are simply too painful to tell. And yet, these stories matter, and without them we can miss the complexity of what God is doing in the world.

I used to think that if I would trust in Jesus and give my life to Him, seeking His Kingdom first, my life would improve, that God would grant me the desires of my heart. That is what I truly believed, and I encouraged others to the do the same. Looking back, that view of the gospel was too simplistic. Through my son's illness, and listening to my friends' experiences, I have learned that problems do not automatically go away when we follow Jesus. Sometimes life gets worse and becomes messier and more painful. Sometimes following Jesus requires confronting pain previously buried in the past, whether I was the one who caused it or the one experiencing it.

Just as being a mother of a son with chronic illness thrust me into navigating a new side of the medical world, worrying about the next fever or infection, and becoming friends with parents who have known tragedy too soon, sharing in suffering with those in my community has opened my eyes to power structures and dynamics, to systems of injustice everywhere in the world, including inside the church. My neighborhood friends have given me an invitation to walk in their shoes, and to see the community through their eyes. I cannot un-see and un-know these truths anymore, nor do I wish to; I must navigate a new and broader worldview.

For nearly two decades, I had believed that God was a fixer of problems, that life with God meant paying some manageable costs in ministry, and as a result, experiencing an otherwise problem-free life. But with this view, there was no place for the suffering present in our world, in my own life and in my friends' lives. There was no place for the sometimes unexplainable, unjust, unexpected long-suffering that Jesus himself experienced and promises to walk with us through.

Yes, I can pray for God to repair the brokenness between me and my friends from the local community, and I can pray for God to heal my friends' pain, so that our friendships can be restored. But I sense that this may not happen when and how I expect it to, because I have learned that God is more than simply a fixer of problems. He is Emmanuel.

He is with me, He is with us. I am able to invite Him into my process as I wait. I am able to trust Him to walk with me and engage with me in my pain. I am learning to feel the moments when my heart is burning within me, so that I can recognize His presence while we are on the road. And as I experience the disappointment and grief from the difficulties of life, I find myself wandering deeper into the mystery of His broken body. My journey with God is one where I am transformed, one where I learn to love more deeply, see and experience pain and be present to it, and continue to hope for healing and liberation of every kind.

❖

A few months after the worst string of hospitalizations, after learning our son's liver condition was worsening, we also discovered I was pregnant again. I felt excited and afraid. How could I be present with my sick son in the hospital while also caring for a newborn? The morning nausea lasted until evening, and I could barely give my son vegetables because I couldn't handle the smell of cooking them. The baby wasn't even here yet, and I was already less able to care for him. My spiritual director gently reminded me that in my humanity, I would never be able to be at every difficult moment in my son's life. She encouraged me to trust that God would be with him even when I was not able to, through everything.

With the birth of our daughter, we have experienced a depth of joy that starkly contrasted the struggle of these last three years—the deep joy of a new life being birthed in the midst of ongoing sorrow and pain. We are able to celebrate in the midst of an uncertain future. We are grateful for every day our son remains well and for every day we get to stay home with him, but we still grieve and pray for his healing and struggle with God in his sickness. Although nights are hard, our house is a mess, and our hands are always full, the emotional burden somehow feels a bit lighter. This new little life who grasps our hands with strong little fingers reminds us that there will always be small victories and respites in the midst of a long, difficult road. Emmanuel is not only present with us in our sorrow, He can also give us unexpected joy and rest during the journey.

I needed this new kind of trust in God for my friendships in the neighborhood, for our church, and for our community, as well as for myself and our family's journey. I needed to trust that as God is still holding the larger story of our family, and our home, He is also holding the stories and struggles within the broader home we all have here in East Los Angeles. While there may be pain and heartache and misunderstanding as any of us journey together, we can hold onto an ever-present hope: the promise of Emmanuel, our God who walks with us.

6

STEP BY STEP WITH JESUS
Claudia Y. Salazar

Claudia Y. Salazar is a full-time case manager at a community mental health center and she previously worked as a case manager in domestic violence shelters and addiction rehabilitation. For six years she served as a youth leader during evenings and weekends and was also a Spanish language translator at New Life Community Church in the Lincoln Heights neighborhood of Los Angeles (a Servant Partners site). She attended East Los Angeles College and was an active part of the InterVarsity Christian Fellowship chapter there called El Acceso. Claudia loves hiking, spending time with friends, photography, and attending heavy metal concerts.

MY MOM AND I live in a small one-bedroom apartment in northeast Los Angeles. For seven years we have had stability. Stability may seem like a simple thing—but it's wonderful, and it hasn't always been this way for us. And I have a job I love, which feels like a miracle. I work as a case manager for a violence intervention program in Los Angeles. Daily I am in the tangle of government systems that have the power to help so many of my clients, but that sometimes also prevent positive transformation for others. I work with families who have seen extraordinary suffering, but who have also beat formidable odds. Working as a case manager can be grueling. Through the years, I've seen deep pain in hundreds of survivors. But I feel deeply connected to this work, and deeply connected to the clients I serve—because not too long ago, I was one of them.

⌗

In 2012 during my third year working at a domestic violence shelter, I learned that we would be getting a new family that day, a woman with three kids. I knew I would be assigned to them. Several of us were waiting outside to receive them, as we always do. They arrived by taxi. The first one to get out was a ten-year-old girl. She had long wavy hair pulled into a pony tail, was dressed in jeans and a hoodie, and was wearing a backpack. She had arrived at a shelter filled with strangers to hide from her father. It was so clear that this young girl was scared and had no idea what was happening. As I watched her, I felt like someone punched me in the gut. All of a sudden, I felt myself fifteen years old again, my long hair in a pony tail, dressed in jeans and a hoodie, with my backpack on— always on the move, my mom trying to settle us again and again after leaving my father.

⌗

Most of my childhood was defined by the fact that my father was an addict who became increasingly violent towards my mom. As I became a teenager, my life turned from being very challenging into hell. I regularly feared my parents would kill each other, and there were a few nights when I had to call the cops. I had difficulty focusing in school because I was sleeping little and worried all the time about home. As I turned fifteen, my parents fought more than they ever had. My home, an apartment in Maywood, was either constant fighting or deafening silence. The only break from this was to leave and go to my aunt's house or my best friend's house.

My mom, like many victims of domestic violence, found it difficult to leave my dad because we didn't have the resources to make it on our own. Though we tried to leave a few times, we always went back to my father. We couldn't find stability with him, so we left. We couldn't make it on our own, so we returned. But each time we went back to him, life was harder and harder. I was an only child, and I was also the only one who could come between my parents and keep the peace—whether calling the cops or literally stepping between my father and mother to save her from his beating. I fought along with them, raising my voice, arguing for peace.

There were a few happy moments in my childhood, before my father's addiction completely took over when I was seven or eight years old. There were moments when my father was able to spend time with me, or when my mother and father and I spent holidays together, when we all got along. I remember a Christmas when my dad bought a fresh Christmas tree. I remember the strangest things about it, like his hands removing the twine wrapped around it in our yard to take it inside the house. We decorated it together. I really loved that tree. A few weeks later, though, he knocked it down when he was drunk. Even the few happy memories have a bit of sadness in them too. But at least, during those very early years, I felt like I had a family.

✳

The first time I learned I could not count on my father, I was barely sixteen years old. My mom and I were home alone when she collapsed by my bed in writhing pain. I knew I had to help her but wasn't sure how. She was in too much pain to drive and I had no idea how to drive a car. I wanted to call 911 but she asked me not to call an ambulance. She said she didn't want the fuss. Somehow, I entered into a kind of adult survival mode and arranged transportation for us with a taxi service. Everything was moving so quickly. Our driver rushed us to the hospital across town, and I checked my mom into the emergency room.

The nurses took her away, and I didn't see her for hours. In fact, I had been waiting so long that I fell asleep on the emergency room chairs in my pajama shorts and one of my dad's old over-sized t-shirts. When I woke up and went to the nurse's station, they informed me that she had been moved to another, nearby hospital. And because I was a minor, now that we were separated, they weren't allowed to let me leave. We needed my dad. I needed my dad. I called home again and again—I must have tried calling home over twenty times—but my father never answered. Technically, they probably should have called Child Protective Services (CPS). I know this is one of the days that someone, something, intervened. At that particular moment in our lives, a CPS call may have made things much worse for my mom and me. Instead, a kind police officer thought outside the box and drove me down the street to my mom's room at the women's hospital.

My mother had had a miscarriage, an ectopic pregnancy. She'd had a hunch she was pregnant a few weeks earlier and even took a pregnancy test, but it had come back negative. It had been wrong. The pregnancy was lodged in her tube, which is why she was in so much pain. It can be very dangerous, but we got her medical care in time. We still couldn't get ahold of my dad. My mom and I were alone, and I had to become an adult. I had to be the adult for my mom and the parent to myself that my father couldn't be. It isn't surprising that a few weeks after her miscarriage, my parents separated for the last time.

The night my mother and I finally left my father, I wish I could say that my mom had it all planned out—that we had an apartment to go to and that things were going to be great. But that was not the case. One night, my mother just couldn't take it anymore. She had gotten into a horrible fight with my dad. She simply told me, *"Agarra tus cosas, porque nos vamos."* (Get your things, because we are leaving). That night I left with only my backpack and the clothes I had on. We didn't tell him; we just walked away. But when we quickly returned later that night for my mom's phone charger, my dad asked, "What happened? What's going on?" Although we had left and come back many times, something inside me knew it was really over. And I told him that: "It's over. We're done." I didn't see my father again for three years. I knew that my mom had finally had enough. And I knew I needed some kind of peace. That night—a terrifying roller coaster ride—was when adulthood began for me. Everything that night and everything in the days to come went so quickly that it is all now a blur—the moments and the memories of them. There was no stopping, no taking breaks, no chance to understand what was happening, to process the past or the next moves. All I could do was to keep going.

❊

I had little idea then that even though my mother and I had left an abusive father, I would meet another father many years later: my Abba. Abba is the name Jesus calls God when He cries out in suffering from the cross. It means "father" in the Aramaic language. Because of my complicated relationship with my father, as I began to learn about God, I couldn't handle thinking of Him as "my father." But I could think of Him as Abba. And in my prayers and my journals, that is usually how I refer to God. Meeting my Abba was how the story of my healing begins.

During my first class on my first day of school in September 2005, I was invited to a Latinx Bible study called El Acceso by a girl I had met in that class. El Acceso, I would learn later, was part of a bigger organization called InterVarsity Christian Fellowship. Going to Bible study was odd for me because they all welcomed me, and I didn't understand why. It was also odd, or new rather, because I didn't grow up in the church and hadn't read the Bible—at all. That first day, I was introduced to Molly Ramos and others in the study. Molly and Abner, her husband, who are both currently on staff with InterVarsity, were ministers with El Acceso. Even as a White woman, Molly treated me like family right away, and I was not used to anyone showing me the kind of love she did.

At my second week at our El Acceso gathering, Abner shared a word. Abner is a great speaker, but I'll be honest, I don't remember what he said that day. But I do remember feeling something as he spoke, something that led me to ask Molly to pray for me, and I remember breaking down in her arms. I felt an ocean of pain, waves crashing in on me as I cried and cried. She held me, prayed for me, and she let me cry. Molly didn't try to fix me or soothe me. I was in awe of how a White woman—and one who didn't know me—could love me so well.

From that first week until the end of the semester, I met with Molly on a weekly basis. I knew she had something to teach me and I was desperate to learn it. During our very first meeting we were in an empty classroom. I started talking about my father, and Molly just listened. She and I had nothing in common except Jesus, and to my surprise that was enough.

I thought my meetings with Molly would consist of her giving me advice or telling me in various ways to "get over it." Instead, she opened our time together in prayer and invited the Holy Spirit. Then she would just see what happened in prayer or conversation. As she prayed for me, usually a memory came up. The memories usually involved my father, and they were always painful. I usually didn't want to think about it and would have the urge to run from these memories. But I would sit with Molly and let the memories come, and I would hear Jesus speak to me and look for where He was in that moment. That was the first time ever I experienced the love of Jesus. It was also the first time I experienced inner healing prayer, which is when we invite God into a painful memory, which essentially heals or begins a healing journey for that memory to heal. I never knew God could be so personal and look into my soul. That's when I wanted to know more about God. I felt known by a God who I had thought was distant, if He existed at all. I hadn't realized that God would care about the life of any seventeen-year-old girl, let alone me. But He saw me, He loved me, and I was desperate to know that love in a deeper way.

✳

Twelve hours after the fight that finally split up my parents, my mother and I had a brand-new life. My father was out of the picture, and we were facing an uncertain future. The next two years of our lives were very unstable. We lived wherever we found space: hotels, the homes of my mom's friends, rented rooms whenever we could afford it and when one became available, and when all else failed we slept in our car.

Finally, not too long after leaving my father, my mom and I found a room to rent. We had a moment when we both thought we were good to go now, and that things would get easier. But the landlady was a nightmare. And we soon felt we were just too close to my dad (he was just down the street)—we had to leave to keep away from him, so we did. For a few weeks, my mom tried finding a new place for us, but she kept coming up empty handed. She was getting desperate and scared, so one night, she told me, "I can't have you be homeless with me. If I can't find a place to live, you will have go back to your father."

I couldn't go back to live with him. I was terrified the next day at school, hoping and praying we would find a place. Years later, I understood this as one of many moments God intervened in my life and gave us a place to lay our heads—by that night, by God's grace, my mom had found a room to rent for us. I was relieved knowing I would not have to go back to my father. But I was also tired. Another move. No idea of what the future held, where we would be, if we would have a place that was safe and clean. If we would be able to stay and settle in.

Mom and I had been there for a few months, and we were finally starting to experience some stability—a sense of home after months of being uprooted. One day, I came home from school to find firefighters in front of our complex. A fire had broken out in the garage, and many apartments had caught fire. Almost all the apartments had severe damage. We lost our place to live and most of our belongings: pictures and memories and the few pieces of furniture and clothing we had purchased or been given since leaving my dad. Once again, we were left with nothing.

I was in shock and I couldn't really feel anything. Maybe I was just used to being hit with wave after wave of trauma and disappointment. I was learning to ride those waves and take a breath whenever I had the opportunity to do so, even if those opportunities didn't come around too often. The fire was perhaps the most dramatic bearer of the message I regularly learned as a teenager: everything I held dear, I lost.

The city put us in a hotel for two weeks and we had to figure out what to do quickly. My mom frantically tried to find a place for us to live. She found a room in the house of a family, but we didn't stay for very long. I got involved with a boy related to the family we were living with. I was desperate to be loved and accepted. I couldn't find that acceptance in school, and my mom could only do so much. I turned to this boy to try and fill the very painful void I had inside. It didn't work, and the void only got bigger. By this point, I was already getting used to the constant change. Our relationship with the family was strained, and my mom moved us to our next house within months. I used to say "our next home," but with all the transitions I went through, I stopped calling places home.

✳

Three months after first attending El Acceso, and meeting Molly and Abner in December 2005, I went with a friend of mine to his church. It was a big Latino church and they were offering to baptize new believers that night. There are many different beliefs about baptism, that it is important for salvation or that it is an important marker of the seriousness of your intention to journey with Jesus. I didn't know about all of that. I just knew I loved Jesus and I wanted to give Him my life even though I didn't totally understand what that meant.

The church had us put on white gowns and they had the baptismal pool built into the floor up in front. When it was my turn, I didn't realize the pool had steps and I'm kind of clumsy anyway, so I slipped getting in, nearly hitting my head. The pastors reacted quickly and caught me before falling right into a head injury. They lifted me up from the water and quickly dunked me. Alive in Jesus! Literally! It was pretty funny actually. It's also how all of my faith life has gone: a desire, an intention, and then the next thing I know I am sliding into baptism, or faithfulness, or ministry—then figuring out the details as I go along. That night with only my one friend from El Acceso as a witness, I was baptized. I told my mom the next morning and decided to start figuring out the details of what it meant for me to follow Jesus.

I continued to meet with Molly into 2006. She had walked me through so much healing, and now I was ready to learn how to live my life as a Christian. At this point we had built a rapport, and I knew Molly's input would only make my life better. I was seeing my life change as I followed everything she advised me to do. I learned I had to be responsible and start earning a living, so I applied for my first job at Taco Bell. I learned that to get closer to God, I needed to spend time with Him. The bus was the only time and place I had, so I carved out a spot in the very back, listened to worship music and read my Bible. I was putting down roots with Jesus. My mom and I also moved to Bellflower around this time, where we would stay for several years while I went to school and worked in Monterey Park. Daily this commute took at least two hours each way, every day. I was determined to grow, and work and school were crucial to the life I was trying to build. I found the best way to use those two hours—praying and studying the Bible—and as it turns out those were some of the sweetest moments I had with Jesus.

❄

When I was a teenager, I didn't fully understand why we had to keep moving around. I would learn in years to come that we weren't only living the struggle of a woman trying to hide from an abusive husband, but also of an undocumented woman trying to stay under the radar.

After the fire and the brief stay with the family, we ended up in Watts. I felt scared and lost. I had always lived in the inner city, but Watts was not like Maywood. Growing up, I had heard about all the violence that took place in Watts, and that fear grew after my mom was mugged and physically assaulted by a woman on drugs across the street from where we lived. Because of this, in Watts, my mom didn't want me going out of the house, talking to people, or making friends. Somehow, despite it all, I graduated from high school. The summer that followed was the worst season of my life.

My mom was just trying to survive, literally to keep us physically alive. She didn't know that her teenage daughter was falling through the cracks. I was alone, sad, and insecure. Soap operas and boys were the only methods I knew to help me deal with the pain. In my head, no one really loved me, and I had to figure out how to survive on my own. I got involved with another guy. Once again I was trying to fill the many voids left by my father, by the chaotic life we lived, and by the isolation of living in a dangerous neighborhood. Unfortunately, this guy was worse than the last. It felt like life was just pain and more pain. As a seventeen-year-old, I didn't realize the many messages I was taking in from the world around me, from the men I was learning to depend on, and even from soap operas which reinforced that having chaotic relationships was the only way to feel complete.

As I continued in this new relationship, I got very depressed and considered taking my life. One night, I was ready to do it. I planned to slit my wrists, and I had the blade ready to end it all. I had fallen so far that I thought suicide was the best option. Something stopped me. I didn't do it and instead took a shower. That night I went to bed like a zombie, but I woke up alive. I know now what I couldn't understand then: that something was God. He was present in my life long before I understood anything about Him, long before I chose to say yes to a life walking closely with Him.

As the summer came to an end, the only thing I knew for sure was that I was alone and that I had to learn to fight for myself. It was in that spirit that I started college at East Los Angeles College (ELAC), and my life would quickly take a new direction. It wasn't just a huge step forward in figuring out what I wanted to do, and gaining the skills to do that, it's also when my healing journey would really start. The path wasn't going to be easy for me, but for the first time in years, I was hopeful, and I started to believe that maybe there was a future for me.

✳

Compared to the chaos of my teenage years, after becoming a Christian, life wasn't necessarily easy, but it was starting to feel like a life worth living. I was establishing routine and finding peace. Except that in the fall of 2007, my father stumbled back into my life. It had been over three years since I had seen him.

I was on a bus just going about my day and there he was, on the bus, going about his. I covered my face with my hair and tried not to be noticeable. It was obvious he was still very much an addict. He passed me and sat down. People were leaving and coming, I thought my trick may have worked. Then I heard footsteps coming toward me. I recognized them. I didn't know you could recognize the sound of someone's footsteps until that moment. He tapped me on the shoulder and then sat down. Though I remembered the life I left behind, the reasons we ran away, I still had hope he could be a father to me and maybe things could change. Well, I had hope...and confusion. He asked for my phone number, and I gave it to him. I didn't know what to do or say—he was my dad. From the time I was twenty to twenty-one he was in and out of my life. But he was falling deeper into his addiction, and I was being taken along for the ride all over again. The disappointment was so painful, all I could do was run to Jesus. The wounds got deeper, but that time Jesus was showing me I didn't have to do it alone anymore, and I shared the pain with my community. I had to take him out of my life again. I knew if he stayed, my life would spiral out of control again since I was still trying to get out of the spiral of my adolescence and my parents' separation in 2003.

During all my years of mentoring with Molly, I cried out in anger, disappointment, and frustration, but in this season, there was even more. I learned through those times that Jesus was with me through community. Molly and my friends were there in my pain. They heard me, they challenged me, and they helped me believe that hope in God was never lost. They reminded me I had a perfect, heavenly father who loved me and wanted to fill the hole my father left. By mid-2008, I cut my father out of my life to regain some stability, and I kept moving forward. I worked hard at East Los Angeles Community College while working part time for Taco Bell. I kept learning about Jesus and trusting that somehow what I was doing would lead to something. He had something greater for me and I could trust that. Then the next significant trial came into my life.

My mom was laid off and had a difficult time finding work. At first, I thought it was because jobs are tough to find. Then she told me the truth: she was undocumented. So, I started providing for the household. We had always lived paycheck to paycheck, but this was even more extreme, every cent was counted. I wasn't able to go out or live a life resembling a normal adult in her twenties. Overnight, I started paying the bills on my part-time Taco Bell income while trying to survive in school, hoping school would eventually open a door to a better future.

In this crisis, I learned the power of community again. Molly met with me every week to pray and cry out to God for change, for open doors, and for the eyes to see He was with me in this storm. God did give me those eyes to see what He was up to—and He was up to a lot. My friend, Caroline, went with me to help my mom look for any work she could find. Though we found nothing, I was still trying to find a way out, so I considered dropping out of school. My El Acceso community was there to make sure I didn't make that decision. They saw the bigger picture when all I could see was the current crisis. And in that crazy year my mom and I had landlords—who were also caterers—and who cared for us by bringing us food left from events whenever we needed it. And we had a mechanic who fixed our car even when we couldn't afford to pay him. My mom found small odd jobs here and was able to get some small money to put gas in the car and buy some groceries for the house. By the grace of God and the blessing of community, we made it through somehow.

Around Christmas 2008, that miracle job for my mom finally came. My boss saw my stress and listened to my story, and decided to give my mom a chance. On New Year's Day, she started working. In a matter of months she was a full-time employee at one restaurant and a part-time employee at another. Some might wonder, "How is that answered prayer? The woman was working two jobs?!" But when you grow up in the inner city on minimum wage, two jobs is the norm, especially in a single parent household. My mom never was afraid of hard work, only of not being able to work.

✵

In 2009, my view of God shifted. For many years it was all about me and how God could work in my life, but that would begin to broaden. I was invited to go to the Middle East for the summer, but I turned it down out of fear. Molly and Abner offered me the opportunity to go to Urbana (a missions conference) in 2009 to learn more about the world, what it means to be missional, and to figure out what I was passionate about. So I worked extra hours during the majority of 2009 and I saved the money to go to Urbana.

It was my first big conference, my first flight, and I got to go with two of my closest friends. But the ticket was expensive and all the money I had set aside went to the hotel. To be honest, I was broke the entire time I was there. So were a few of my friends. At Urbana, breakfast and dinner were provided, but lunch was on our own. So those of us with limited resources had a few choices. We either shared what we had so we could eat lunch during the conference, or we swallowed our pride and let other friends buy us lunch, or we would save the majority of breakfast and use it for lunch. But even with these challenges, we knew Urbana was still worth it. And going to Urbana confirmed what I already knew: we could not love people from a distance. Being a Christian meant purposely making hard choices in order to love others. I learned about children around the world who were being abused and exploited in hard labor, and my heart broke for them. My eyes were opened, and I knew I wanted to be part of change. I wanted to work with women and children.

Upon my return, I was invited again to go on a summer mission in 2010. Again, I was scared and I said no. My fear of losing what little my mother and I had gained financially was bigger than trusting God and serving Him in a different country. Finally, 2011 came around, which was my last year at East Los Angeles College. That year, I was given the opportunity to go to the Middle East, and I knew I couldn't say no. I didn't want to say no. I said yes, and I trusted that God would provide.

As it happened, a second team was being sent that summer to Ghana in West Africa, to work with a school. I had wanted to go to Africa for as long as I could remember. So I asked if I could go to with the team to Africa instead. Of course, the process was longer and much more expensive. When I panicked at the costs, my leaders shared all the options for summer missions and their costs: the Los Angeles Urban Project would be local and a lot cheaper;

the trip to the Middle East was the trip most students in my Bible study had done the last few years, and it was expensive but previous participants of that trip were ready to give; and then there was Ghana, which had not been offered for some years and was the most expensive. But I prayed, and I knew that Ghana was where God was calling me to go. I would be the only one going from ELAC, and I had no idea what the road to Africa would entail.

Summer missions require a large amount of money—plane tickets, visas, vaccines, housing, and transportation, and usually a gift to the host ministry—which is usually raised by the person going. So I started the journey to fundraise, and what a journey that was. I had no home church, no resources, and no one from my college or from any community college was going on this mission. I had to raise $5,000 in four months. So, I got to it. I made a list of people to invite to be donors, and I used the skills I had to work odd jobs, so I could use that money towards my financial need for the trip. I was afraid I wouldn't make it, and that my connections would not be enough to fundraise $5,000. In my mind, what I was attempting was crazy and out of my league: there was no way a poor community college student could raise that much money.

But it seems that the "impossible" is exactly what God does. He takes the most impossible situations and says, "Watch me work." Donations came pouring in from people. I had some donors give hundreds of dollars and others who were willing to hire me to work. It was amazing. But still it wasn't enough, and I feared I would have to keep fundraising after I returned from the trip. One night as I was looking at my fundraising, I told God simply, "I need $1,000, Lord." That same week, I received an email from one of the Ghana team leaders. The email informed me that a donor had given $1,000 to the organization we were working with, and they wanted the entire amount to be credited to my fundraising. Just weeks before leaving for Ghana, that secured my funds. God worked in my weakness and showed that nothing is impossible for Him. He can and He will use a poor college student. His resources are always more than enough.

In Africa, God confirmed what I already knew: I had passion to love women and children, in every part of the world. I loved being in Africa and was convinced I wanted to be a missionary there. But God challenged me. As I was praying, I heard, "You can love Africa, but can you love Los Angeles?" I could love people halfway around the world, but could I love people in my home, in the city I'd lived in my whole life? I felt a deep conviction that being missional didn't always mean leaving to a foreign country. This time it meant staying in my home and working to see God transform a city I had lived in but never loved. I finished my six weeks in Africa and went home knowing I had to make some big changes.

⁜

I knew that serving Jesus meant being in the lives of kids and caring for women struggling with addiction and in abusive relationships. So in 2012, that's exactly what I did. I gave myself completely to ministry as I struggled to find a stable job in my field. In the midst of finding my way in this ministry, I was also trying to look for work in my field, as I was in a temporary job as an administrative assistant, which God had provided. This job allowed my mom and me to move into our first apartment since separating from my father in Lincoln Heights. All our other places had been rooms in someone else's house or apartment. It was then that God blessed me with a job in my field, which allowed my mom and me to stay in Lincoln Heights. For the first time in a decade, I was able to call a place and a city home. That became my life. I worked as a drug and alcohol counselor in a treatment program for women and children every day, and every evening and on weekends, I volunteered with our church's youth ministry team and helped on Sundays as an interpreter for our worship service. I left for work at 5:00 a.m. every day and began work by 6:30 a.m. It was difficult, but it paid the bills and allowed me to continue as youth leader in the evenings.

During my first week on the job, I was introduced to my first client. Amanda was addicted to meth, had a lot anger issues, and did not listen to authority. She was also aware that I was new. When I started working with her, she blew up at other residents and challenged my authority any chance she got. At one point when she screamed at me, I was forced to put her on a contract which meant that a similar repeat offense of screaming at staff or residents would result in her immediate removal. I found myself frustrated all the time as I worked with her. Every time we met and she had an outburst, I felt defeated. This wasn't what I imagined. Where was the breakthrough? I felt like I was losing her and failing miserably as a counselor.

Then one day, I was sitting at my desk and Amanda came to me to talk. I was worried, especially after she said, "Something is wrong." I panicked. I thought she was going to tell me that she'd gotten into a fight or used drugs. What came out of her mouth shocked me. She said, "I feel happy. I'm not angry, and I'm not used to not being angry. This is new." I started to smile and told her it was a good thing and that the work she was putting in was producing results. She was changing. Two weeks after that, I came into work one morning and found that my client board was empty; Amanda had been discharged. She had relapsed and tested positive for meth. She was kicked out. I never saw her again.

If you look at the way success is defined in my field, ministry, and even society, Amanda failed. She relapsed, and all her hard work went out the window. But I learned something new with her—that although she failed in her goal of sobriety, there were small successes. She learned to be happy and let go of her anger. She learned that she didn't have to be angry all the time. A seed was planted, and if and when she was ready, she could build on this success. She changed my definition and understanding of success and helped me see that working with people is never black and white. Real change takes time.

Working with Amanda was also the beginning of my own process in facing my trauma as a child victim of domestic violence. My work began a new layer in my healing journey. For a life that continues in tragedy, it doesn't mean that the successes and hopeful moments are insignificant or don't happen; we simply haven't gotten to the end of the journey. I became open to seeing the beauty of people and their struggle on a daily basis—to cheer for the little successes even if the big one was not there yet and may never come. My work brought me face to face with many who are tangled up in all kinds of brokenness and pain. Most importantly, I began to understand how loved by God they all are, even in the midst of making choices that have destroyed their lives and the lives of their families. Following Jesus into the dark places of our own and other's lives is muddy, uncomfortable, painful, and will always expose our pain and limited ability to love. But God is truly in the darkest of places, and we have to learn to see it. We all have access to grace.

⁜

That family with the ten-year-old girl who arrived at my workplace in 2015, with the long wavy hair in a ponytail, hit too close to home for me. Seeing her brought up sharp pain, and I knew that I couldn't care for them the way I needed to. I couldn't be their case manager. I pulled the therapist and my supervisor aside to explain my situation. They assigned the case to my coworker, and I knew I had some internal work to do. It took a long time to shake the image of that girl getting out the van. I saw her, and I saw myself. That day was the beginning of a new and on-going season of healing. That experience did something else besides shake me up; it deepened my desire to fight for the rights of women and children. It reconfirmed that I wanted to empower women to thrive and live lives free of addiction and abuse.

When I started in my early twenties as a counselor and case manager for people struggling with substance abuse and survivors of domestic violence, I used to say it was because of my father. And although I do not want to be close with him or have an active relationship with him, I want to acknowledge and celebrate that he has become a Christian and has been clean and sober for ten years. Forgiveness and wanting good for my father's life, I have had to learn, does not necessarily mean I can be close to him. After the life my mom and I lived with him, and experiencing how difficult it was to build a new life, I simply don't have the capacity to have a close relationship. Like the evil one, addiction steals, kills, and destroys. Addiction destroyed my family, and it tried to destroy me when my life was just beginning, before I had the chance to flourish. I've learned to accept that as part of my story.

I have also learned that not everyone will want or be able to change right away, if at all. And that success cannot be measured by who graduated from a certain program and who didn't, or who became a Christian and stuck with it and who didn't. Success has many different definitions. As we fight for total transformation, we need to remain flexible and willing to see what did change in a positive way rather than only seeing the failed milestone. We need to be realistic about the bumps on the road to success, even while trusting that we are fighting with an unchanging and faithful God on our side. Of course, I still have doubts. I get frustrated. I wonder if I will ever see transformation. Will I see His promises to me fulfilled? When I want to give up because I am feeling too tired or hopeless, my Abba always takes me back to this verse, "Have I not commanded you? Be strong and courageous. Do not be afraid; do not be discouraged, for the LORD your God will be with you wherever you go" (Joshua 1:9, NIV). The Lord's work takes time, patience, work, perseverance, prayer, and community. We will never fully see God's kingdom come until Jesus comes back—but every small part we do get to see is worth it. Every small success is a step along the way.

The sobering truth is that often, we see more darkness than light. Often we see and experience more heartbreak than success. I don't want to sound hopeless or discourage anyone from the work of transformation. But I also want to be honest that this world is dark. We are fighting strong forces, and we will see those forces fight back. So yes, life can be dark and exhausting and hopeless. But we have Jesus. And He knows the weight of darkness because He carried the sin of the world on the cross. He also resurrected, and He gave us a better way. We can move forward every day, even in the darkness we face, because Jesus has given us hope.

Today, now in my thirties, after eight years of doing this work with those struggling with addiction and survivors, I continue because there are a lot of people like me whose lives have been destroyed and who need hope. Even a little. Their road will be long. It took my mom and me more than ten years to find stability. There are many people who need a case manager and counselor who are not willing to give up the fight, even if it takes ten years. I consider myself that type of person.

For individual clients and for my community, I refuse to give up the fight for transformation, even if it is long and complicated and filled with only brief glimpses of hope. I refuse to believe that a life cannot be changed, and when I lose sight of that, I look back at my own life. I look back at the many people who have built me up and reminded me of the real Claudia. I look back at the lives I have impacted, and after eight years of grueling and exhausting work,

I realize I have touched hundreds. This is why I do it. I either get to see bits and pieces of transformation or I get to plant seeds. My mentor, Molly, invested in me for six years despite many ups and downs. She could have given up when I seemed to be moving backward, but she didn't, and she saw me transform before her eyes. Even when the milestones of wholeness and stability were far off, she celebrated the small successes, and she stayed with me through the many bumps in the road. I want to be that same force in the world—in my workplace, my community, my church, and anywhere else God leads me.

7

FINDING MY CENTER
Rachel Christine (Chrissy) Braithwaite Davies

Rachel Christine (Chrissy) Braithwaite Davies has worked with Servant Partners for ten years as a ministry coordinator, worship leader, host, and community mom. Chrissy is also a certified doula. She enjoys not only assisting in childbirth but also in the birth and growth of justice, new ideas, and personal development which is why she also became a certified lay counselor focusing on storytelling. Previously, Chrissy worked in campus ministry with InterVarsity Christian Fellowship at Oregon State and Portland State Universities. Along with her husband Trevor and their three exuberant and beautiful daughters, Keira, Jordan, and Ashlyn, Chrissy lives in Johannesburg, South Africa. She enjoys singing, green spaces, and gathering people over food—if she can do all three at once, all the better!

GROWING UP IN THE predominantly White suburbs of Seattle, Washington, I was always one of about four Black kids in my school. I knew I was different, and why I stood out. If by chance I forgot though, my mother made it clear to me that I was at a disadvantage every time I walked into my school. She would say, "you have two strikes against you: you are Black and you are a woman, so you have to work twice as hard as everyone else to be seen, to be treated well, and to succeed." The thing is, I kind of did forget sometimes: I blended, I assimilated. Sure, sometimes I joked about being the speck of pepper on the cheerleading team or in the choir, but my difference wasn't in the forefront of my mind.

Being different didn't become real to me until I went to college. I had become a part of InterVarsity Christian Fellowship on campus, and I was leading a Bible study in my dorm. My fellowship decided to start exploring racial reconciliation, and as one of the few Black people around, I was asked to pioneer a Black student Bible study.

I was so fearful. These were supposed to be 'my people' but because I had grown up in a White context I had not really learned how to be with 'my people.' I was anxious I would get more of the kinds of comments I'd heard as a kid from the Black folks who, literally, lived on the other side of the bridge from where our family lived. Comments like "Why do you talk so proper?" or "Why are you tryin' to be White?" The thing was, I was comfortable being around White folks. And up to this point in college, I had not participated in—or even been to—the Black Student Union activities. I felt very out of place there. I was sure everyone in my Black student Bible study would see right through me. But I agreed anyway, and I decided to just do my best.

I found myself wanting to introduce myself to everyone in my new Bible study in a way which would allow me both to blend *and* to just be myself, which in this particular case, was probably impossible. Anyway, who was I to lead my people, when I had had a completely different experience? I looked like them but that seemed to be all we had in common. How could I lead as a Black woman when I wasn't sure they saw me—despite my complexion—as Black? God led me to the stories of Moses and Esther, and I can't get into it all right now, but I'll say this, if you have ever struggled with these things like I have, spend some time in their stories.

Knowing that I couldn't achieve both my goals of blending and being myself, I decided to just go ahead and come clean from the beginning. I told the folks who showed up to Bible Study who I was, where I came from, and that I was actually afraid to lead them for fear that they wouldn't accept that my story was different than theirs. And that act of vulnerability gained the trust that so many future relationships were built on. I couldn't be anybody but me—a lesson I would continue to digest and metabolize for years to come, in each new season, in each new place.

CALLED TO PURPOSEFUL PARTNERSHIP

AFTER GRADUATION, I decided to become a campus minister with InterVarsity Christian Fellowship. I loved investing in and leading students at such a formative time in their lives. Our fellowship had continued pursuing racial reconciliation and working towards reaching out to the students of color at our school for a few years by then. Our desire was to come to a place of seeing and understanding one another's experiences as best we could, so we began a series of facilitated conversations (called "Race Matters") around issues of ethnic identity. We wanted to pursue relationships with each other across differences of skin color and background that were real and intentional, embracing and acknowledging each others' struggles, values, and gifts.

My role during this beautiful and turbulent time in our fellowship was to lead us in worship. My heart was, and still is, for worship. I love communicating with Jesus in song; it's the way my heart speaks and expresses itself best. As the worship leader in these challenging and often awkward times, I knew I was a learner myself, and I wanted to bring our fellowship along with me in the journey of getting comfortable with being uncomfortable, in terms of worship styles and languages different than our own. Doing ministry this way made me feel alive. As difficult as it was, it felt right. And there was something startlingly real about this journey and learning about crossing cultural, ethnic, and language barriers that helped us all to discover how Jesus felt about "the other" or the stranger.

It was during the beginning of the new movement toward racial reconciliation in our fellowship that I met Trevor Davies, who had recently come on as intern staff with InterVarsity. Our first real conversation was quite intense. We had just finished having a "Race Matters" conversation with the students who made up the Bible study leaders team. Trevor had shared honestly with that group that as a White man from South Africa, growing up under apartheid, his only interactions with Black people had been with the people who worked in his home or who were in a service position. His vulnerability about the true functioning of his country, and his acknowledgement of his place in it, struck me. So did the reality of it.

Later when we were all finished eating dinner, I was cleaning up and went around the room picking up plates. When I took his plate I had the thought, "does he expect me to do this...to serve him...because I'm Black?" So, I went ahead and asked him. It led to an intense conversation about all this, which is how we began to get to know each other. And no, for the record, he didn't expect me to clean up after him, but I started to get a picture of what life must have been like for him, as well as for Black South Africans.

Later, Trevor and I led a Black student Bible study together. We became close friends as we navigated the joys and pains of cross-cultural ministry on a predomi-nantly White college campus. As our friendship began to move into new territory, but before we officially started dating, he informed me that "if we date and it gets serious, you need to know I'm going back to South Africa." It was an intense pre-dating moment, but as a result, I started seriously considering if this was what God had for me. Was God actually calling me to South Africa? Because as much as I was starting to like this guy, it didn't seem wise to follow him to a faraway land, right? What if it was a horrible experience, and I wanted to go home? It clearly had to be God and not Trevor that took me anywhere.

SHIFTING IDENTITIES

In 2004, I did marry that White South African man. In 2008, Trevor and I, along with our seventeen-month-old, Keira, moved to Johannesburg, South Africa, with plans to minister as bridge builders in an informal settlement—which is a more contextual and appropriate term for what some might refer to as a slum—called Zandspruit. We wanted to continue on this path of God's call to us to be peacemakers and reconcilers across ethnicities and the economic divide, by ministering in this historically broken and deeply segregated country. We wanted to see what God was up to there. I was fearful to leave home, but God had given me love for a man who loved God and God's purposes. So I took the leap to follow what God had ignited in our hearts.

I felt compelled to follow God to where I could see and interact with His heart in a very practical way, to displace myself and see how God might use me to be a blessing in a place and to a people I didn't know. And it didn't seem too complicated. I thought, sure, we can have Bible studies and work in the community. I could continue to learn in the area I had loved so much in college, leaning into God's heart for every language, ethnicity and culture. And practically, I was trained as a doula (which is a certified birth coach), so I thought I could work with local mammas and do some birth coaching. But no big shift, no matter how ordained by God—into marriage, becoming parents, or moving to another country—is without its share of bumps and turns and surprises. Bumps and surprises, yes, that was certainly the case for us.

EXPECTATION VS. REALITY

There were the cultural surprises, like how dressed up everyone seemed, even in the informal settlements. Or how red the dirt was, just so red, it was a struggle just to keep my pants clean. Yet everyone around me looked like they were dressed for a party, pressed and clean—while wearing white—as if they weren't walking around on the same red dirt that I was.

Then there were the ministry surprises, like what we would be doing exactly. We always knew we wanted to start by having an extended season of listening and learning. Our deepest desire was to be a part of reconciliation work here in South Africa, helping people do the heart work that might shift perspectives so that folks could reach toward each other, even cross culturally. We had planned to work with a community center within Zandspruit and had hoped to build relationships and partner with organizations and individuals in the community through the center. They had an after-school program and an ante natal (which is known in America as "prenatal care") clinic going already. We hoped to lead Bible Studies and discussion groups there and within the community. It seemed like a great place to learn and listen, and do some helpful things along the way.

During our first years, I was intimidated by the overwhelming need in our context, and not sure how I could fit. It had seemed simple in theory, but it felt harder to get specific and to sense what the Lord actually had in store for us and the community. Trevor loves to explore and be in new places and figure out how they work, so he spent long days walking the roads of Zandspruit, having conversations and getting to know people. But with Keira strapped on my back and a baby on the way, doing ministry that way just didn't feel normal or natural—it just wasn't physically or emotionally feasible for me. And I wasn't sure what kind of work I could do once I was a mom of two.

Initially, I had hoped to focus on being a doula, connecting with the ante natal clinic at the community center and in the neighboring community where we lived, Cosmo City. When we planned our move to South Africa, I had no idea that we would be expecting a second baby just six months into our time here (let alone a third not too long thereafter). Nor did I know that, despite being a doula and trained to be helpful in labor and delivery rooms to birthing mothers, I would find I was not a welcome presence at government hospitals.

My first client as a doula here in South Africa was Mapule, a young woman from my township. It would be her second child, and she wanted to know someone would be with her the whole time, so she asked me to help. She was giving birth in a government hospital where they are underfunded and understaffed. When I arrived with her, the nurses and midwives were not going to let me in. They shouted at her in Zulu, "We are the midwives, who do you think you are, bringing your own midwife here?" I tried to explain that I was there to help, not take over, that I only work from the waist up. But to them, I was only an intruder there to take away their authority. Mapule, at that point, didn't care what was being said and kept her death grip on my hand. So, I just kept gently, consistently, pushing the hospital bed toward the delivery room because, well, it was time! This situation was common. It was not easy feeling like a burden, feeling unwelcome. But as I remained, I was able to be helpful.

So, I had to learn really quickly how to be comfortable with being around even when people didn't want me to be there. And I was trying to do more than just be there, but to truly be present. There is something significant and prophetic about being present where you are not wanted but do have something of worth to offer.

Connecting to the community and conversations around racial reconciliation did begin to happen quite early. We had developed relationships with folks from Zandspruit as well as a pastor of a White Afrikaans church, and we decided to bring these groups together to have discussions about what it meant to follow Jesus in South Africa given its history. Here we were, being the bridges we had imagined. It seemed like we might be starting to see the first glimmers of possibility in our larger vision for our work here. We hoped and prayed that this group would go far together and be a light on a hill. But it didn't. After only two years it dissolved and we had to take time to grieve and learn from what God had done in us and among us. In many ways, it felt like we had failed at what we came to do. We had wanted to come with a direct approach to something that was dear to our hearts, to God's heart, but it wasn't fully received. We learned that we needed to understand what capacity people had for this work.

These peaks and valleys continued all while our family was growing, first three of us, then four and then five. In hindsight, what felt like a season of failure and confusion at the time, was really a season of learning and growing.

WHAT IS A MISSIONARY ANYWAY

I CAME TO SOUTH AFRICA first and foremost as a learner. When we enter different cultures, no matter who we are, I believe we should enter being aware that we do not know much and allow ourselves to be led and taught. If we have anything to bring of value, any words or knowledge, I think it should come after a season of listening and learning. So that's what we tried to do. But as we have worked and learned together with the friends that we have made in the different parts of South Africa, regardless of my intention or posture, or whether I see myself as being a learner, I've realized that others may not always perceive me that way. There are a number of reasons for that.

In South Africa, we have two very different worlds living side-by-side, in tension, all the time. The Black South African world and the more Western world brought by the Dutch and British colonialists. It necessitates a nuanced dance that plays out daily. For example, when our context is more western or White South African, I, as a Black woman, often have to fight to be heard, taken seriously, or given authority. For instance, I spent time getting to know a predominately White organization that I had an interest serving in. I had built trust and relationships during that time, and so I offered some suggestions about how to allow for their leadership structure to be flexible and more accommodating to the community they were trying to serve. It took a full year before they took the advice, and only after the ideas were endorsed by another White person.

However, when I'm in a predominantly Black South African context, with my title as a minister and an American,

I am usually struggling to give back authority, in order to empower and make space for others. In the informal settlement where we work, there is often an assumption that I am going to come and lead a conversation or event, rather than simply participate; in fact, I might just show up and in the moment be asked to address a crowd at an event I'm simply attending but have no role in. So, to remain a learner, I have had to be very conscious of putting responsibility and leadership back in the hands of those I'm working with, even as I try to be helpful and offer the gifts and skills I do have. For Black South Africans, although I look similar, there is a set of privileges granted to me because of the deference given to westerners, and western thought, and titles like "missionary."

And I am, after all, a missionary. But, to tell you the truth, I really don't like being called a missionary. In history, Christian missionaries and colonialism have been allies, and so much culture and domination has been mixed up with the mission of spreading the good news. Presently, here in South Africa, I've seen missionaries focus on big crusades, on the conversion at the altar, and on teaching a set number of practices that legitimize one as a Christian. In the community where we serve, I've seen missionaries come and spend more time and energy counting the sandwiches they hand out so they can report good numbers back to their own organization than I have seen them building relationships and actually seeing and getting to know people. And to be direct, none of those are things I want to be a part of.

But I can't seem to get away from the word missionary, because when it comes down to it, the life I hope to live here—or anywhere God chooses to take me—is an intentional, missional life. A life with a purpose and a mission. A mission to serve Jesus and look after the things of His heart—like justice, mercy, and humility. A mission to connect people to each other and to Jesus. A mission not so much to lead people toward or to count decisions at the alter, as it is to walk with people through their whole lives, in their context, as they wrestle with what it means to be a follower of Jesus in every decision, the best that they can.

I have wrestled with Jesus a lot about what my best is. For a time, I thought I needed to do it all: preaching the gospel, making disciples, developing leaders, building community, organizing and fighting for justice and reconciliation, sharing resources like food and clothing, developing and delivering education, and so on...(along with everything I am doing to just make it through daily living). Obviously, this isn't healthy, possible, or true. I knew I could not be in the center of all that is happening in community, but I have definitely battled with these internal and unspoken expectations of myself. I am not the center, rather I choose to pursue God as the center of my ministry: He is the hub. All spokes of my ministry need to be centered in Jesus. When I live in a way that reflects this truth, I am able to bring a proper humility to the work, and in turn, I am more able to bring the actual me. Even in my messy vulnerability, living with Jesus as my center allows God to use me in the work He is doing in this place.

AN UNUSUAL FAMILY

When we decided to make the move to South Africa, I wasn't prepared for what I would experience as a Black woman, nor as the mother in a biracial family. I didn't realize that once again I would be put in the position where I would need to defend and explain my existence, my background, and why I was there. I also didn't have the experience to know just how different race relations in South Africa were. Aside from more recent immigrants, racial groups in South Africa are understood as Black, White, Indian, and Coloured. Coloured people are a multiracial group whose heritage comes from many different people groups (African, Asian, European) but who now are seen as a racial group in their own right, different and distinct from someone who is bi-racial. Socially, people tend to stick with their own racial group. It is uncommon to see people my age together with people of other races except in workplaces where there may be some mixing and some friendships made. Apartheid was not that long ago—it only ended officially in 1991—less than thirty years ago. And its effects can still be seen and felt.

As a Black woman, I was grateful there were some places that I blended in. Because I am Black I can basically look like any other African woman here. And then I speak. Or someone speaks to me, in one of the eleven languages represented and realize the conversation can only go so far. I either become the American celebrity, "Aye ke! a Black American, wow, neh! I've always wanted to go to your country, can you take me with you? You know Beyoncé?" Or, I am an anomaly, "Wait, you're American? Oh, you are just visiting, right? Oh, you live here? Why would you leave there to come here?" The first response is usually from Black folks, the second is usually from White.

These dynamics can be hard, but mostly it's just uncomfortable to have my difference called out over and over. The times I find the most unsettling—where I really have to work hard to remember that I'm a Christian spreading the love of Jesus—is when people approach me about my children. Trevor and I have had three beautiful children who, as biracial kids, are all too often the subject of much unwanted conversation such as "Wow, these kids are beautiful, neh, the mother is White?" In Johannesburg (and most of South Africa) it is very uncommon to see an interracial marriage. And since many families, Black and White, have nannies, people assume that I'm the nanny... to my own children. I usually pause and gather a calm that can only come from the Holy Spirit before I explain that "no, I am their mother." And yet people often still argue with me, and I have to tell them again "yes, I truly am their mother, let me tell you their birth stories."

I knew that being in an interracial marriage here would be hard, but I had definitely underestimated the daily challenge of standing firm in who God made me and who He gave me to love. Knowing who I am and being grounded in how God sees me has never been more important to me. In my early days of being here, those kind of interactions would ruin my day. I just wanted to blend in, so I didn't have to defend who I was and the fact that my children are my own. But after a while, I decided this might be much like it would be for a Black woman in America, amongst a predominantly White community. There, as here, I would also have to be the educator. I would have to justify my lived experience even when I perceived surprise or disdain.

So now, I try to use these interactions as an opportunity to explain that I see God doing a lot of new things here in this country (including bringing a family like mine together). Then I ask what they see God doing. And then I explain to my children why people assume that I'm not their mommy, and I affirm that they are beautiful, reminding them of how God sees them—and reminding myself at the same time.

A MINISTRY SHIFT

DURING OUR EARLY YEARS in South Africa I often struggled with the question of when to challenge culture and when to adhere to it. Once I was sitting in a group of people, in my own home, where I found the discussion interesting. After some time, I looked around and realized it was actually a group of men and I, the only woman, was receiving strange looks from them as I tried to share my thoughts. I scuffled to the kitchen where the rest of the women were sitting around chatting or gossiping. This type of situation, which seemed to repeat constantly, was when I felt the most American. It was so hard for me to realize that it was time for me to leave and to feel I wasn't welcome to contribute my thoughts and ideas about what I found to be interesting and relevant conversation. It took so much discernment to decide when to push back in these situations and go ahead and share, and when to accept the culture and ask what else God had for me to do.

In time, I learned to take the opportunities I did have, even if they weren't the ones I wanted. I would try to start meaningful conversations in kitchens with the other women. And I tried my best to be present and helpful how, when, and where I could. For example, I hosted a lot of meetings in our home as a way to minister to others through hospitality. I shifted from being in charge of leading meetings to just trying to make people feel welcome. Both while hosting and at other times, I tried to have as many one on one conversations as I could. But to be honest, I was discouraged. This wasn't how I wanted to do ministry, and I wasn't seeing the kind of fruit I had in previous ministry experiences. I had organized and led conferences that were rich learning and connecting opportunities for students. In addition, I spent significant time with students, often walking with them through bad choices and encouraging them toward good life choices. But our context was simply different.

As a missionary in South Africa, I really struggled to find my place. Not only could I not lead in the way I had learned in my six years as a campus minister: upfront, visionary, and strategic—I couldn't lead, period. While it may seem obvious, I learned that success as a leader in one context and season of life doesn't automatically translate to a new context or season of life. Being a leader as a single person on a college campus in America and being a leader as a missionary in an informal settlement in Johannesburg, South Africa with a husband and three children are, as it turns out, two completely different animals. This season of life was not conducive to ministry as I had known it. But neither would the ministry I'd known and led in during college be helpful for our context here in an informal settlement in South Africa.

I had realized after having my second child I couldn't do ministry the way Trevor was, talking to the people he would meet during those long walks through the community, setting up meetings to strategize about how to develop our plans for ministry and reconciliation. It became clear that I would need to lead in a different way. But I didn't know that soon I wouldn't feel able to participate in our ministry much at all. By the time I was juggling two and then three children under the age of six I was honestly just barely making it. I struggled to plan or be strategic or have vision for our own lives, let alone our work. My mission was to keep my children alive and reasonably happy for another day. And even that I was winging almost completely! As the mother of these three beautiful girls, who had me absolutely running for my life, I was easily overwhelmed. I had quickly entered a season where I could only be present in the moment.

After around six years on the field, as a team, we'd generally felt like there hadn't been a vast amount of fruit in our first season. Many relationships were built and foundations were laid but there was no huge fruit hanging off those branches. And I didn't feel like I personally had done any real or important work at all. But—regardless—it was time to prepare for sabbatical: a season where we would step back from our primary work within our community in South Africa and into year of reflection, to connect with those who were supporting us in our ministry, and to ask God what He wanted to do inside of our own hearts.

Just before we were about to go on sabbatical, a young woman named Portia came to my house and said that she wanted to talk with me. Portia worked at the home of some friends of ours that lived just down the road, so I saw her now and then. I didn't know her super well. We had had a few conversations and one time, when she was desperate for child care, I took her baby to come play with my girls so she could work.

I invited Portia in from the heat of the day, and she sat down. She told me that she was planning to move home with her parents who lived in another city so she could start studying psychology. She told me she wanted to develop herself and her family. She was excited to begin studying to learn new skills and be able to have the kind of career and resources that she felt would help her be the mother and wife she wanted to be.

I was happy for Portia. I wasn't totally sure why she wanted to share this with me, but I was happy for her—she was excited and seemed to feel purpose and clarity. But then, she began to thank me for all I had done for her. Huh? She said I taught her about being a good mom and how to look after herself and her family. I was confused. I kept thinking, "Is this my mommy brain, what have I forgotten?" I couldn't remember having any of these kinds of conversations with Portia. I was sure she had me confused with someone. So I said "I'm so glad to hear about this next step for you, but did we have some chats that I'm forgetting about?"

Portia laughed. "No, no, I just watched you with your kids and listened to how you spoke about your husband and family and I wanted that for myself. So I thought about how I could get there, and I made decisions!" I was dumbfounded and started crying. I have this way of crying just sort of silently where tears stream out of my eyes endlessly, like rain dropping into a puddle. Portia laughed at me, in a friendly way, for being so emotional about it.

Here I had been thinking, for years, "*all* I can do is host meetings in my home, but I'm not making any real impact on anyone, except maybe my kids." The pace of ministry for me had seemed to slow to a crawl. And then along comes this woman, Portia, who just watched me bumbling through my life from afar and decided to change things in her life because of what she saw! I had been completely unaware of how God was using me. The Spirit was using me in a deep way here. It strikes me now that this is often how God works, in extreme mystery, almost undercover. I don't have to strive to be "important," I am an instrument, I can let God use who I am, at every stage of life. The interaction with Portia drove home for me that ministry does not always look how I think it is supposed to look. Life and following God's leadership—seeking to lead others here in South Africa—would be very different than it had been before. I never expected this change of pace, or this shift in my perspective. Portia helped me to see that there were beautiful areas in my life and ministry where I wasn't doing much, but where God was bearing fruit.

It was then that I began to understand the ways being around as a mom to my own girls, while doing the little ministry I could, was sometimes a blessing to the broader community as well. Rather soon after moving to South Africa, our house became *the* neighborhood house that all the kids came to. Every day, I have a contingency of young boys that come over to play with me and my girls or to just hang around the house. On a regular basis I have neighbors ask me if I run a crèche—which is the term here for daycare.

Initially, I was often surprised that these kids kept coming back—because I have rules and expectations at my house. Most parents are working when their kids come home from school. So while some kids here have nannies who look after them, some kids just run free until the sun sets. When children come to play at my house I have two expectations: one, they must greet me when they come in, and two, they must be kind and play fair while they have fun. Everyone gets three chances. If I have to speak to one of the children three times about their behavior, then I ask them to go home and try again tomorrow—because the Lord gives us new mercies every morning.

There are many stories I could tell about children who have played at my home, the lessons they have learned, and the lessons I have learned from them. But one boy has a special place in my heart. Tshepiso, who lived down the street, was five or six when he started playing at our house. Sometimes he would be locked out of his own house when he returned from school, or he would be hungry because there wasn't enough for him to eat, and he would show up at my gate. In fact, he basically showed up every day. Whenever he was playing here, I would have to go and break up fights, facilitate apologies, and help the children forgive each other. Tshepiso inevitably would use up all of his three chances, each time he came. I would walk him to our gate, give him a hug and tell him "I know you can do better, and I hope to see you tomorrow."

One particularly difficult afternoon, Tshepiso had been starting fights and swearing at his friends, and I had to ask him to leave. He had been really ugly to another child, so I raised my voice, and I was really firm with him. As I walked him out that day, he hugged me so tight and said "I love you Mama Keira." (African mothers are typically called by their firstborn's name, so I am Mama Keira.) I realized that day when he hugged me so tight, that for Tshepiso, discipline and consistency meant love. I had a unique opportunity every day to create loving boundaries at my house that weren't present in the same way in the homes of many of these boys. Before that day, I had been feeling like I was missing an opportunity—that I should be leading a children's Bible study or a homework study group, or something. I knew, though, that I didn't have the capacity for those things in that season. Instead God used me, for a few hours everyday, to be a mother to many. The little I gave—my home, my love, and my clear boundaries—made a big difference. God is always faithful to take the little we have and multiply it. My role was to love with boundaries and call out how I saw God within each of them. That I could do—and that, as it turned out, was powerful.

STRENGTH AND VULNERABILITY

NOWADAYS, MY CHILDREN are not quite as young, not nearly as dependent on me as they once were, and so I've had a new challenge: trying to rediscover parts of my identity, to differentiate from my roles as a mother and wife, and find lost parts of myself again. Now that all of my children are in school, I'm coming around sort of full circle, getting involved in ministry in a more upfront way again, although not exactly in the way I had imagined. Now I have the benefit of time and experience, a clearer understanding of the way that I lead. And I'm more rooted in the reality that God uses whatever training and knowledge I have.

One of the programs that our team had started in our community was a ladies' gym called Kaofela Retlakgona, which in English is "Together We Can Do It." As our new teammate, Jen, joined our team she looked for a meaningful way to connect and serve. She started interviewing a lot of people, specifically looking for something called positive deviance: behaviors that were outside of the norm in a positive way. She found many women had a desire to exercise but didn't feel safe running within the community on their own, because it didn't feel safe, especially in the evening after work. Sexual harassment and violent crime are very real possibilities for women walking alone. So she started Kaofela as a safe place for women to exercise. This ladies exercise group, which soon became a small gym, used group strength to foster more safety for all the women there.

Our hope with the gym was to not only create a safe space to exercise but a place to build relationship and a community of trust, health and wholeness. I have had the opportunity to work with the ladies at the gym, building relationships, and encouraging their leadership. Through this program I've seen these ladies learn to work together, encourage, and challenge each other. They have become a support for each other when times are hard. As we developed the feeling of community in this gym, all the women who took classes together began learning that vulnerability and empathy are not signs of weakness, but rather that they are needed within their community of women. Although they are taking baby steps into sharing life differently, they are taking steps! It has been so encouraging to watch and be part of their stories.

As my children got a little older, I began to stretch my wings a bit and tried learning more about storytelling. I had attended the weekend Story Workshop at The Allender Center in Seattle during sabbatical, and I loved it. The way they (and I) are using the word storytelling is the practice and ability of looking at the deeper themes in one's own life: asking questions of our own stories and figuring out how to live them more fully and walk through our pain to get to our healing. I enjoyed the weekend training so much that I decided I wanted to learn more about how it might be useful in our context. So I did something that at the time felt kind of crazy, I returned to South Africa from our sabbatical, only to turn right back around and go to Seattle with Trevor's blessing, leaving he and the girls in South Africa for a few months, to do work towards the Lay Counseling Certificate through the Allender Center. I wanted to learn more and look deeply and specifically at the big and small traumas in our lives, and how to be present in someone else's story. The program taught me so much about how to sit with people in their stories, how to listen, how to create space for them to work out the particularities of their memories and experiences and see what larger themes there might be. I was grateful for the experience of sharing in other people's lives in this new way.

After so many years of ministry shifting because of my primary job as full-time mom, I was finally finding life again in the midst of this new passion and feeling Jesus work in me and through me in a new way, though I now see the streams connecting all the things I had been learning. Twelve years ago I was trained as a doula, supporting a mother in her pain and struggle as she labors to give birth. Creating places for people to tell their stories and share their joys and pains is, sadly, not a normal part of our culture, and often when we do share there is often not the kind of support or emotional safety we need. I can see now how both my doula work and my work as a storytelling facilitator involve supporting labor—only the latter is an emotional labor. As I create space for people to be safe as they share their stories either one-on-one or in a group, I'm providing a space that is rare and valuable. It almost always ends up being life giving to myself and others. I am still working on adapting this concept to our context, finding ways for sharing among the women in our community that doesn't re-traumatize those who share their stories and their pain vulnerably.

For years, I had done all that sitting, in so many kitchens, with so many women, chatting and trying to have conversations that were deep and meaningful. I never really succeeded, no matter how well the women knew each other, I found that the depth of relationship didn't feel to me very deep at all. At first, I thought no one was interested in deeper topics. Eventually, I learned the real reason why they were not sharing much. There was a dynamic of reluctance to share vulnerably because the community would gossip and use your words against you. There was very little trust and safety.

In this context, I have found that so many lives around me are marked with severe trauma. So many lives and so many experiences, in fact, that the conversation and feelings around it are numbed. Trauma is practically a cultural experience, a normalcy. To be sexually harassed, to watch a loved one die from HIV, to take in a child because their parent has left or died, are just a few of the things I regularly hear my friends dealing with. Most people, though, keep it below the surface; it's rare for someone to even discuss these challenges. So much of my heart wants to see my friends and those around me rescued from the situations and from that pain. But my heart and my training tell me that healing comes from walking with Jesus gently through the pain, not from making it less than it is with "silver lining" encouragement. Sometimes as a lay minister I have the chance to help people who are hurting to engage with their own stories and sometimes, among groups, by engaging with each other's stories and letting them crack us open.

Recently I had such an opportunity. The women's ministry of my church hosted a tea with our ladies' gym group. I wasn't so sure about how it would go, as my church at the time was a predominantly White church and most people with privilege or money do not readily find themselves in the informal settlement like Zandspruit, and are generally uncomfortable with the idea of being there. So I had pretty low expectations for the time. As is the tradition in the women's ministry at our church, someone will share a testimony from their life, or a story that gives insight into how God has shaped them. Lesedi, a woman from the gym, was asked to be one of the people to share.

Lesedi is a bubbly and talkative woman who was newer to Kaofela, our ladies gym community, and the experience of sharing was also new for her. She closed her eyes and began sharing some things which she had never spoken about in her life, about the horrific and terrible evil that had been done to her, and she shared her journey in meeting challenge after challenge that was set before her. While she spoke, eyes closed, I glanced around the room at the other women's eyes—almost none of which were dry.

After the time of sharing, I went to check in with Lesedi, and she told me that she hadn't expected to share all that she had. She felt very exposed. I hugged her and reminded her that she was loved and not alone. Shame would keep us hidden and trapped by fear of not being seen. Lesedi's vulnerable sharing was a kick in shame's face. She had no idea why she shared all that she had that day, but in later conversations she figured that it was just time to tell the truth about her story. I thanked her for her vulnerability and acknowledged the way that it likely blessed many others. When we share vulnerably we give others permission to see us, as well as permission to share vulnerably with others in that same way. And her sharing did open up a healing space for both her and others in the room. Later, the gym ladies spoke about wanting to have more space to share stories and speak more deeply with each other about their lives. I had experienced such a general lack of trust between women during my time in South Africa. What a gift Lesedi brought that day, opening a door for others, marking the beginning of a path forward. Given that this was all fairly recent, my hope is that the ladies in the gym can continue building on this experience by starting story groups where we learn together how to sit with one another in our pain and see the beauty that is also present, holding both together, Jesus sitting right there with us, bringing healing.

DESPITE MYSELF, CONTINUING TO SAY YES

IT'S BEEN A DECADE here in South Africa. I can honestly say I never foresaw this as my life. Not to be a bridge builder in college nor as a campus minister. Not going to South Africa, marrying cross-culturally, or raising three daughters overseas. Yet this is my life. And it is a good life. But I do, still, have deep moments of doubt, moments that are full of questions. *Should we be here? Should we be on the field? Is it worth it to open myself and my family to the stresses and tension we face daily? Am I able to serve Jesus in this way long-term? Do I know too much now to turn back?* Among all the questions that arise though, I am most challenged by the idea of home. *Where is my home? Is it where I've lived the longest? Where I've raised my kids? Is it up to me to teach them about my home and our people there, about African American history and culture? Is it my responsibility to make sure that they also feel at home among their people in America?*

Home has become even more complicated as America no longer feels like the respite it used to. Watching from afar the continued problems of brutality against Black people, my heart feels lost. Returning there has been even harder, feeling scared in a way I rarely remember registering as a young person. Teaching my children not to question the police for any reason if we are pulled over and to keep their hands visible felt awful but necessary.

And as I do this, it's gone—the sacred safety of home is gone. *Maybe home is just where my family is together? Or is it simply the places that are life-giving? Or is it heaven that I long for, the both sober and joyful thought of being with Jesus, in peace for eternity? Where is home?* I don't know.

All these questions rise up in me from time to time and demand fresh assurance. The one thing I consistently hear from Jesus in those regular times of doubt and questions is to "stay in the tension." Still, I look to Him for certainty. But Jesus invites me to walk the line between comfort and challenge, to lean into discernment, to continue to go deeper with Him, with myself. All I can do is to try to say "yes" to the invitation, over and over. That's how I've made it to ten years on the field. I've said yes, in the midst of the tension, in the midst of the struggle. Over and over again I've tried to choose the holy shift God invited me into: into sharing from my true center, into the unexpected marriage, the unexpected calling, perhaps slowly receiving the unexpected fruit of a slowed-down pace of life, and continuing to shift back into Jesus as my only center.

Though my life often feels frantic and messy and broken—listen, I know it is frantic and messy and broken in *every* other life and place too—I know that God can use my little efforts to do beautiful things here in South Africa. When I manage my expectations by bringing into perspective the reality and struggles of life, and when I take time to breathe in the truth of the God of the Universe and His sovereignty, I am able to see more clearly and say yes more wholeheartedly. The world doesn't need perfection, the world needs men and women who are as in touch as possible with Jesus, people who can embrace all of who they are—the beauty, the ugliness, the power, the weakness—offering it vulnerably and then trusting God with the fruit.

8

GIRL, YOU NEED JESUS!
Janet Balasiri Singleterry

Janet is a Thai-American woman who grew up in Indiana. She worked on staff with InterVarsity Christian Fellowship for eleven years: on the Indiana University campus for seven years and then as the national Global Urban Trek Coordinator for four years. Janet also directed the Trek teams of college students headed to Thailand to live and serve alongside the urban poor in Bangkok for many years. She now lives in San Jose, California with her husband Andy and their informal foster daughter Nayeli. She and Andy are on staff with Servant Partners as the directors of the San Jose site leading an internship of young urban ministers as well as pastoring a young church plant, Shalom Iglesia, a bilingual congregation in their low-income Latino neighborhood.

IT'S 1996 AND I AM sitting in the stadium seats at the University of Illinois Champaign-Urbana, but I am not attending a college basketball game. Instead, I am worshiping Jesus with tens of thousands of other people singing, "I have a Father, He knows my name. Before even time began, my life was in His hands," the first verse to the worship song "You Know My Name," and tears are streaming down my face. I am aware, I am realizing, that I do feel known and loved presently, by my father: God the Father. My actual father died when my whole family was in a car accident a few years ago, and my life had since tumbled in directions I could never have anticipated. The first of which, of course, is how this culturally Buddhist, Thai young woman became a Christian in the first place.

My parents, Jarunee and Tanunchai, who immigrated to the United States in 1970, opened the first Thai restaurant in the entire state of Indiana. To get ingredients, we had to travel monthly in a cargo van to Illinois to get groceries from Chicago's Chinatown. On one such trip in 1992, after we finished shopping and made a stop to celebrate my mom's birthday over dim sum, my parents and I headed back to Indiana. I was fifteen years old. I often slept on the journey home, and that day was no different. I was sleeping soundly when the van swerved out of control, and I awoke to a booming pop near my head. The tire burst, and my dad was trying to regain control. I looked around, trying to make sense of the noise, and saw an array of Kikkoman soy sauce, Tiparos fish sauce boxes, and bags of jasmine rice flying through the air like socks being tossed round and round in the dryer drum. By the time we came to a stop, the van had flipped over with its wheels spinning toward the sky. I was trapped underneath boxes, broken bottles of oyster sauce and dented cans of young corn. Other drivers screeched to a halt, coming to the van to help dig me out. My mom was just hanging there, upside down, from her seat belt. She was screaming my name at the top of her lungs because the boxes were blocking any view of me. Light started to break through as the strangers moved things off of me until, finally, I could slowly crawl out onto the grassy median. I was reunited with my mom, and we began searching for my dad, since the driver's seat was blocked by boxes that had shifted from the cargo area.

I think I knew my father was gone at the scene of the accident because the medical crew on the scene had made a wall between us and his body after they pulled him out of our van. They didn't want us to see them making their final efforts to revive him. When the doctors at Jasper County Hospital came to the recovery room hours later, his death was confirmed, as they declared to my mom that there was nothing more they could do to save him. The thin fabric curtain separating my mother's bed from my own could not shield me from their words. I swung open the curtain and ran to my mom, to hold her and weep from the depths of my gut. The months that followed, without my father, meant massive change: a new apartment, a new school, and a new way of life. My mom could no longer commute across Indianapolis to work, make sure I had what I needed for school, and be at the restaurant all day and into evening while worrying about me being a half-hour drive across the city. My mom found an apartment that was located less than a mile from the restaurant, which allowed her to check in on me whenever she chose to do so, and I began attending a new school nearby.

Part of being Thai meant I grew up culturally Buddhist. Another adjustment after losing my dad was that I came to find out that my mom wasn't sure that dad was going to heaven. I was pretty shocked by this realization: how could we not be sure of his fate after death? Since his life was taken so suddenly, there was no way to be certain that his "good" outweighed his "bad." In its simplest form, that is a Thai-Buddhist understanding of how one achieves entry to heaven. Later in life, as people grow old and nearer to death, even nominal Buddhists actively "make merit" by donating to charities, and they "do benevolence" by serving the less fortunate in order to tip the cosmic scale to good. That way, when they die, they can be more certain that their good deeds outnumbered their bad deeds, and they can go to heaven.

According to our family—and not just my mother—no one had any level of confidence that this was the case for my dad. This began a journey of questioning for me that introduced me to the good news of Jesus Christ. A friend in my homeroom class was going on a ski trip with her church youth group, and I invited myself along, likely the easiest evangelism she had ever done. It was music to my ears to know that Jesus was perfect and had never done any wrong, and so if I believed in Him, I was then forgiven for all the wrong in my life, and I was guaranteed to go to heaven. This seemed to make much more sense to me than all the uncertainty that was swirling around me, and the complex equation of heaven I had grown up with. I couldn't earn my way to heaven with merit and good deeds; I needed Jesus. I chose to follow Christ that day, six months after my dad had passed away. My understanding of salvation has continued to deepen, since then, but I have never looked back on that decision.

Three months after I became a Christian, I went with my new faith community to Matamoros, Mexico, on a classic "build-a-house-in-a-week" type of mission trip. In that time, I got to use my limited school Spanish to share my testimony, and through that, a leader in the slum community where we were working in came to Christ. That experience sparked something new in me and—I know now—set the trajectory for my life. I went on three other cross-cultural mission trips during high school, and on my last trip, just as I was about to enter college, I felt that same spark from my first missions trip grow into a flame. The flame was strong and hot enough that I needed to let my mom know that I wanted to change my career path.

My plan to this point had been to study chemical engineering. And my acceptance into an elite engineering school, Rose-Hulman, was not just a big deal for me; it was also a historical one for the 120-year-old university: I had been accepted into this college of engineering as part of the first class of women Rose-Hulman was accepting. Changing my career path to an unknown path serving the Lord would likely lead away from engineering, away from worldly success, away from the near-guarantee of monetary stability. I shared my desire with my mom and was rebuffed. There was no convincing her. My honest confession of a desire to transfer schools and consider a new path of education was met with crying and screaming about what an ungrateful child I was. She literally stormed out of the house, crying in anger, as she walked back to the restaurant.

My parents had moved here from Thailand and built their life up from nothing. Mom took whatever job she could as a maid or cook until my dad could finish school. They worked harder than I can probably imagine to make ends meet as they brought me into the world. Their dreams for me included a life without concern for money. Not wanting to disappoint her and all the aspirations she held out for me on behalf of herself and my deceased father, I went on with the original plan and started Rose-Hulman in the fall of 1995.

During that first year, I went to class, studied hard, and made the grade as a good student and a dutiful daughter. But what excited me wasn't the chemistry, it was the late-night conversations debating faith and science, on and off campus, and the conversations in the Bible study I led—the first woman to do so at Rose-Hulman. In that time, I had the privilege of leading two of my best friends to life under the Lordship of Jesus.

One night at the large group gathering of our fellowship, the speaker was sharing about life in full-time ministry in Papua New Guinea, and how it had shaped and formed him. As he spoke, my heart began to beat faster and faster, and I could feel it ringing in my ears with each thump. I felt hot with that same flame I had felt when I went on my first missions trip. I had to get up and walk to the bathroom to get some air. My best friend Dawn, whom I had met in the first weeks at Rose-Hulman, followed me, knowing that something strange was happening to me.

In front of the mirror, so I could face myself, I confessed that I felt God's strong and unwavering call on my life, and it was not to sit on a chemistry lab bench all day for the rest of my life. In that moment, I had made my decision. Tears ran down my face as I processed the gravity of it all. There would be my mom's disappointment in me. And then, there were my own fears of this call—that still seemed both totally certain and totally unclear, to which God was beckoning me—this strong call to a yet unknown life.

But I did it. I told my mom, and she took me to a psychologist because "hearing from God" sounded like I was "hearing voices" in my head. I started the paperwork to transfer from an elite engineering school to a large public university. Then, I finished out the remainder of that school year at Rose-Hulman and transitioned to Indiana University to study secondary education with a focus in Spanish.

At Indiana University (IU), I got involved in InterVarsity, though it was intimidating since it was three times as big a group of people as the Christian fellowship at Rose-Hulman had been. The fellowship at IU encouraged me to go to Urbana, InterVarsity's missions conference that happens every three years with college-age students from around the world. I made plans to go, though ironically, I would spend as much time with my Rose-Hulman friends as I did with my new friends from the IU fellowship. Even as I had already made costly and life-altering decisions, I still had one foot in each boat. My heart was conflicted, with different parts of myself in each place. This calling that I was trying to figure out was unfamiliar and uncomfortable, and I deeply needed the confirming presence of God in my life.

So here I am, at Urbana '96, sitting in this stadium seat. I am weeping. I am singing. I am hearing myself say the words, "I have a Maker, and He knows my name," as I sing. And I feel the presence of God. I am certain in this moment not just of the fact of my heavenly Father's love, but of His call on my life, and His guiding hand in the choices I have made.

Confirmation of God's call in my life is reassuring in this moment, but to be honest, as I move back into my day-to-day life, I will still be asking, "Where will this call take me, exactly?" Certainly away from the trajectory I have been on for my life thus far. But for the next few years, as the what and where remain unclear, I will hold onto the surety of this unknown calling even as I walk directly into it, step by step.

✳

Fast forward. Today, nearly twenty years after trying to respond to that initial calling on my life, I'm in California. I'm married, and I live with my husband Andy in the Guadalupe Washington neighborhood of San Jose, just south of downtown. It's over two thousand miles away from Indiana, and it is a long way from the life that I had known.

The smell of *al pastor* meat being grilled and cut for savory tacos with a splash of pineapple *sabor* wafts through the streets and hangs in the air, along with the sounds of gunshots and helicopters circling overhead at night. Our neighbors on all sides have two-bedroom apartments being shared by multiple families. Where I grew up in the Midwest, a two-bedroom apartment was an appropriate and affordable space for a single individual. Here turnover is high because even with that many people contributing for rent, it's often impossible to afford Silicon Valley rent unless you have a Silicon Valley tech job at Google or Facebook. I myself shed many a tear during my own housing search, as Andy and I looked at apartments that are smaller than the two-car garage that I owned (attached to the four-bedroom home) in Indiana.

Being worlds away from that suburban, spacious, Midwestern life, I often sit on our front porch with friends in the neighborhood who work hard at their jobs, but despair after hours of low-paying and back-breaking work, that they are not able to put food in the mouths of their children or scrape together enough to pay for the roof over their heads. We sit together, we cry, and we pray for God's provision. Even though Andy and I can afford to rent our house with just our two incomes plus a housemate who pays a portion of the rent, not two or three whole families needing to pitch in, we feel the challenges of this housing market alongside our friends. We're lucky enough to have a landlord who was a former pastor of our church, who has been generous enough to freeze our rent price for the last few years. Every day, we live in the reality that our present life would not be possible without the grace of God and the support of community. No one said the call would be easy.

After I finished my degree in education and graduated from Indiana University, I started my student teaching semester in a high school Spanish class. All the while, I wondered what was next. Was this the call? Or where would this calling lead me? During this time, I was invited to return to my college fellowship at InterVarsity and speak at the "Back to School Retreat" about how to discern God's will. I spoke about stopping often to ask God where He was leading, and not just relying on what you thought you heard Him say so many years or even months ago. I also, upon hearing myself, had to sit down and take my own advice. I reconsidered where I was going in life. Close to that time, my former InterVarsity staff worker who had invited me to come and speak at that event asked me to apply to come on staff with him to lead and disciple college students. After some thought and prayer, as well as working through the trepidation of my own self-consciousness about being good enough or my ability to connect with cool college kids, I applied and was provisionally appointed to come on staff with InterVarsity at Indiana University. Now the kicker: fundraising.

My mom had made one thing very clear when I went on my first trip to Mexico with my youth group at church, and that was that I was not to ask anyone in our family for support. And I complied. But I did have a few of her friends on the list, whom I felt close to. Unfortunately, that didn't go well, as they called to ask her why she couldn't pay for her own daughter's travels. Raising funds to support myself for salary, benefits, and ministry expenses on a regular basis, as opposed to a one-time trip, was a formidable challenge for me, especially knowing that my mom still did not want my family or any of her friends to be contacted. I came to know Jesus through Faith Church in Indianapolis, and they sent me off to college with a good foundation. Many of the congregation there had children who had also been involved with InterVarsity, and they were overwhelmingly supportive as I went into full-time ministry.

I moved back to Bloomington to start working to rebuild the struggling chapter of InterVarsity at Indiana University. Early on in college, I had experienced joy in building community through small group Bible studies. Once I was on staff, I had the privilege of leading young people through many inductive studies of scripture, and also creating a place for them to belong—on a campus of over thirty thousand students. I would write personal notes to students, sometimes with candy attached, and place the notes in their campus mailboxes to encourage them, so they might feel known in a sea of loneliness at IU. I was getting to do what I loved.

My second year on staff with InterVarsity Christian Fellowship led me to the Global Urban Trek, a program which takes college students to live and serve among the urban poor internationally, at various sites, for six weeks every summer. The first year I led a trip, and every June thereafter, for many years, I'd pack up my bag full of clothes appropriate for the hot and steamy season in Bangkok, Thailand. It was a privilege to help students through this experience, to help them process their understandable dissonance with sleeping on a thin mat, on top of wood slats which did not fully cover the sewer water underneath the homes—homes that were built quickly, in the cracks of society, with little oversight or regulation. The danger of water snakes and rats was real, and the stench was even more real. They laid down as well as they could on those thin mats and tried to block out the vivid sounds of cats fighting, motorcycle rumbles, and the resounding conversations of those who had consumed a few too many beers. There were so many moments and experiences to process as students struggled through language barriers with a genuine desire to relate and love those around them in the slum community.

About seven years later—building the fellowship of students during the school year and taking some of those students to the slums of Bangkok during the summer—I came to California to take a short sabbatical. I ended up meeting Andy Singleterry, who would become my husband. When we met, we quickly discovered that we both loved manuscript Bible study, and we both felt called to ministry among the urban poor. Some of our first evenings together were alongside the guests of the Emergency Housing Consortium, our local homeless shelter, at their monthly game nights where we hung out and played Scrabble. Andy's love for games and ease ministering to all kinds of people quickly made it clear to me that he would be a good partner in ministry, life, and faith. As a result, my short sabbatical trip to California ended up becoming a big move.

In the fall of 2009, Andy and I were about one month away from our wedding date. On a Tuesday morning, I woke up and found I no longer had control of my legs, from the knees down. My brain would try to communicate to my toes to move, but my spinal cord would not pass those messages along. As it turned out, I had a spinal cord injury and ended up in emergency surgery to try to correct the issue. After two surgeries on my back, acute physical therapy, occupational therapy, and recreational therapy—on my wedding day, one month later—I was somehow, with a little help, able to walk down the aisle to the altar to marry my husband.

I took almost a year off of my work with InterVarsity to focus on my healing journey and deal with the grief from the losses in my body. It takes a whole year of physical therapy to even get a sense of what kind of mobility is possible after an injury such as mine. There were a few unexpected byproducts of this year on leave from full-time work. There was space to consider what kind of turn my life might be taking. I took stock of the losses I was experiencing and grieved them. Though it was likely that I could physically bear biological children, I began to picture my future toddler running into the street and me, with my present reality, not being able to chase my toddler and provide protection from oncoming traffic.

These concerns about family life were accompanied by discernment of God's call for me to leave InterVarsity and transition to Servant Partners (SP). Andy was already on staff with SP and was hoping to plant an internship of young adults engaging in incarnational urban ministry in San Jose. For a couple of years, Andy had been inviting me to consider the possibility of joining him in this. But I was a "company man," meaning I intended to be loyal to InterVarsity until the day I died, so I had resisted, instead assuming I would take a new position with InterVarsity in California. However, the life circumstances of my injury brought me to a point of needing to consider an abrupt shift. I could no longer trot the globe as freely as I had done in the past. In a year's time I had made a lot of progress—I had moved from a wheelchair to a walker to a cane to being able to get around using only braces on my lower legs—but I was still not as mobile as I used to be.

Andy's vision for us to partner together in urban minis-try did sound appealing. The transition would definitely allow me to pursue a calling to work with young peo-ple who were exploring their call to urban ministry. And instead of six weeks, I would have nearly two years of working side-by-side with emerging leaders in our neighborhood, helping to develop them to minister alongside the urban poor. Also, Servant Partners was an organization very much connected to my current work. In fact, it was started by a few InterVarsity folks who were transitioning off staff life in the 1990s pursuing their own call in urban poor missions. In the spring of 2011, I applied and was accepted to Servant Partners staff and transitioned from my work with InterVarsity.

Later that fall, we started with our first class of interns in San Jose. The home church we joined had been investing in this area for about seven years at that point. They had purchased property for a community garden across from the vibrant and community-involved local school, Washington Elementary. The garden was a place where folks from the neighborhood could maintain plots to grow and harvest vegetables and flowers, while also building community with those around them. At the school, church members had hosted after-school tutoring programs on and off over the years. The school had also graciously allowed our church to host week-long Bible camps.

When I first engaged God's calling on my life during my first year of college, and I switched from chemical engineering to major in secondary education in Spanish, I had no idea I would be wrestling with the Word of God in this foreign language weekly. I'll never forget seeing my friend Rosa's eyes light up when she heard me speak her native language for the first time. At this point, I feel certain that the Lord did know even back then what He was planning. God knew what a joy it would be for me to sit with these neighbors who had been going to mass all their lives, but had not had the opportunity to open the scriptures for themselves, to read it, to discuss their thoughts and questions about it, and to consider how it applies to their daily lives in their native tongue of Spanish.

In addition to the Spanish Bible studies, activities in the neighborhood with the interns were moving along at a reasonable pace. We had plenty to do with the Bible clubs and the parents' groups, but we lacked dedicated Latino leaders who could join us in the work and devote their lives to the vision. This would not only limit the work going forward, but buy-in and input from neighbors were critical to the vision itself.

Then, in the spring of 2013, two years after we had begun, we heard from a couple who were long-time friends of Andy's from his many trips to Honduras. Jairo and Lourdes Sarmiento were being sent out from their home church, Iglesia en Transformación, in Tegucigalpa, Honduras to minister to Latinos in the United States. Their call to church-planting was specific, but like my call had been for so long, they did not yet have a specific location. Jairo and Lourdes already had thirty years of church planting experience under their belts—they would be amazing teammates and assets to our Servant Partners site in San Jose. After processing with God and working with SP on sponsoring them for a religious worker's visa, the Sarmiento family arrived in San Jose simultaneously with our second class of interns that fall. Our bilingual Bible study had been going for about a year at this point, and it was chugging along just fine, but with Jairo and Lourdes on the scene it was like adding jet fuel to a model T car. Things started to pick up rapidly due to their experience, their cultural aptitude, and their passions in evangelism and discipleship. Their partnership in the neighborhood was a gift from God. A Jesus community was now growing rapidly right before our eyes, meeting in different homes in the neighborhood throughout the week.

Our interns were spending time getting to know kids from the neighborhood at the Washington United Youth Center located next door to the elementary school. There was one young girl, Nayeli, who was eleven when our interns, Lizzie and Cayla, met her. At first, she ran away from them because she didn't want these "strange White girls all up in my business." Nayeli's main point of reference for White people at the center were the county officials who would check on the programs and effectiveness of the center. Being that government officials made Nayeli nervous, she couldn't let her guard down until she realized Lizzie and Cayla weren't part of the government. They were faithful to show up twice a week to attend the Young Women's Empowerment Group, or "group" as participants called it, so Nayeli began to understand they weren't going anywhere and they weren't county officials.

Many of the girls in the program needed help with school and homework, and Lizzie and Cayla had the skills to help them. Nayeli started to ask for their help with schoolwork, and over time she also opened up about the stress of family and life on the streets. As Nayeli and her older brother were also beginning to get more involved with the Shalom Iglesia church ministry, Nayeli's grades were improving from Ds and Fs to Bs and Cs. She no longer felt alone carrying the burdens of her academic struggle, unstable home life, and the draw of drugs and gang life. It's not as though these realities went away, but she had people who consistently asked her how she was doing, and who walked alongside her, helping her to see new possibilities for her life.

During Shalom Iglesia's Sunday bilingual Bible study, Lizzie and a few other SP interns started to gather the girls from the empowerment group and other neighborhood teens together for an informal youth group in their home at the same time. After the study, their group would join our adult group, and we'd all have dinner together. At that point, she was one of the most consistent youth showing up at our Shalom youth events. It was Christmas time in 2014 when I first met Nayeli. She seemed stand-offish to anyone who had not yet earned her trust, so she stuck close to Cayla and Lizzie. A few weeks later, she had a long report to write on a British monarch, and I was recommended to her as one who could help her through it. She came over with Lizzie and the three of us worked on the report. Though she was understandably suspicious of outsiders, Nayeli and I got to know each other a little that day and perhaps I built a bit of trust. She and I didn't know then that there would be many more nights working on school reports together in our future.

Shalom Iglesia was growing into a stable church body, so the leadership team planned to move the Sunday worship service to a church building in January 2015. The folks who would gather for Friday night prayer, Sunday bilingual Bible study, and informal youth group were all waiting for church to "finally start." But Jairo, our pastor, needed to have a quadruple bypass, so we needed to delay, not only for the surgery but to allow for Jairo to slowly heal and recover. Waiting has never been easy for me, and now leading others in the waiting would be even more difficult. It would be many months after January of 2015 before we could begin the move to formal worship services.

We decided to use the unexpected time to invigorate the work in the neighborhood. We invited the head pastor from New Life Church in East Los Angeles, a Servant Partners church plant, to come to Guadalupe Washington and spend some time with us. Pastor Chris brought Tavo with him. Tavo was a believer who had had serious anger issues growing up, similar to many men in our neighborhood. Nayeli's brother lived by the law of machismo, with few healthy outlets for the anger and frustration that came to the surface during crisis and struggle. But Tavo had encountered the Holy Spirit at New Life Church, and God had begun to do a work of transformation in his life. Here he was with us, just a few years later, testifying to God's goodness and praying with Holy Spirit power as he ministered to our small church plant, gathering as we were waiting to finally start our new Sunday service.

One Saturday during Chris and Tavo's visit, we hosted a barbeque lunch at our house for our interns and the whole New Life ministry team. Nayeli and her brothers came to our backyard gathering to meet up with Lizzie and Cayla. But they were all heavy of heart—they were all meeting up to go to a funeral fundraiser for a good friend of theirs, because fundraisers like community car washes are how most burials are paid for in our neighborhood. The boy who had died was twenty years old. He had just been visiting Shalom Iglesia's youth group the Sunday before, celebrating Nayeli's birthday. Lizzie and Cayla were the godmothers to his newborn child. Tavo and Pastor Chris offered to pray with the whole group who was headed to the funeral fundraiser, each of them individually. Nayeli and her two brothers all received prayer that day. She told me later that she remembered experiencing the presence of the Holy Spirit tangibly in her life for the first time that afternoon, and she grew hungry for more. We learned that day that even though our church may someday soon be in a more formal building, no building or lack of one could limit God's power to work within our little growing church. On April 12, 2015, we launched the first Sunday worship service for Shalom Iglesia. Families we had been working with informally for years gathered to sing praise and hear the Word of God preached in Spanish, the language of Heaven, as Pastor Jairo refers to it. God is faithful.

Right around that time, in the spring of her seventh-grade year, Nayeli's family was evicted from their home, which was just a few doors down from our house. Housing scarcity in San Jose is one of the areas in most need of systemic change. No family members nearby were able to take in all six members of her family because they felt their houses were already filled to the max. Staying in their van was an option, but a dangerous one that they had experienced in previous years. After a few nights, Andy and I took in Nayeli's mom, boyfriend, and two younger kids while Nayeli and her older brother went to stay with our interns. This was a short-term solution while we helped them to search for housing. After a few weeks, they were finally able to land somewhere, but it was not an ideal situation, so they made longer-term plans to move about an hour south, just after the school year finished.

The Lord kept bringing Nayeli to mind. She had been invited to become a student leader at her school during the eight grade, and her grades had risen dramatically. She was on a trajectory to succeed, and the thought of her moving to a new area during the final year of middle school was unsettling in my heart. Whenever I thought about other households in the neighborhood, I knew ours was emptier than most. I often wondered what my own mom and my mother-in-law thought about not having grandkids yet. I kept asking the Lord how to pray and what to do. Nayeli's mother and I got into a conversation about what might be best for her daughter. Her school bus stop was just around the block from our house. I had a proposition: for eighth grade, would it be good for her to stay here at our house during the week and go to Salinas on weekends to be with her family? Her mother and family agreed that for academic reasons, this would be the best situation. The night before the first day of school, she brought her one blue Rubbermaid bin full of clothes, and moved into our home.

The first six months of grafting our lives together were an adventure with some very high highs and some very low lows. Andy and I do not have any biological children, so parenting was all kinds of new for us. I knew that breakfast before school is helpful for any child's ability to learn during the day, so I got up each day and made her a breakfast sandwich. None of us are morning people, so not very much was spoken in those wee hours of the morning. It took a few months for her to say that she would rather not have a breakfast sandwich in the morning because she didn't eat a lot before school. Apparently me waking up to send her off to school was weird, and too much attention for her. It made sense that going from being one of six kids in the house to being basically an "only child" could be a rough transition.

The other major stress on her was that though she had shelter and food to eat each day, the rest of her family was not always guaranteed those privileges. For example, the first few months she was with us, Nayeli's oldest brother slept on the streets at times, and wasn't eating because he didn't have the money to buy food. She would save up her allowance to buy him a meal. My heart broke knowing that she still carried so much stress and pain on her young shoulders, and I know the weight of the privileges she has been given will likely haunt her into her future.

Inexplicable anger and frustration would surface from all this family stress, and I would have to constantly remind myself that I had done nothing wrong, and that her pain and distress were not caused by me. My heart would cry out to the Lord on her behalf, and I prayed that He would comfort her where she was not yet able to let me in to comfort or pray for her in her internal distress. If someone asks, I tell them that my parenting style is prayer alone. Those prayers seemed to chip away at the stone of hurt around her heart, and she began to open up to me, and for that I give God all the glory.

That winter, we asked her middle school for an independent study week, so that she could miss school to travel with us to the Midwest. She would experience flying for the first time, as well as the culture shock of my home state of Indiana. On this trip, she met my mom and step-father and my dearest family friends, attended my home church where I came to know Jesus, went sledding in frigid temperatures, and pulled clay pottery for the first time. She was afraid and anxious at most of these new experiences, her brow would furrow and her body would stiffen, but most of the time she would trust us and try it. In the moment, it was difficult to tell if she was actually enjoying the experience or if she was just humoring us. But in retrospect, she always speaks of these times fondly, and wants to make them a tradition that we do again. It is a discipline of faith for me to push through those unreadable facial expressions and grumbles of fear and uncertainty. Just as in most disciplines, the pay-off comes in a surprising moment much later.

During this winter excursion, Andy and I knew that we needed to discuss the possibility of Nayeli staying in our lives and our home longer than the originally planned eighth grade year. And if we were going to do so, we would need to pursue legal guardianship, since the past few months had been tricky with doctor's appointments and school form signatures. Her mom always had to come by to sign permission slips, and she had to make the calls for doctor appointments that came up. As we spoke to friends who were parents and who know us well, we asked them what they thought about the prospect of inviting Nayeli to stay with us for the next four years of high school. One of them aptly responded that it would not just be the next four years of high school, but that we were making the decision to invite her into our lives for the rest of her future. No turning back. We needed this truth to settle in, but the more we discussed it, the more we wanted to ask her and her mother and grandmother to consider this permanent step with us. In January, after a few lengthy conversations, they agreed that this would be the best option for Nayeli. We were committed to making sure she had continued weekly time with abuelita on Mondays and visits to see her mom and siblings as often as we could make them happen. We did not want to take Nayeli away from her family, but we wanted to walk alongside them to offer her the best chances to succeed in her future. As Nayeli and her family will also attest, this kind of arrangement was messy and difficult. We sadly even had a number of people asking whether it would be better to cut Nayeli's family out of her life to make things "simpler." Simple doesn't always mean good.

On Easter, Andy, Nayeli, and I celebrated Jesus' resurrection with Shalom Iglesia, and then grabbed a bite to eat and boarded a plane for Long Beach. Nayeli had the week off from school for spring break, and I was asked to teach a seminar for graduating seniors from Cal State Long Beach and some other colleges in Southern California. But just as we were getting aboard the boat to our final destination, Nayeli's fever was at a 103-degree high. She had been feeling lousy as we traveled, and I sent a number of emails to our intercessors for her healing and relief. She was a trooper as we went by plane, car, and boat to get to Campus by the Sea. Beautiful Catalina Island was the setting for this week-long InterVarsity camp. Though breathtaking, one of the hurdles for Nayeli would be the lack of Wi-Fi and telephone reception. I taught eight hours a day, so in that time, Nayeli explored the island and took in all the magnificent views. She found huge rocks by the ocean on which to sit, ponder, and begin to read her Bible on her own. One night in our cabin, she exclaimed, "I think I prayed for eight whole minutes today!" She was pursuing God and encountering the Lord in a personal way for the first time. At lunch on the third day of camp, she brought in her Bible and asked what blasphemy meant, since she was starting to read the book of Mark. Wanting to talk to me and discuss theological terms from scripture? Win! In many ways, this trip to a small island off the coast of California was a turning point for Nayeli and her personal relationship with Jesus. She began to pray out loud that week more often than she would deny that she could. She testified to God's faithfulness in her life, amid struggles and temptations, to small groups and even to large crowds. I teared up and welled up with unspeakable joy each and every time she shared.

Back at home, over dinner conversations, Nayeli would ask what it really meant to be a Christian. She wasn't perfect, she still did bad things, she still was tempted and desired to do bad things. So she would ask, "How could I be a Christian?" We discussed the idea of faith, and how it wasn't dependent upon our own deeds but on Jesus' death on the cross. She was beginning to grasp this, so when her sister or her sister-in-law felt hopeless for various reasons, she would tell them, "Girl, you need Jesus! That's the only way I make it through all this shit in our life." She knew the bottom line of the gospel: we are all bad, we are beyond helping ourselves, we need Jesus. Finally, in November of 2016, she chose to be the first person to be baptized at Shalom Iglesia. Aptly, she chose Job 10:12 (NIV) as her life verse, "You gave me life and showed me kindness, and in your providence watched over my spirit." Job, a man who endured much suffering and still chose to follow God and have faith in Him and His purposes, was the biblical character she wanted to model her life after. She couldn't have made a more fitting and profound choice. Her life, like Job's, is truly a testimony of trust in the Lord and His providence even through suffering.

Throughout my life, the calling of God has been meandering and uncertain at times. I am here today living in an inner-city neighborhood under the rumble of propellers and the bright lights seeking to spot the "gangsters" we call friends. Each of them has a name and a face and a story more complex than I can imagine. People on the outside of our neighborhood say that these "gangsters" can make the choice not to quit school, not to sell or do drugs, and not to join a gang. But those who live here know that those choices are clouded by the constant fear of abandonment, the pressure of poverty, and the desire to be loved unconditionally, to name only a few. At one point in my life, I thought living out this calling of God to the city meant giving up the "American dream" into downward mobility. I thought it would look like being a good example for young people "less fortunate" than me.

I stand corrected and now believe my calling is not as much to be an example to anyone here in this neighborhood, but instead to learn from their example. I daily learn to love the one God has brought into my life and into my home, including all the chaos and mess that come along with that decision. When she asks me why I put up with her family and all the drama and messiness when I'm not even related to them, I am reminded of Ruth's commitment to Naomi in scripture. Though we are not blood-related, I have decided: Nayeli's people are my people. No turning back. I have been called to learn from her unconditional sacrifice to her family, from her faith which goes beyond her circumstances, and from the beauty that can be formed only through the refinement of suffering. For this calling, I am eternally grateful.

9

FROM ZIMBABWE TO THE WORLD
Beauty Gunda Ndoro

Beauty has been working in urban poor communities since 2004. In 2007 she joined Servant Partners as a missionary, moving with her family to Mexico in 2009 and to Nicaragua in 2015. Beauty advocates for women and other vulnerable populations and wants to see justice for them. Walking alongside the hurting and facilitating the process of healing is one of the ways she uses her gifts. Beauty also enjoys pioneering projects for empowerment and personal development. She loves thinking of new ways to facilitate spaces for growth—using creative facilitation techniques and dynamic exercises to make education successful and fun. She has captured some of this in training materials she has developed for healing recovery groups and is working on publishing them as a book. Beauty loves singing and worship music, swimming, watching Korean dramas, learning new things, and teaching. She lives with her husband Phillip, son Tadi, and daughter Tino in Managua, Nicaragua.

I COME FROM ZIMBABWE. And, I am a missionary. A missionary *from* Africa, not *to* Africa. I share my journey for those who may never have had the chance to see God working in such a way. But I also share it for those who come from any place in the world that might be seen as a place to go for missions, not *to be sent* out from. If we are following Jesus, we are called to make disciples, to the ends of the earth. So you, beloved you, whoever you are, wherever you are from, hear me: God has something for you to share with the world. He is doing so much more in so many more people from so many more places in the world than any of us can know. Our narratives about places and people and God can be so limiting, our lack of imagination diminishing what we can see of God's glory. But let us remember this scripture from Ephesians 3:20-21 (ESV): "Now to him who is able to do far more abundantly than all that we ask or think, according to the power at work within us, to him be glory in the church and in Christ Jesus throughout all generations, forever and ever. Amen."

HISTORY, LEGACY, BLESSING, AND
CALLING: BECOMING A MISSIONARY

ZIMBABWE WAS A British colony that became independent on April 18, 1980. Consequently, my culture has a noticeable British influence—and sadly our people have failed to fully retain their native cultures. English is an official language, along with Shona and Ndebele, the two most common languages. My husband Phillip and I are both from the Shona ethnic group, and we both speak Shona—though different dialects. Phillip also speaks six other African languages. And though we have taught some Shona to our children, Tino and Tadi, our following of Jesus has taken us far from home, so our children are now actually more comfortable with Spanish and English.

Both my mother and father came from big families and showed great love to their extended families. Before I was born, my parents were already taking care of the necessary school fees for other kids within our extended family who could not afford them. My parents also opened their doors and reached out to the needy; my mom and dad never let anyone pass by our home without eating. They taught us that food is to be shared with the hungry. They clothed those who needed clothing. Sometimes people without a home would come and my parents would give them shelter for days. My mother raised a number of orphans from within the extended family: from infant twins to high school students who needed to continue with school after their fathers had passed away.

I grew up Catholic, but even so, I didn't understand why my parents cared so much about other people, why they sacrificed to accommodate those who needed shelter, and why they fed those who were hungry and often bought clothes for children who would visit. As a child, I did not understand why my mother loved other children as much as she loved me, even though I was her biological daughter. It was not until years later that I began to appreciate how my parents showed me human kindness, what it takes to connect with others and to live in community with one another, something I would later emulate in my own life. I made a decision to have a personal relationship with Jesus in my second year in college through FOCUS Zimbabwe, a student ministry on campuses connected to IFES (International Fellowship of Evangelical Students).

My relationship with the living God led to a call on my life to love others, to follow in the footsteps of Jesus by offering sacrificial love to others.

Before my husband Phillip and I became international missionaries, we met a teenager who had no home. I was pregnant with our firstborn, but we both felt God wanted us to help him, not only with a place to stay in the short term but also by helping him grow in his faith, and working to find a family who could love and care for him for the rest of his life. He ended up with a wonderful Christian family who has adopted him as their own. Through that experience and others, I began to realize that my upbringing was a kind of sovereign foundation for the missionary life I would be called to as an adult, first at home in Harare, Zimbabwe, and then in other places in the world.

It wasn't just my family that was this way; my culture in general is social and not individualistic. Shona culture revolves around others and seeks to live in community with each other, not partially, but wholly. This is represented in the Shona word, *hunhu* which means "correct behavior." Because our culture is communal, correct behavior is defined by a person's relationships with other people. *Hunhu* refers to behaving well towards others, or acting in ways that benefit the community as a whole. Such acts could be as simple as helping a stranger in need, or they could be much more complex. It is quite similar to the Golden Rule: "Whatever you wish that others would do to you, do also to them" (Matthew 7:12a, ESV). Hunhuism says that *"munhu munhu nevanhu,"* meaning, "a person is a person through other people." My humanity is co-substantively bestowed upon the other and me as we interact well. A person with *hunhu* knows his or her place in the universe and is thus able to interact gracefully with other individuals.

This value, this phrase, has a deep meaning of humanity and was very much a part of the cooperative understanding behind the liberation of our nation in 1980. The same value was an inspiration to those in South Africa in the 1990s and was used to guide the transition from apartheid to majority rule. In South Africa, it was known as *ubuntu*, likely from the Zulu language, though the word can be found in many bantu-based languages throughout the southern part of the African continent. The idea of *hunhu* or *ubuntu* is known to the broader world through two of modern South Africa's most influential leaders: Nelson Mandela, the late, first Black South African president, and Archbishop Desmond Tutu, a Black Anglican cleric from South Africa best known for his human rights and reconciliation work in the aftermath of apartheid.

Sadly, because Zimbabwe has become very influenced by other cultures with a stronger value for individuality, it's become more difficult to sustain the value of *hunhu*. Yet *hunhu* has been an influential value in my life, and I have been grateful for experiences all over the world where people have shared in and lived this value. This type of loving-kindness can make any place a home for those who live there, and those who are traveling through. Yet beyond how *hunhu* can help people live graciously with one another, I am grateful for the gospel, the saving grace that brings each of us as sinners to our true spiritual home of forgiveness and our heart's renewal, so we can abide in peace with ourselves and God. This is why I follow Jesus, to make disciples, even unto the ends of the earth, like so many from different countries who have come before me, all of us sinners, all of us in need of God's forgiveness, grace, and continuing renewal.

MISSIONS IN AFRICA AND AFRICAN MISSIONARIES

WHEN WE AS BROKEN and sinful people do our best to follow our understanding of God's call on our lives, there is sometimes a mixed result. Our imperfections often get in the way, and sometimes we simply do not have the kind of servant love that Jesus calls us to demonstrate as his disciples. The complex legacy of Christian missionaries in Africa has had repercussions to this day.

In southern Africa, most of the leaders who participated in the fight for independence were educated in schools built by missionaries. Many missionaries built clinics and brought in immunizations that saved lives, as well as medicine that decreased the rate of infant mortality. European missionaries, especially from Portugal, France, Britain, and Germany, went to Africa under the premise of converting the locals to Christianity. While some of them stuck to their mission of simply bringing the hope of Christ, others aided in the colonization of Africans by Europeans and assisted their governments in the subjugation of Africans. Because of this, in many cases Christian conversion looked more like cultural conversion to capitalism and westernization. The countries sending missionaries plundered African resources and turned the indigenous Africans into slaves in their own land.

Even the missionaries who truly came to share the love of Jesus often brought with them the attitude that all things European were superior to all things African. They often failed to distinguish between Christian biblical principles and the principles of their countries and cultures, and they misused biblical passages to further the causes of their colonizing friends. European missionaries to southern Africa during the nineteenth and twentieth centuries played a strangely complicated role in the history and affairs of the region. On one hand, they were driven by a strong desire to genuinely serve the Lord and humanity while bringing about material and social changes which would improve quality of life. On the other hand, they were possessed by a moral self-righteousness which led them to make hasty and uninformed judgements upon indigenous mores, norms, and values they were seldom equipped to understand. It has been noted by several historians that a famous statue in Victoria Falls, Zimbabwe, of David Livingstone, a European missionary to southern Africa, shows the mixed legacy of missions in Africa: he holds a Bible in one hand and an axe in the other.

After most African countries received their independence from their colonizers, some countries, like Zimbabwe, have continued to receive Christian missionaries. With missionaries and local ministers, Zimbabwe has experienced continued Christian revival and seen the extension of the gospel—some 85 percent of the population is Christian. Even though there is not much written about missionaries from Africa to other parts of the world, it's a new era in the history of Christian mission. African missionaries from different tribes and tongues and nations are being called by God to serve overseas. I know of one brave Zimbabwean young lady who stood up and said yes to her call to serve God in Somalia. It was difficult and challenging for her, but she made a difference during the time God had her there. My family is also one of the many African families God is raising up for cross-cultural missions.

My husband Phillip and I have been ministers of the gospel since we were married. He worked for FOCUS Zimbabwe, which is a college Christian fellowship similar to InterVarsity, and connected to the international missions organization IFES (International Fellowship of Evangelical Students). At his local church, Phillip served as a youth pastor and missions director, and we both reached out to the poor in neighborhoods in Harare. At the end of the day, we would go home to our very comfortable, middle-class home. When my husband's term of work at FOCUS was up, his supervisor and mentor gave him and our family some options within IFES to consider for ministering next, including Tanzania, Mozambique, or South Africa to help re-pioneer the student ministries, which would provide some help for us through a grant. We also had a fully funded offer to serve with a missions organization in the Philippines. In all these opportunities, we would live in a middle-class setting, while continuing to serve the poor as we were able. But then, unexpectedly, we received a letter from Mexico inviting us to join Servant Partners to live and minister in an informal settlement (often referred to as a slum) in Mexico City, as fundraising missionaries.

We took time in prayer and discernment to determine whether this was what God wanted of us. The Mexico City option was the only opportunity where the primary strategy for ministry was not only holistic (caring for the whole person, as we had been doing throughout our ministry), but also incarnational, where we would live amongst the poor whom we would serve. Phillip knew more quickly than I did that this is where he felt God calling us. I took the time I needed to also hear from the Lord, praying and waiting on God until I had that peace and conviction to follow Jesus in this way—to the other side of the world, away from the culture and comforts I had known.

FROM GOD'S CLEAR CALL TO CLEARING CUSTOMS: EARLY PRACTICALITIES IN MISSION

AFTER THIRTY-TWO HOURS of travel, Phillip, Tadi, Tino, and I finally landed in Mexico, a great relief to be off the plane. Well, it was a relief for a few minutes. Once we remembered we were in Mexico, our anxiety heightened again. There was so much to learn, so many adjustments to make, and so many details to attend to, the first of which was going through immigration while only knowing how to say *hola*. A kind immigration officer led us through the immigration processes—though we didn't understand a word of what he was saying. Somehow, we received the necessary clearance and were sent out to baggage claim. We were relieved to see a couple from our new team—who later became dear friends—waiting for us. After spending a few weeks with our teammates in Mexico City, we left for the six-hour journey to Oaxaca to learn Spanish.

"Puedo tomar una foto con usted/sus hijos?" ("Can I take a photo with you/your children?") was one of the phrases we had to get used to very quickly. Many people were curious about us. My six-year-old son Tadi enjoyed the fame from the start. He would eagerly prepare himself to take photos with strangers and loved the attention he was getting. However, my three-year-old daughter Tino didn't like it at all. In the beginning, we pressured her to be nice to people—we were missionaries after all. We didn't realize right away the emotional stress it put on her, but in time we learned to create stronger boundaries around her. Maybe because they were little and cute, our children received most of the comments wherever we went—well, comments and hair touching. When I would feel exasperated, I thought to myself, "This is probably what the White western missionaries had to go through when they were ministering in my country as well."

Usually, the rest of the conversation would continue like this:

"De dónde eres/son?" ("Where are you/your family from?")

"I am from Zimbabwe."

"Donde?" ("Where?")

"Zimbabwe, in the southern part of Africa." If I didn't mention that it's in the southern part of Africa, they would often think that we were from Cuba, Haiti, or the United States.

"Ah! Africa! Waal, you are from Africa?"

After their initial surprised reaction, we were able to talk more deeply about this Africa. I was amazed to find how many people thought Africa was a country. People had heard different stories about Africa, but since they were interested in the subject, talking and educating about Africa was one of the ways I could engage with my new neighbors. Nelson Mandela said, "Education is the most powerful weapon which you can use to change the world." Here I was from Zimbabwe, as a missionary in Mexico, and I knew I might be the only one who could teach them about Zimbabwe and, more broadly, Africa.

As my Spanish slowly improved, I would tell them, "Africa is not a country, but a continent with many countries that speak many different languages that were colonized by many different European countries." I would explain to them that Zimbabwe is one of the fifty-four countries on the African continent, and it is in the southern part. I often shared about the different climates throughout the continent, as there was often an assumption that all of Africa is very hot. This was especially important to clarify since they thought it was because of the heat that we were Black. It was difficult to explain melanin, especially as we were not yet fluent in the language. Another assumption was that we lived among animals in Africa. I had to explain that we had to pay money to go to the zoo, or pay to go on a safari trip to see most of the animals.

Often we were asked, "Why Mexico? Why are you called to serve here? You are coming from Africa...why here?" Some of this is pure curiosity that any missionary would get: what would lead us or any person to make the crazy move into a totally unknown land—their land—to share the love of Jesus? But more generally, their concept of missionaries was that missionaries were White people; therefore, they were amazed to receive Black African missionaries like ourselves, who were sharing with them about the work of God. I would share as politely as I could, "Well, God wanted us here, and here we are." We had come from a comfortable middle-class community to minister to the poor, but our Mexican friends were always concerned about the assumed poverty of Africa as a continent.

Then, we were often asked, "You like it here, right?" And without waiting for a response, both strangers and friends of ours would say, "It's better than Africa, right?" It was confusing to know how to respond, wanting to honor their country but also wanting to share about my own country and the broader continent. And it was often clear they only had one story about Africa. They would share that their understanding of Africa was as a place of greater need, that it is poor, and that all the people, especially the children, are all hungry. They had a single story of Africa, not dissimilar to the single story most westerners have.

Having my whole continent made into a stereotype—poor, helpless, starving, sick—had only one upside. It helped us understand how it feels to be reduced to a single idea of a place, a single story of a people, and so we didn't in turn want to have a single story of Mexicans, rich or poor. We wanted to embrace them and actively seek to learn and understand their nuanced culture and individual lives. Living right next door to those we ministered to, now as neighbors, in a slum, would certainly help us do that.

My family and I may have initially been typecast as people coming from a poor continent, but that was not actually our story. As I mentioned, we had just left a very middle-class Zimbabwean life: a three-bedroom house with a beautiful driveway, electric gate, a nice green lawn, and a garden. Our lot also had a maid's quarters because, like most middle-class people throughout Africa, we had a domestic worker. Phillip and I both worked, and our maid washed and ironed clothing, cooked and cleaned, and occasionally helped with the children. I had rarely in my life had to do any house cleaning or caring for the clothing. The area we lived in, like many areas of Harare, was very nice. I say to people that if you were blindfolded and dropped into a wealthy suburb in any part of Zimbabwe, you would be forgiven for assuming you were somewhere in Europe or the United States.

This starkly contrasts to where we would minister in Mexico City: a poor, informal settlement, what many call a slum, by the name of Chimalhuacan. Chimalhuacan is a community with very little vegetation. Everything is dusty; the atmosphere always seems grey. There are dogs and dog droppings everywhere. Houses are small and have simple concrete floors, and they are crammed full of too many people living together in one space. Running water out of a tap is a luxury. Water has to be drawn from underground stores on each property several times a day. This is how our new neighbors all lived, and now how we would live as well, by call and by choice.

CHALLENGES OF LIVING IN A SLUM

FOR THE FIRST TIME in our lives, we were living amongst the people we were serving. We were living in a Mexican *barrio* (a common Spanish term for slum) and able to withstand this drastic downward mobility because of our conviction to live and minister amongst the urban poor, together with a team of likeminded believers. We were looking forward to doing this and anticipating enjoying the experience, as well as growing in what God wanted to teach us. But I had no idea what awaited me in the process. I thought that since we were called to this, everything was going to be smooth. I was wrong.

I hadn't thought about the possible health challenges until we were living in our slum. Our house in Chimalhuacan had two bedrooms and a common area that was a combined kitchen and living area. It sat right on the main road, which was not paved. Most of the dust from that road came inside our house. This led to a need to sweep all the time, and worse still, the dust caused health issues because our house had a poor ventilation system. I had asthma attacks almost every day. I was also diagnosed with gastritis at nearly the same time. During our first eight months in Mexico, I was sick all the time. I had to stop eating the delicious, spicy-hot food so common in Mexico, and we had to find a place to live that would not aggravate my asthma.

During that eight-month season, being often incapacitated by sickness, God took me through the basics of faith again. It seemed like I had to learn everything anew in this context, even how to be faithful. Lying on my bed,

I would take time to pray for myself, intercede for my family, my team, and my community.

Before we left Zimbabwe, it seemed that moving to Mexico with a three-year-old daughter and a six-year-old son was not too much. But in Zimbabwe we had had a domestic worker who helped me with the upkeep of chores every week, and that would not be true in our new context. So, when we started planning for our move overseas for missions, I had already started brainstorming how I would manage without house help, while parenting my children and doing ministry at the same time. But when we arrived, the big shift in our lifestyle was quite challenging. I was with my children all the time except when they were in school. I learnt to do all the house chores by myself with a little help from my husband when he was there. After all that, what was left of my life meant I could only work half-time doing ministry. It was a different life. But as my neighbors continued to be curious about our lives, where we come from, our family, and the choices we made, it provided us an opportunity to share our lives with them, love, laugh, and care for them, and they cared for us in return. Out of these talks, many relationships were birthed and many intentional conversations were initiated. God has used these to pave the way for all of us to receive more deeply from Him and each other.

The first week in our house in Chimalhuacan, we celebrated my birthday. I threw a birthday party for myself and invited my neighbors. It was a simple party, especially in contrast to the elaborate parties that my neighbors often throw, with food and music, even in very poor communities. Their hospitality is amazing. I tell you, Mexicans know how to throw a party, and they serve food until you sin against God by eating too much!

When all my neighbors came for the party, we welcomed them. They realized that our house was not very different from theirs. We too had concrete floors. We too lacked running water and used buckets filled from an underground reservoir to bathe. The simple birthday party opened doors for me to be invited to their homes. Since they had been in mine and seen that it looked like theirs, it made it easy for them to come knock on my gate and converse. It opened doors for their kids to come knock and ask to play with my kids. My Spanish became fluent as I intentionally connected and had conversations with my neighbors. I learned a lot from my neighbors about their culture, and I loved spending time with them. Our neighbors' daughter offered to help my son with his Spanish homework whenever we didn't understand it. I was grateful for these growing relationships, and I was settling in, learning what it took to keep up the house and minister part time.

NEW LIFE OUT OF SUFFERING

DESPITE THE CHALLENGES in our early months, we did our best to stay close to Jesus and to follow God's leading for us in Mexico. He was gracious to make things grow. We hosted our church's praise and worship practice in that little house, and a women's Bible study group was birthed while we were living there. The Bible study started with four women. Two of the women had no church background. The other two, Lupe and Marta, had a Catholic background, meaning they were raised Catholic and took their faith seriously, but they had not had an experience of really studying Scripture or interacting with God. I invited the women to bring their Bibles, and together we would read, discuss, and pray. They asked to start reading the Bible from the beginning, starting with Genesis.

When we came to the third chapter of Genesis, they had an epiphany. Upon reading about the fall, they realized the Bible didn't say that the fruit that was eaten was specifically an apple. They asked, *"No fue la manzana?"* ("It wasn't an apple?"). They were surprised because their grandmothers had told them, "Do not eat an apple, it's cursed—all because of Eve." They realized they needed to read the Bible more to understand God's story with humanity. Lupe and Marta gave their lives to Christ, were baptized, and are now serving as servant leaders in one of the churches we planted.

Though there was so much joy in our new friendships, building cross-cultural relationships is challenging. In Mexico City, the *barrios* that surround the city are filled with people from all the different states of Mexico, coming to look for a better life in the city. As a result, most of my neighbors' relationships with each other were new as well. And as such, in our slum, I found that people didn't really trust each other. Rather than dealing with problems, many in our community spoke behind each other's backs. Sometimes it was evident we had been the subject of such chatter, because someone whom we had never met would greet us by name. It was a little uncomfortable, but we chose to use it as an opportunity to start conversations with them and make new friends.

When neighbors came to us wanting to gossip about others, I told them I was only interested in gossiping about Jesus. I shared with them wonderful news and everything Jesus was doing in my life. As some of these neighbors became friends and church members, I was able to talk about how Scripture teaches us not to gossip, but to speak directly with anyone who has hurt us. What the enemy intended to use to divide people, Jesus was able to use for good as we focused on Him and His goodness and not the perceived faults of others. Amazingly, two of the ladies who were great gossipers were Lupe and Marta, the women who became a part of my first Bible study group. Then Lupe became a trainee and a co-facilitator in a women's group, leading hurting women through a process of recovery and healing. The Lord Jesus transformed their lives before my eyes, and they in turn were participating in calling others in their community into the same kind of Christ-centered transformation.

These women's groups we hosted in our community that focused on recovery and healing were amazing. Many women, young and old, were transformed. Some received Christ and invited Him to heal them from terrible memories, and He did, while others had their understanding of their identity as God's beloved children restored. Some were delivered from a spirit of fear, while others received God's love rather than a sense of His rejection. Some were given a new purpose in life that came from God's love for them and others.

Apart from working with the healing groups I had pioneered in our community, we also worked with a pastor who had several churches close to our neighborhood. We started arranging inner healing trainings for his church pastors and leaders to help them break free from pain. Pastoral couples and their leaders narrated their stories of pain. The experience of hearing stories of pain and bitterness shared and brought before God, and then witnessing people asking for forgiveness from each other, was one of the most beautiful things I have ever seen. I experienced the power of prayer as I saw people set free from pain, bitterness, and anger. Masks were pulled off of many faces, and chains of bondage fell away as Jesus set His people free.

I used my own experience of pain and suffering to connect with participants. I shared how my father had passed away when I was seventeen years old and how devastating this experience was in my life. I explained that it was a long process of healing, yet Jesus met me in that place of pain. We taught about how Jesus is able to identify with us in our pain and suffering, as He Himself went through the same; we also taught about how His death gives us hope for healing and deliverance from our pain and suffering. We all felt that Jesus was with us, and we all felt His permeating love and embrace. Realizing that God wants us all to know that He loves us and can help us go through any suffering led many people to a saving knowledge of Jesus Christ and a personal relationship with Him.

Many people need a safe place. One's color or gender does not make a difference. Just as God was able to use me as I experienced His healing in my own life, God can use you to be a safe person for many who are hurting as you let God heal you. During this season, I simply listened to people's stories. Working with women who have been abused or ill-treated and never given an opportunity to express themselves taught me to listen—not just with my ears but with my heart—and to try to be there for them with love and empathy. I have heard stories of pain that I never thought would happen to anyone regardless of context or background. People came to me and felt safe to talk about all that had traumatized them and hurt them, revealing their wounds to me. God used my difference, my uniqueness, to bless people who were heavy-laden.

I worked with women who had never been listened to, or whose voices had never been heard before. Women who have never had an opportunity to express themselves because someone has always told them not to express themselves. In Mexico, many women are taught, *"Calladita, te vez mas bonita,"* meaning, "Quiet, you look more beautiful." The concept of beauty was twisted up with the added punishment and emotional weight of being told not to speak about any horror or trauma they had endured. So they stopped airing their voices, and they became voiceless. Then, when they felt they had to speak, for example to tell about sexual assault, no one believed them. Many women I met were silenced and denied justice, even by their own families. In many cases, only what the aggressor said seemed to matter. They had been told loudly and clearly that they could have nothing to say, and that they did not matter. Of course, these lies from the enemy became their "truth" and affected them daily. When they could hear from Jesus that they did matter, that they could speak, and that God and others would still love them when they did so, they finally had a safe space to break their silence and receive God's love and healing.

WAITING ON THE LORD

AS I LOOK BACK to where I came from, I am amazed by God's goodness and faithfulness. By God's grace, after beginning to follow Jesus, I had the opportunity to serve amongst marginalized communities on the outskirts of Harare, our capital city. Then I was given the opportunity to serve in the outskirt slums of Mexico City. But even as I was leaving my country, my safe place, my comfort zone, my family, my friends, and my culture, I had no idea how our journey in Mexico was going to unfold. Every day we relied on God's mercies. All I could hold onto was the promise that God was with us.

God knew I would be different from the people whom I was called to serve, and yet He called me anyway. Why? This was one of the questions I found myself asking when I was frustrated or angry, or when things were difficult or didn't go my way. Why did you bring me here, Lord? Why? Now I understand He wanted (and wants) me to be in community and fellowship with others of different ethnicities, cultures, and all the labels we have created to discriminate us from together being and becoming the image of God. God wants to be shared amongst everyone, and I had a role to play in the extension of His Kingdom here on earth. The good news of Jesus Christ of Nazareth that was shared with me now needs to be shared through me, wherever and to whomever I am sent.

When our five-year commitment with Servant Partners in Mexico City was coming to an end, we started a process to discern where God would lead us next. However, before we had even put much thought into our next call, a friend from San Diego came to visit us. She was going through her own process of discernment. When we were praying together, she said, "I hear Nicaragua, I hear Nicaragua," so Phillip and I thought that God wanted her to go serve in Nicaragua. Little did we know then that God was actually telling *us* through her that *we* were being called to go to Nicaragua after our time in Mexico. It took us a year and a half after that prayer time to realize that what our friend heard from God was actually for us. One day, when we were talking with Servant Partners leadership, they shared with us that one of the sites that needed pioneering work was Nicaragua. We decided to visit the country in 2014. There, we felt God confirming He was calling us to Nicaragua. What a sense of humor God has in using others to speak to us!

When we first came to Mexico it was such an adjustment, so difficult to settle in. I couldn't have imagined that when we would leave, my kids would speak Spanish fluently, have a deep love for Mexico, and have so much love for the people and their friends. God had truly paved the way for us to go there, and He was with us as we followed Him and served in that community.

Now in Nicaragua, I continue to work with women as well as children. Tadi loves to play soccer, so he helps with a soccer ministry we have in our community, reaching out to young boys. Tino helps with our kids club at church. In this new place God has us, my children continue to grow physically, mentally, spiritually, and socially. They have a better understanding of our calling and they are discerning their own calls, which could be different from ours. We are happy where we are because we feel a clear sense of our purpose and calling, and we feel God's hand in our lives. But not one of the four of us has a sense of quite how long we will be here, and we do not know where God will lead us next.

Over these years, we have planted many seeds on the mission field and have experienced many difficulties, including the difficulty of waiting for growth. Jesus describes this experience of sowing seeds in different kinds of soils in Matthew 13. A good number of my seeds have not fallen on good soil. Instead, they fell along the path, or in rocky soil, or began to grow but among thorns where they were stunted. I have had to wait on the Lord and trust that He will cause the seeds that were planted in people's lives to begin to germinate and bear fruit in due season, if that is what He intends to do. In the waiting, sometimes I have doubted whether I had done it right, or whether any of the seeds I had sown were planted in good soil. I often ask, "Did I do it right? God, what did I do wrong? What more can I do? I have given my all, but why is there no change?" And usually when a seed grows, when transformation starts to take place, even that can be hard to believe. But it is wonderful and worth the wait.

Mariana is one of the people whose transformation was worth the wait. She and her husband had a terrible relationship, and she would send her child to our house at midnight for help because their fighting had gotten out of control. Mariana went through our healing recovery group, joined a Bible study, and became a member of our church, but she still struggled with her identity in Christ, as well as depression. There were days when she seemed happy and productive, but the following week she would fall into depression again because of problems at home—she had come to faith but her husband had not. She was still in this cycle of dramatic ups and downs when Phillip and I were called away from Mexico to Nicaragua. My heart remained heavy for her, and she was often in my prayers. A few months after we arrived in Nicaragua, a friend visited our old community in Chimalhuacan and spent time with Mariana. My friend sent me a picture of herself with Mariana and she said, "Your work was not in vain. Mariana is here in church with her husband." At church with her husband! It was not a simple process, neither was it short. But healing was continuing in her life and in her household. My heart rejoiced that her husband had chosen Jesus and that deeper growth and transformation were in process. These things sometimes happen over years—not days, weeks, or even months. And they are always worth the wait.

I consider myself blessed. Even when I was afraid to go to Mexico, I knew where I was going and why, regardless of not knowing the details of how my journey would unfold. I knew God was going to be with me. Even so, the work of serving as a missionary is often overwhelming, and if I were doing it on my own strength, I would crumble in no time. We must not frustrate ourselves in thinking that because we are there, things will change rapidly. Yes, we plan and come up with strategies, but it is always God who causes the work, and us, to grow in His time. We must not give up because we are not patient enough to wait for God. Let us continue to water the ground, and in due season we will be surprised to see a new sprout shoot up and grow. The center of all we do has to be Jesus—not ourselves. We must not serve others so that they can love or appreciate us—in fact it is best to assume they won't and may even gossip about us. Rather, whatever we do we must do only for God.

WHOEVER YOU ARE, BELOVED, IF YOU ARE CALLED: GO

YOU MIGHT NOT BE an African woman doing missions in Latin America, but you may be a woman of color thinking about doing missions somewhere in the world, maybe even on the African continent. You will face some of the challenges I faced, and you may face some different ones, but I want to encourage you: you are not alone. You will never be alone. God who promised never to leave us nor forsake us, who called you to serve Him in whichever nation, is faithful. He will be with you, all the way. I love the passage in Isaiah 43:

> But now thus says the Lord, he who created you, O Jacob, he who formed you, O Israel: "Fear not, for I have redeemed you; I have called you by name, you are mine. When you pass through the waters, I will be with you; and through the rivers, they shall not overwhelm you; when you walk through fire you shall not be burned, and the flame shall not consume you. For I am the Lord your God, the Holy One of Israel, your Savior. (Isaiah 43: 1-3a, ESV)

Fear not, sisters (and brothers), we are called by the most high God.

You will have challenges. It might be learning a new language and experiencing the frustrations of not saying what you want to communicate and not hearing correctly what others are saying. It might be adjusting to new context, new environment, new cuisine, and even suffering sickness. It may be working hard but not seeing fruit immediately. Some of these challenges are to build up our faith, to mold us into the image of Christ, to take away impatience and plant patience, to take away pride and give us humble hearts. Some of them are just natural consequences of the call. For me, in all cases, I have had to learn to totally rely on Jesus. I have had to learn after praying, planning, working, and having done everything I could, to let go. I have had to tell Jesus that I will trust Him—even if I don't understand what's happening or why.

Sometimes we fail to see challenges as opportunities because of our own limitations. Fundraising, for example, is difficult for many missionaries, but it is especially difficult for missionaries coming from the developing world. The challenge is real. I have a heart to see missionaries from the developing world cared for more deeply, but fundraising and missionary work is never easy. We have to look beyond our limitations and not see fundraising or any other aspect of missionary life as a barrier. It's an opportunity to see the faithfulness of God. As we trust God to make a way, He uses that experience to prepare us for the work ahead. So, take on the mission of God wherever He sends you: go! Beloved, I urge you, taste and see that the Lord is good; blessed is the one who takes refuge in him. (Psalm 34:8, NIV).

The goal of serving on the mission field is not to fix people, or solve people's problems, or be their messiah. Neither is it to do everything for the locals you came to serve. Rather, involve people in their own healing and in the healing of their community. You can work together to clearly see and face their challenges. Brainstorm together ideas about how to resolve those challenges. Working and involving locals that you came to serve is a blessing, not just to them but to you as well. You become part of that community, and you have an open door to influence and invite people to the One who transforms lives—Jesus. You have an opportunity to disciple one on one or a group of people together. You have an opportunity to notice leadership skills in people, to instill a value for servant-hearted leadership, and encourage them to lead—even to have them take over your own work, in time. You have an opportunity to see God transform lives as you walk amongst and with. Ministering Christ to people one on one, in their homes, through Bible study, fellowshipping over a cup of coffee, food, laughter, tears, art, and dance—in many ways, you can be a part of the community. It is a wonderful experience.

As a missionary woman of color, I have seen love expressed to me in beautiful ways as I serve God in marginalized communities in Latin America. I have seen His love through children who run to hug and kiss me, who greet me by name; through youth and women who smile as I walk by or who stop me for a short chat. I have been invited to delicious meals in so many homes—served by the people I came to serve, because we are truly friends. We sit down in their homes and open our Bibles to learn together about Jesus. The love of God is made manifest as we pray with people and as we embrace each other. Love has been expressed to me as people open up their lives and homes and confide in us, sharing their tender hearts.

God's love penetrates everywhere. One does not need a certain status to be qualified by God. God's love knows no color, race, gender, nationality, or class.

My fellow Africans and women of color from every nation, if God is calling you overseas to serve Him in another nation, speaking a language you do not know, far away from home and your culture, obey. Do not think that missionaries are supposed to be only White people. I think of Abraham, who was born Abram. God told him to leave his country and his father's grave, and go to a land that the Lord was going to show him. He took off by faith and the journey, just like mine, was not easy. But it was good.

I am a proud Zimbabwean woman—proud in the sense that I don't wish to be of another culture or country. I know who I am and where I come from. I know who I am before God and am open to what He wants me to become as He molds me more and more into a person of Christ. I have flaws, and I make mistakes. But God helps me to work on my mistakes, and I have seen and experienced the mercies of God as new every morning. Knowing who I am in Christ and accepting that is sufficient for me. I don't and neither does God define my humanity by my skin color. Who I am is more than my skin color and gender. I am important and so is my neighbor—in Zimbabwe, Mexico, Nicaragua, and the world. We are all equal before God, and we are all sisters and brothers in Christ Jesus.

10

PRIVILEGE, FRAGILITY, AND GRACE IN THE MARGINS
Jennifer Chi Lee

Jennifer Chi Lee was born and raised in Hawai'i as a child of Korean immigrants. She has been working with Servant Partners since 2005 in several capacities. First working with the Internships Department in South Los Angeles, Jen trained young adults in a practical theology of urban ministry. Eventually, she moved to Johannesburg, South Africa, where she founded and directed a holistic health and fitness program for women in a township community. She also serves as a member of the Learning and Collaboration Department, supporting staff and site teams with training and development. Jen's interests are in the tensions between justice and reconciliation, privilege and marginalization, and stress and resilience. She holds an MA in Conflict Transformation from the Center for Justice and Peacebuilding at Eastern Mennonite University and is an instructor with CJP's Summer Peacebuilding Institute. Jen also loves cooking and sharing food, hiking and group fitness classes.

FOR THE PAST SEVEN years of my life, I have lived in a township in Johannesburg, South Africa, alongside hundreds of thousands of Black South Africans and foreign African nationals. If that statement had been made by one of my neighbors, it would not be unusual. But I am a second-generation Korean American woman with a university degree and a salary paid in American dollars, not South African rands, so there is much about me that sets me apart from my neighbors. Navigating the disparity that reverberates between my background and experiences and those of my neighbors has been the site of tension, growth, and in many ways, integration in the better part of this last decade.

ROOTS

I GREW UP about as far away from South Africa as one can get, on the other side of the world in Hawai'i, which is nearly the opposite point on the globe from Johannesburg. Learning about my island background almost never fails to elicit gasps of delight from people, but before we get carried away with visions of a picturesque, idyllic life of leisure, allow me to clarify how I came to be born and raised there. My parents, both immigrants from South Korea, met and married in the mainland United States. Having come from a relatively monocultural country, they had struggled to fit into the more diverse Black, White, and Latin American neighborhoods in which they had lived in Chicago and Atlanta.

On the mainland, my dad had been compared to Bruce Lee (who is Chinese, not Korean), and my mom had been called by her first name by the young children she nan-nied (which is disrespectful and unheard of in her culture). But when they moved to Hawai'i, the state with the largest population of people of Asian (mostly Japanese, Chinese, and Filipino) ancestry, they no longer stood out. Every-one referred to them respectfully as Mr. Lee or Mrs. Lee, people took off their shoes before entering homes without having to be asked, and Asian grocery supplies abounded. It was a breath of fresh air after the isolation and racism they had encountered on the mainland.

I grew up hearing stories from my parents about how they had struggled as Asians and as immigrants in 1970s Chicago and Atlanta. But as a second-generation Korean American born in Hawai'i, I grew up in relative cultural comfort as one of many in a sea of Asian or part-Asian faces. For the first two decades of my life, I labored under the mistaken belief that the so-called melting pot in which I had grown up occupied an advanced state of racial rela-tions that the rest of the country had yet to achieve. In fact, when I first arrived on the mainland for college, I brushed off discussions about racism as outdated and obsolete. I was still embracing a falsely glamorized view of race in Hawai'i, and I had not yet realized how much I had inter-nalized a sense of my own ethnic and racial inferiority. It took most of my first year in college for me to begin to acknowledge my own deep-seated self-loathing of my sec-ond-generation, person of color identity, which stemmed in part from the prejudices I encountered growing up. There had been as much racism, classism, and sexism in Hawai'i as anywhere; I had just never really acknowledged it.

Unlike in many other areas in the United States, the majority culture of Hawai'i isn't White.[29] While the original colonists in the islands were White people from Europe and the United States, as fields of sugar cane began to flourish in the rich soil of the islands, more people were needed to work the growing plantations. In addition to the Native Hawaiian people, these laborers were generally people of Asian descent, as well as Portuguese from the islands of the Azores and Madeira. Many residents of Hawai'i today trace their heritage to these early plantation workers, and generations later, the local culture of Hawai'i continues to be strongly influenced by the cultures of the Japanese, Chinese, and Filipino people who came as plantation workers.

Other people of color in the United States may have had experiences of being compared unfavorably to White people, but I did not. Because of the dominance of Asians as a racial group in Hawai'i, as a child, I didn't feel my worth was diminished because I wasn't White. (Interestingly, within the first few days of attending university in California, I began to recognize how much the world was built for White people, and I quickly began to internalize my relative inferiority as a person of color.) Growing up in Hawai'i, however, I did not desire to be White or even to be associated with White people.

White people in Hawai'i are called "haoles," which literally means "foreigners." The term can often take a derogatory turn, and implicit in it is an assertion that White people are clearly outsiders in the land. Generations after the colonization of Hawai'i, haoles continue to be seen in this light. This was the central focus of my self-loathing, because in essence, if not in name, my parents were also haoles—foreigners. As immigrants not only to the United States but as newcomers to Hawai'i, they were outsiders, and I feared that I too would always be seen as an outsider. There were many aspects to local culture that I had to figure out and then teach them, and as a child, navigating a world my parents didn't understand made me feel vulnerable and ashamed. As a second-generation Korean whose family was new to Hawai'i, I didn't wish I wasn't Asian, but I did want to be a different kind of Asian, someone who seemed to belong in Hawai'i, like my fifth-generation Japanese friends. At the time, it did not occur to me that the plantation workers had originally been foreigners and outsiders as well.[30]

I spent much of my childhood attempting to assimilate to my perception of local culture. I took Japanese as my foreign language for six years in school; I learned to make butter mochi using my friend's mom's recipes; I ate poke and rice (before it was appropriated as the latest food trend by mainlanders); and I joined the outrigger canoe paddling team for a season. I even learned to turn on elements of a slight pidgin (Hawaiian Creole English) accent to sound more like an authentic local. But I felt awkward and uncomfortable when other people pointed out elements of my Korean identity because it meant I was different and weird, and I felt ashamed of my parents for speaking English with an accent—and not a pidgin one—and stumbling over their words, because many of my friends' parents did not. Many of us in Hawai'i grew up making jokes about each other's and our own cultures, but I never felt comfortable when Koreans were on blast.

I could never completely roll with the jokes because they hit a little too close to home.

FAMILY TIES

MY PARENTS, as immigrants, have always been outsiders. The model minority myth in America today is sometimes rationalized by the success of certain immigrants from Asian backgrounds (generally East Asians) who come on study visas to get their PhDs or MDs; these Asian Americans and their children often make more money than their White counterparts, thereby defying statistics about the wage gap between Whites and people of color.[31] But this myth is destructive and harmful because it silences the stories of struggle and marginalization for many other Asian immigrants and Asian Americans, usually those of Southeast Asian descent.[32] My parents, though East Asian, fell into the category of immigrants who come to the states poor, with limited skills and education, who work long days in tiny stores or large factories to scrape together the resources to survive and hopefully send their kids to good schools.[33]

My parents were born during the Japanese occupation of Korea, which ended in 1945. Despite formal Japanese occupation having ended while she was still a toddler, my mother bitterly recalls having been forced to take a Japanese name, Yoshiko. My father remembers his father forbidding his family from speaking even a word of Japanese in their house as an act of resistance against their colonizers. Japanese rule in Korea ended due to the global powers at play toward the end of World War II, with American and Soviet forces occupying the Korean peninsula, but even after the war officially ended, the destructive repercussions of that war continued in Korea as the Americans and Soviets jockeyed for influence in the region. My parents were young children when the Korean Armistice Agreement was signed in 1953, enforcing a stalemate to halt hostilities between Soviet-influenced North Korea and American-influenced South Korea. They grew up in its aftermath and have long borne the trauma of physical and cultural occupation.

When I have shared photos with my parents from some of the Servant Partners sites I have visited in slums and squatter settlements around the world, they have regarded the images with a sort of sorrowful nostalgia and recounted stories of their lives growing up in war-ravaged Korea. In a way that I can never understand, they know—viscerally—the experience of a life on the margins. In the states, where my parents eventually met, my father worked as a semi-skilled laborer alongside other people of color, while my mother was a live-in nanny for a wealthy White family and then a cook's helper in a Chinese restaurant.

And yet, several decades later, by American dream standards, they have made it. My parents eventually owned and operated a small mom-and-pop printing shop in Hawai'i, and with that income, managed to buy a house and send me to private schools. In a twist of irony, they have become foreigners who own property and make a profit in another colonized land, with little appreciation for the reality of what has been taken from and forced upon Native Hawaiians.

BRIDGE BUILDING 101

WHEN I LEFT the United States for South Africa in 2011, I had little sense of how my childhood experiences or family background would impact my life in Johannesburg. In fact, before I left for South Africa, I revelled in the uniqueness of my Asian American origin and what it would mean for ministry in this context. Here, where there are fewer people of Asian descent, I believed I would be in great position to be a bridge builder among diverse groups of people. Since I was neither White nor Black, I imagined I could stand in the gap among people of different backgrounds.

My theology around reconciliation was informed by a holistic view of God's work of ongoing redemption both in and through those who follow God (2 Corinthians 5:18). For God's kingdom on earth to expand, there must be healing and wholeness among individuals as well as groups of people. The ministry of reconciliation that God imparted to us includes the crossing of all kinds of borders—physical, geographical, historical—in order to build the bridges necessary for restored relationships. As I discerned my call to the ministry of reconciliation, I believed God was in the process of transforming South Africa, and I was eager to join this work.

I joined a small but diverse team who helped me envision the potential blessing of being Asian in the work of reconciliation in South Africa. As an obvious outsider without the associations of being Black or White, I could be a person who might provide a less threatening entry point for people of all backgrounds to dialogue about race, privilege, and justice. My lack of foothold in any particular culture could win me entry into a variety of circles that others would not be able to access so easily. I loved this idea and fully embraced this identity as a bridge builder.

And this has been true, to an extent. I face less suspicion, in many ways, than my White friends do, and I am not as easily dismissed as my Black friends are. However, I had not taken into account a crucial component of building bridges: it only works when people want to cross to the other side. I have, at times, found my intentions unwelcome and learned that people don't always want the bridge I'm offering. Of course, they have the right not to cross it, and in fact, maybe they shouldn't, if they don't perceive me to be a safe person or if they feel I am demanding they do it on my terms rather than theirs. But as a well-meaning missionary engulfed in my own first-world privilege, it took a long time for me to come to grips with that.

Informal settlements and townships in South Africa are dense, crowded places. The community in which my team works is an informal settlement of about a square kilo-meter in area that is home to upwards of 200,000 people. Every election year, politicians come to make promises to expand service delivery, to build more houses and roads, and to improve the general conditions, but every year after elections, politicians fail to keep their commitments. Once, an outcry arose in the community over the govern-ment's decision to build a large pedestrian bridge when what people actually wanted were houses. Money had been earmarked for a bridge, and it would have made crossing the multi-lane highway safer, but it would not have met a deeply felt need for land that had been long promised and long awaited. Tempers flared, demands were made, and eventually residents took to the streets to protest, blocking off major thoroughfares, burning tires, and expressing their deep discontent. As Dr. King said, "A riot is the language of the unheard,"[34] and this protest was a riot against politicians who failed to hear, see, and take into to account the voices of those they claimed to serve. Similarly, I have often failed to hear others well because in my privilege, I have listened poorly. I have wanted people to cross bridges not of their own choosing.

A core value of Servant Partners is that of incarnation. We draw from John 1:14, "And the Word became flesh and dwelt among us" (ESV). In taking on human form, God became accessible to us in a new way; by living life among us, we were opened to the glory of God in Jesus, full of grace and truth. The ultimate bridge builder, Jesus transformed himself into the path upon which we walk to draw nearer to God. This is our model in Servant Partners, and it has always inspired me. As an organization, we hope that by following God's example of incarnation, of dwelling among and with, perhaps others can behold the glory of God in our lives. We assume, of course, that the bridges we are building are desirable, that they are bridges that God is building through us. But sometimes these bridges are our own idea, built on our own strength, borne from our own arrogance in assuming we understand what people need and how God is moving in their midst. Though God hears the deepest cries of our hearts and understands our needs, we, as fallible humans, are imbued neither with omniscience nor unconditionally abounding love and wisdom, and we can make mistakes of discernment in how we relate to others.

In moving into an informal settlement, learning the languages of my neighbors, and eating the food they serve me, I have already done far more to cross cultures than most non-Black South Africans have. But going through the motions of daily living does not necessarily equal incarnation, and it certainly does not approximate what Jesus did in His incarnation among us. When Jesus became a man among humans, He was infinite God becoming finite human. When I live among people on the margins of society, I am just another finite human, often too caught up in my own significance, trying desperately to live in a way that helps rather than harms other finite humans. I cannot replicate that downward movement from divinity to mortality, but I can seek to live as Jesus did, building relationships that matter, making my life accessible to those around me, re-centering the margins, and speaking prophetic truth to power.

PERPETUAL FOREIGNER

UNDOUBTEDLY, THIS IS all well and good and noble sounding, but the daily, lived-out experience is less so. Bridges must be stepped on to be crossed, and soon enough, I began to tire of being trod upon. When I first moved to South Africa, I spent a couple of months living with my teammates Trevor and Chrissy and their children in their small home in the township suburb adjacent to the informal settlement in which we work. Unlike the informal settlement, which is basically a long-standing squatter camp, this is a planned settlement with mixed levels of housing for people of various—though mostly lower—incomes, with paved streets, legal water, and electricity meters.

Several times a week, Trevor and I would walk across a large field from his house into the informal settlement to visit people we knew, go to our Setswana language classes, or walk around getting to know more of the community. On these walks, Trevor, a White South African with blond hair and blue eyes, and I, a Korean American who looked like a "China" for all intents and purposes, drew many stares and comments. When I walked around with Trevor, or any other White man, I was almost never catcalled, but if the man I was walking with was African, he would invariably receive praise for his presumed romantic conquest, this "China girlfriend" he had managed to obtain. In my early days of ministry in a South African township, this was still a novel experience, and while I was irritated, I was also often drolly amused.

I grew restless living with my teammates, and since our work was primarily in the informal settlement anyway, I believed that as a single person unencumbered by spouse, children, or mortgage, it behooved me to move into the squatter camp in order to more fully live out our value for incarnational ministry. A few months into my time in South Africa, I did just that, renting a room in a government-sponsored house from the mother of a new friend. Prior to my move, another friend who had lived most of his life in the informal settlement warned me: "You know you're going to be proposed to every day, right?" By "proposed to," he meant propositioned. I shrugged it off as a necessary discomfort, a cost to be paid to do the kind of incarnational ministry I had done since joining Servant

Partners. After all, it had always been my intention, in moving to South Africa, both to live and to work within the informal settlement itself.

Within a couple of months, I found myself fielding a steady stream of both propositions and proposals, demands for money, and misinformed racial taunts (imagine fake Chinese-sounding gibberish and requests for martial arts demonstrations). There were also many children who ran after me to hold my hands and stroke my hair. They were used to light-skinned—generally White— NGO and missions workers coming into their community, offering candy and hugs. In fact, children in the community were all too familiar with well-meaning do-gooders who paraded through their streets, often to take photos of them for their newsletters and fundraising mailers.

White folks, whether South African or not (although, you can always tell the American missionary teams and youth volunteers by their zip-off hiking pants and Tevas), were accorded automatic privilege in townships. White folks were almost always NGO or church workers bringing foundation money, food parcels, or job applications. In the informal settlement, I was perceived sometimes through the lens of NGO privilege—essentially as a White person, a lekgowa (in Setswana) or umlungu (in isiZulu), with resources to spare and connections aplenty—and other times as an exotic foreigner. The onslaught of these experiences, particularly the ones where my female Asian features targeted me for attention, frayed my nerves, making my emotions fragile and my soul weary. I prayed frequently for a reprieve, especially in times when I felt more vulnerable, but it never really came.

During a particularly emotionally fraught time, after a meeting at my teammates' house, I remember asking God to spare me from comments and catcalls for the fifteen minutes it would take me to walk home. I texted a friend to ask for prayer, steeled myself for the battle ahead, and set out into the streets. I was about halfway home when two young men muttered comments about my race and laughed as I passed them. Tears filled my eyes, and I was glad I was wearing my large sunglasses—which I had begun wearing every day, in part because I believed they hid my eyes and facial structure, my most Asian features. (This, by the way, is not an effective strategy). When I got home, I threw myself facedown on my bed and screamed into my pillow in misery (a thing I had previously only seen in movies). I prayed, *This was such a small thing that you could have done for me, God, to give me fifteen minutes of relief today, on a day when I feel I could have really used a sign of your care and protection for me. How much do you not love me that you would refuse such a small request?* I thought of the man whom Jesus healed of his leprosy, who had begged of the Lord, "If you are willing, you can make me clean" (Luke 5:12-13, NIV). I was not begging for healing, but I was begging for protection, and it seemed the Lord was not willing, in that moment, to grant me this. Of course, God had protected and cared for me in many other ways; God just had not acquiesced to my particular demands that day. In time, I came to realize that God would not provide peaceful circumstances under the guise of protection. Instead, I would need to become a person of peace in turbulent circumstances.

Of course, in this, I have the luxury of choice. I chose to live and work in South Africa and in a township setting.

Unlike my neighbors, this is a choice I can unmake relatively easily. I can leave whenever I want to. Many of the challenges I face are ones of my own choosing. That's not to say I think it's my fault that men catcall me or that I should be fine with racial stereotypes, but rather to point out that for many of my neighbors, these kinds of challenges are everyday occurrences that cannot be avoided. I can move back to Los Angeles, sit in a coffee shop in Koreatown, and never have anyone assume I am Chinese, or think I don't know English (if anything, they might wonder if I can speak any Korean), or wonder if I know any martial arts moves. Getting away from men who take advantage of women is more difficult, but there are spaces in the world where I feel relatively safe as a woman. This is all thanks to my American privilege.

For the women I have met and spent time with in the informal settlement, harassment is an inescapable reality. When I walk with Black women through the informal settlement, we stare straight ahead or look sideways at each other as we chat. We steadfastly ignore or yell back at men who ogle us and always quickly pass the taverns with groups of men drinking. Non-township spaces are not that much better. In those spaces, Black women from informal settlements or townships endure the demeaning gaze of wealthier White people who ignore, pity, or underestimate them. In those spaces, I may be misunderstood at first glance, but my American accent and money buy me passage in ways inaccessible to them. I am not ignored, pitied, or underestimated by those who are wealthy and White because I am the "right" kind of person of color—one who can speak fluent English, one who is financially stable, one whose choice of words and defense of her opinions reveal she is university educated, and one who is self-confident enough not to be easily dismissed. There are few spaces that afford a Black woman from a township in South Africa genuine respect and dignity. I am cognizant of the luxuries of choice my privilege affords me, and these must be navigated well if I am to live an incarnational life among people who are more marginalized than I am.

That being said, part of navigating my privilege required that I first grapple with the limitations of my identity. As an Asian American woman, I was an anomaly who fit into precisely zero of the categories of people that South Africans were used to encountering. I could discuss race in Black and White terms, but I struggled to make sense of my experiences as an Asian American in South Africa. In the informal settlement, if I wasn't assumed to be a church or NGO worker, there was an assumption that I was one of the Chinese from mainland China who ran gambling rings. There was always confusion about whether I could speak English, whether I knew martial arts, and especially, what it meant that I was an American, since Americans were White. Sometimes this was amusing, but mostly it got old: death by a thousand microaggressions.[35]

Being seen as an outsider and a foreigner awoke in me the deeper childhood pain of growing up in Hawai'i and being perceived as not belonging. I am not proud of how I once responded to a taxi marshal[36] when he asked me if I spoke English. I lashed back, sneering, "Better than you can!" Thinking back to the interaction, he didn't appear affected; he made no acknowledgement of my rudeness and simply responded by directing me to the right taxi.

We both moved on, but I left ashamed and disturbed by my own knee-jerk reaction of rage. At the time, I could recognize that the level of anger was disproportionate to the level of the offense, but I hadn't figured out the root of the unhealed pain that was causing me to behave unkindly.

In fact, it wasn't until a number of years into my time in South Africa that I truly understood why it was so difficult for me to be seen as a "China." Since the discovery of gold in Johannesburg, Asians of both eastern and southern backgrounds have lived and worked in South Africa. But, as is the case in many places, Asians are seen as a sort of perpetual foreigner, an odd group of folks to whom certain privileges are granted and others are not.[37] In South Africa, while both Indians and Chinese have been here for many years, the Indian population is larger, and because of an additional wave of newer Chinese immigrants in the last few decades, they have continued to be seen as outsiders. Although I resented being called a "China" because I wasn't one, the real issue was what it branded me as: an outsider.

My teammates, Trevor and Chrissy, who are White South African and African American respectively, experienced their own share of frustrations unique to their respective races, genders, and so on, which I myself could not fully understand. Chrissy looked like an insider but was a foreigner, and Trevor was not a foreigner but was an outsider to our community of ministry. The toll it took to be treated perpetually as both a foreigner and an outsider was unique to me. We each had our own unique set of identities, our own unique journeys in cross-cultural mission, and our own unique pain to wrestle through with God.

THE FRAGILITY OF PRIVILEGE

WHEN I WAS FIRST visiting our Servant Partners site in Johannesburg before making the decision to join the team, I asked a missionary from another organization about her time thus far in the country. What had her experience been like? What had she appreciated about life in South Africa, and what had she learned from people she had met here? This woman was able to speak with ease about the difficulties she had faced—the misunderstandings with the local organization she was working with, the challenge of being known and cared for, the shock and strain of differing cultures. But when it came to what she had appreciated and learned, she struggled to answer the question. Eventually, she said, "Well, I just love the people here, and their culture," or something equally feeble.

In the moment, I felt great pity toward her. To live and work in a place God had brought her to, but to be unable to name what she had learned—this seemed pathetic. I vowed, if I returned, that I would approach my life here with intention—not romanticizing missionary life or the people of South Africa and their cultures, not hiding away in wealthy gated suburbs, but instead having a full, rich tapestry of relationships and experiences. I was determined to retain my sense of awe and wonder at the work and people of God here. And yet when I eventually came to South Africa and attempted those very things, I found it was not as easy as I had anticipated.

Before actually moving to Johannesburg, I had been safely ensconced in the affirming, encouraging context of my life in Los Angeles, with a relatively diverse community of friends who understood me and appreciated my quirks. I hadn't realized how much I had relied on and been protected by both knowing and understanding the world around me, as well as by being known and understood by others. From a place of safety, I could envision most of the aspects of my multiple identities— single, female, second generation, Korean American, from Hawai'i, well educated, practical—as assets to the ministry I was headed to in South Africa. I could imagine that they would make me both insightful and disarming and that I would thus be well received as a prophetic voice. But as it turned out, it was these very intersections of my identities that betrayed me.

Once I was in South Africa, in my struggle to find my place in a new context, I found I surrounded myself with simplistic, dualistic discourses that didn't make great sense of my situation and were instead harmful to my sense of well-being. I would tell myself, "South Africans don't get what it means to be Asian American, so I will never find real friendship here," and "It's fine to binge-watch a whole season of Scandal at a time because #selfcare!" Even as I recalled my attitude toward my former missionary friend, I couldn't even bring myself to feel shame for my judgment and lack of empathy—such was my own self-pity. I did not know how to make sense of being a person holding both privilege (lighter skin, American, education) and marginalization (female, single, non-White). Those intersections of my identities are the axes along which I navigate life, and they affect my own worldview as well as how others view, understand, and relate to me.

Intersectionality is the idea that the whole picture of a person's identities is greater than the sum of each one put together. It also contains the acknowledgement that these intersections of a person's identities can, in certain contexts, create the perfect storm for oppression and marginalization. Kimberlé Crenshaw, the scholar who pioneered the concept of intersectionality, explains it this way: racism is usually understood through the lens of the kinds of experiences commonly suffered by Black men (versus women), and sexism is usually understood through the lens of the kinds of experiences suffered by White (versus Black) women. But the strategies and conversations that arise from those separate discussions are insufficient for Black women, whose experiences are neither the same as Black men nor White women. When a person has multiple marginalized identities, the overall effect is a different level of oppression that is more than the sum of the parts.[38] I am not a Black woman, but I understand feeling dissatisfied by dominant narratives on race and gender.

Living in South Africa was not my first time of exile from a safe space, but it was certainly my longest. I felt physically exhausted all the time from the mental, emotional, and spiritual work of navigating a new place and culture. Because I felt so destabilized and often attacked in my personhood (as a woman and an Asian American), I wallowed in the slow burn of my resentments as a coping mechanism without considering what was coming apart in myself as I was dwelling in bitterness. What I had not considered in these reactions was something I now understand as "privilege fragility."

I came to understand this by considering how I have seen racial privilege play out in White communities. "White fragility"[39] is a term used to refer to refer to the relative inability of White people to undergo even small amounts of racial stress without reacting defensively because they have not developed the mental and emotional muscles necessary to do so.[40] For example, this is exhibited in the White person who contends that "all lives matter" in response to the rallying cry of "Black lives matter," the one who says, "I worked really hard for my (insert achievement here), it's not because I had white privilege," and the one who says, "I grew up poor, so I didn't have privilege." Of course, these are straightforward examples, but white fragility goes deeper. It's also in the well-meaning, progressive-leaning White folks who say, "I just want to be helpful; you should be grateful for it." It's in those who claim to be allies, insinuating that their motivations and degree of commitment are beyond reproach. It's in those who, when confronted with the possibility of having to do real work to confront their privilege, will slowly fade away because they just have "too many other commitments" already.

What I have realized, from my own experience, is that there is also a fragility that goes beyond whiteness, that extends to all of us who experience privilege in some way: "privilege fragility." As our eyes are opened to our own privilege and power, we face the question of how we will respond to this new awareness, and there is a tension we face in this awakening. Will we make the choice to close our eyes to that knowledge, or will we keep them open? Privilege fragility shows itself when we choose to let our fear, our apathy, and our defensiveness close our eyes.

Privilege fragility reveals itself in all of us who believe we are "woke," who believe we are among the most progressive and enlightened, when in fact the state of being awake is not at all static. One single moment of being awake matters less than the ongoing process of awakening.

In the moment of tension between staying asleep and opening our eyes, there is an invitation to choose to take risks and continue to grow. But this invitation doesn't come with a map; there isn't a specific path or a checklist of tasks to accomplish; this ongoing process of awakening is messy and unclear and at times quite painful. For me, it wasn't just my trusted friends gently challenging me who helped me to see my own fragility. It has often been in situations where people challenged and confronted me not as kindly as I might have liked, when I reacted first with defensiveness, that I have learned to keep my eyes open to my own rough edges and places of needed growth.

HOPE IN BROKEN JARS

DURING MY SABBATICAL year in the states, I witnessed a Church divided. An overwhelming majority of those who identified themselves as White evangelicals elected, to the highest political seat in the nation, a man whose actions defy any sense of awe and humility under God or compassion for the poor and downtrodden, particularly minorities and immigrants.[41] Many Christians of color began to reckon with the extent to which white supremacy has rooted itself in our beloved body of Christ. Perhaps I hoped that White evangelicals as a whole would begin to work to heal the divide of race and class. Instead

I observed many people who earnestly believed they were following God with their political choices even as those very choices deepened racial prejudice and systemic injustice. Instead of opting to do justice, love mercy, and walk humbly with God (Micah 6:8), the western Church has largely chosen the same kind of fearful self-protection and stingy defensiveness that came so easily to me during my fragile first term of work in Johannesburg. This fearfulness and defensiveness is a manifestation of the western Church's fragility, and it has been deeply grieving to behold.

I have wondered what a creative response to the tension of awakening is. I have wondered what soul work the Church needs to do to reckon with its past, present, and future, and what soul work *I* need to do to better hold the tension between meeting my own needs and pulling together the parts of my life that I want to integrate more fully. I have wondered how I can return to the place of viewing the intersections of my identity as a gift and a source of potential. And I have wondered, for the Church, whether we can embrace humility in order to welcome creativity, whether those who hold the most power within the western Church can embrace the growing pains of awakening to their privilege, rather than retreating behind their fragility.

It is a salient question to be asking because underlying the question of whether people of privilege can lay down their defenses and do the soul work is a question of safety. I teach group fitness classes, and those who have attended one of my classes would tell you that one of my favorite cues is, "Brace your core!" With participants in my kickboxing classes, I sometimes tell them instead, "Imagine someone is about to punch you in the stomach." It's another way of saying the same thing, and it's relevant here as an example of how our bodies intuitively know how to respond to situations of danger. The current rhetoric of the evangelical Church in America is that we are unsafe, that we should walk around with fists clenched as for a fight, ready to perceive any challenge or question as a threat. Thus the body of the western Church has come to clench its gut at the slightest provocation—even when there is no danger—even when it is God who is calling us, even when the invitation is to embrace God and God's purposes anew. Sometimes, unclenching our gut when we feel unsafe is a matter of faith.

Unfortunately, even for those of us who love and follow Jesus (and *especially* for those of us who follow Jesus but hold earthly privilege), it takes courage to admit weakness and allow vulnerability: to inhabit our fallible, limited human bodies without despairing. What would it look like for the western Church to reckon with its sense of superiority and the terror of vulnerability, even if that meant acknowledging that white supremacy, white privilege and white fragility have become built into how we understand issues of power, access, and dignity? What would it look like for the western Church to grapple seriously with its internalized sexism, misogyny, and patriarchy, handed down for generations? What would it look like for the western Church to consider that the systemic evils it has sometimes unwittingly embraced have become part of how we have recreated God in our image, rather than letting God change and renew us?

In the work of the kingdom of God, there will always be mistakes, failures, and shortcomings, because we are humans who cannot help but be influenced by the systems of oppression and injustice in which we find ourselves.[42] In the months since being back in South Africa after sabbatical, I have felt this viscerally, in my body and in my spirit. It seems impossible to escape microaggressions here (from well-meaning White people as well as other unaware people of every creed and culture), and I find my own gut clenching involuntarily whenever someone greets me with the one Chinese phrase they all know (ni hao) or asks me if "that's how they do it in your country." I know that they are never thinking "my country" is the United States (if they were, they would simply have asked if "that's how they do it in the US")—it's usually China, occasionally Japan, rarely Korea. This is a small, even miniscule, affront, I know—but that's the point. It's so small that it seems to warrant no concern, and yet these microtraumas build and manifest themselves in my body.

I find my spirit regularly echoes back this sentiment: *there are no safe spaces.* I have longed for a sense of safety and comfort, and have felt grieved by the lack of it, especially after experiencing a physical lack of safety in a "smash and grab," which is an event common enough in South Africa as to have its own name. In my case, a few men broke the windows of my car as I sat stopped at a traffic light. They reached in, and attempted to take whatever seemed valuable, and I emerged from the event with one less bag, wallet, and two car windows, but mostly physically unscathed, except for bits of glass in my hands from when I'd tried to pull my things back. I didn't fully despair, but almost a year later, I continue to flinch when someone approaches unexpectedly. It has made me wonder about the antidote to despair, the alternative to grief's seemingly inevitable descent into bitterness.

Toward the beginning of my sabbatical, I drew a picture in my journal of a vase falling off a table and being broken, and then of it being put back together but with all of the cracks showing. It was a symbol of the spiritual re-formation I was engaging in at the time, and it indicated a measure of hope for me, that I could imagine wholeness after being broken apart. I shared this with my spiritual director, who paused and took in the picture. After considering the image for a moment, he responded, "Yeah, but it still has the same shape. In putting it back together, you drew it in the same shape it was first in." It was true. At the time, I could imagine being broken and put back together as a spiritual act, but I lacked the moral and prophetic imagination to envision a new creation.

A few weeks after the smash and grab, I had a conversation with a friend who was preparing a presentation on trauma and resilience. She asked me, "What is a passage of scripture that describes the experience of God caring for us in our trauma?" After a moment, two things came to mind—the drawing of the broken vase, and a passage from 2 Corinthians 4:7-10: "But we have this treasure in jars of clay, to show that the surpassing power belongs to God and not to us. We are afflicted in every way, but not crushed; perplexed, but not driven to despair, persecuted, but not forsaken; struck down, but not destroyed; always carrying in the body the death of Jesus, so that the life of Jesus may also be manifested in our bodies" (ESV). These words, written by the Apostle Paul to the church in Corinth millennia ago, speak of the fragility of treasure held in clay jars—much like the fragility of my body, the fragility of my mind, and the fragility of my humanity. And yet there is a sense that this fragility does not have to be borne in a solitary fashion. A very divine God lives in our very human bodies, and the cracks that reveal our fragility can also reveal the grace of God contained within us, light shining through broken jars of clay.

This, then, is resilience; this is safety: God lives within us, and our brokenness can reveal God's glory. Grief and trauma come to us all. In our privilege, many of us are able to avoid certain kinds of grief and trauma, thus being able to forgo the acknowledgement of our fragility and humanity. But in confronting our privilege, we can hope that the inevitable grief and discomfort will not lead only to the vulnerability of our brokenness, but to the hope of God's ability to recreate and reform us. Perhaps, as I discovered with my spiritual director that day, I still cannot imagine what new shapes that broken vase could take—but God surely can, and I am content to wait in the tension of being in pieces as I am made new in Christ.

---

[29] This is not to negate the ways in which Hawai'i is still dominated by whiteness and Americanness. The primary spoken language in Hawai'i is English, as in the rest of the United States. After the 1893 overthrow of Queen Lili'uokalani, the last reigning monarch of the Kingdom of Hawai'i, the islands were annexed by the United States government and have since come under the same larger system of cultural dominance that is true in all of the American states and territories.

[30] I understood, intuitively, that though the descendants of the plantation workers were not native to Hawai'i, they were not in the same category of people as those descended from White people who colonized the Hawaiian Islands, stole resources and land, subjugated the Native Hawaiians, and brought in foreign workers. Even so, it is significant to mention that, as much as I wanted to be seen as an insider who belonged in Hawai'i, I did not aspire to be Hawaiian. Even as I recognized that White haoles were foreigners, I also internalized an implicit assumption of Japanese superiority and a disdain toward the Native Hawaiians who had inhabited

the islands for centuries. Such was the complicated and problematic nature of my own internalized Asian superiority and immigrant inferiority. I acknowledge my own racism in this, and note that this is a consequence of the colonial legacy in Hawai'i.

[31] E. Patten, "Racial, gender wage gaps persist in U.S. despite some progress," *Pew Research Center*, July 1, 2016, retrieved on March 27, 2018 from *https://pewrsr.ch/2LbZ5x2*.

[32] T. Lam and J. Hui, "The high cost of the model minority myth for Asian and Pacific Islander Americans," *Kennedy School Review*, 16 (2016): 61-68.

[33] Despite their meager beginnings, it could have been much worse. They were connected to small but supportive networks of other Korean immigrants (as well as my White American GI uncle, who helped sponsor my dad to come over), they did not have to hazard a dangerous border crossing on foot, and they weren't immediately criminalized in the same ways other people of color are.

[34] L. Rothman, "What Martin Luther King Jr really thought about riots," *Time* (April 28, 2015), retrieved on June 26, 2018 from *https://ti.me/2Lnk2US*.

[35] D. W. Sue, C. M. Capodilupo, G. C. Torino, J. M. Bucceri, A. M. B. Holder, K. L. Nadal, and M. Esquilin, "Racial microaggressions in everyday life: Implications for clinical practice," *American Psychologist*, 62(3) (May-June 2007): 271-286. The term "microaggression" refers to insensitive comments that are often made in passing that reveal hurtful or harmful assumptions that the commenter holds, whether intentional or not.

[36] A taxi marshal is a person who organizes the queue of minibuses called "taxis"—the main form of transportation for poorer South Africans.

[37] F. Wu, Yellow: *Race in America beyond Black and White* (New York: Basic Books, 2002).

[38] K. Crenshaw, "Mapping the margins: Intersectionality, identity politics, and violence against women of color," *Stanford Law Review*, 43(6) (1991): 1241-1299.

[39] The editors of this collection made the decision to capitalize the first letter of the words "Black" and "White" and all other racial or ethnic identifiers throughout the book when used in reference to people who are identified via those terms. I have made the choice to not capitalize the terms "white fragility," "white privilege," "whiteness," and "white supremacy" because they are in reference to concepts, not people groups.

[40] R. DiAngelo, "White privilege," *The International Journal of Critical Pedagogy*, 3(3) (2011): 54-70.

[41] G. A. Smith and J. Martínez, "How the faithful voted: A preliminary 2016 analysis," *Pew Research Center*, November 9, 2016, retrieved on July 7, 2018 from *https://pewrsr.ch/2myeuZQ*, and K. Shellnutt, "Trump Elected President, Thanks to 4 in 5 White Evangelicals," *Time* (November 9, 2016), retrieved on July 7, 2018 from *http://bit.ly/2L85cSZ*.

[42] In his letter to the church at Ephesus, the apostle Paul describes how God has placed Jesus as the head over his body, and all things on earth below his feet (Ephesians 1:18-23). There is a spiritual reality here for the body of Christ having authority over the powers and principalities, including the systems of oppression and injustice of this world. At the same time, we must acknowledge the reality that as humans, we do not always live in the spiritual reality of the kingdom of God. We live in a broken world as broken people, and we are pulled in every direction by these worldly systems (Ephesians 4:14).

11

CALLED TO REMAIN
Emma Silva Smith

Emma Silva Smith has been with Servant Partners for fifteen years and serves as co-team leader for Servant Partners' Manila, the Philippines. She grew up in the railroad squatter community of Balic-Balic and has returned to Manila's slums to bring the hope of Jesus to those without hope. She has an MA in Christian Counseling and is a visiting professor at Asian Theological Seminary for the Masters in Transformational Urban Leadership program. Emma helped plant Botocan Bible Christian Fellowship, a vibrant church in the squatter community where she lives with her husband Aaron and two boys, Zach and Ezra. She is actively discipling teenagers and women and has seen the Holy Spirit transform lives. She also serves her community as a counselor focusing on violence against women and children, and as an instructor for the high school equivalency exam preparation course.

GROWING UP IN A SLUM

THE HOME I GREW UP in is normal for most people in the world, although probably not normal for most of the readers of this book. It was a one-room wooden shanty in the heart of Manila along a small creek surrounded by thousands of similar homes in a bustling slum. It did not have a bathroom. That's also normal for most of the world, even today. We had to go on newspapers, in a bucket, or in the creek. As you can imagine, the creek water was— well, let's just say it was gross. One morning when I was about six years old, I was holding onto the railing doing my thing over the creek when I lost my grip and fell in. I didn't know how to swim so I sank in the sewage water. Luckily the water was only up to my waist. Thankfully, one of the neighbors across the way saw me and came to my rescue. Life was hard, but it was home, where neighbors cared for each other like family, even if it meant fishing each other out of sewage.

Right before the start of sixth grade, a fire spread through our community. We lost everything. My brand-new school uniform, all of our clothes, our baby pictures, and every single possession my family owned was burned. The creek area where we lived is adjacent to some railroad tracks, and that is where we moved after the fire. We just changed from being squatters near the creek to being railroad squatters in a community called Balic-Balic.

At one point, a group of missionaries, mostly Americans and a few Filipinos, moved into our new community with plans to plant a church in the area. I was very intrigued by this group of people trying to survive in a squatter community. Usually, missionaries would just come into the community for a few hours and then leave. Also, most missionaries lived comfortably, in big houses far from their ministries. But this group didn't only visit, they lived in the squatter area just like us, experiencing the same things as we were experiencing. They would go out to talk to people, build relationships, and share about Jesus. My mother was very interested, and she became involved in the Bible studies and started attending the church service. My sister Marie and I also began attending Sunday school class. In our old church, there was not a special service for the children, so we just went through the motions. But in our Sunday school class, we could study the Bible with other kids, and the teacher took a genuine interest in getting to know each one of us.

When I was eleven years old, the teacher asked if we wanted to receive Jesus, and I responded yes to the call. The three of us—my mother, my sister, and I—were some of the first members of the church along the train tracks, which had been named Balic-Balic Christian Church. We were all baptized at the same time. We started attending Sunday school and other activities in the church more regularly. Marie and I enjoyed attending Sunday school because we liked learning about Jesus...and we got free food when we went. We were also treated to a fast-food restaurant as a reward for memorizing lots of Bible verses and scoring high on Bible quizzes. Even though my father and my brother would sometimes go to church with us, I couldn't see any real transformation in their lives.

❦

My father worked with his relatives as a professional demolisher, tearing down houses and other buildings in preparation for rebuilding. Even so, my father didn't really have a regular job for many of the years I was growing up. Sometimes he looked for work and found it, but often he just had to wait for work to become available. We often had rice with salt and water for meals, or rice with some sugar and water. And when we got tired of that, we ate rice with oil and soy sauce. We used to imagine that it was adobo, a fragrant Filipino dish cooked with pork or chicken in oil, soy sauce, garlic, and onion. If you had enough to eat, you were one of the privileged few. As a child, I suffered from chronic hunger and malnutrition. My growth was stunted at four feet, seven inches, so I am even smaller than an average Filipina woman.

Even when my father didn't work, he still managed to drink alcohol, smoke, and gamble with his friends by borrowing money. Then, when he found work, most of his paycheck went to paying back the creditors for loans that had a very high interest rate. The average loan shark in Manila charges 20 percent over a thirty-day period, or 240 percent annual interest. That would mean that if you took a loan of $100, you would have to pay back $120 within thirty days.

The lack of money and my dad's vices meant a turbulent home life. My mom would get mad at my dad's irresponsibility and shout at him—so he would drink more. My parents would constantly fight. One time after they quarreled, they both left in separate directions. At that time I was twelve, my sister was ten, and my brother was eight. We were on our own for a whole week.

During that week, when my parents left us alone after their argument, the actions of the mission team showed they loved us. They checked up on us, kept us company, gave us food, and made sure we were okay. As the oldest child, I was responsible not only for myself, but also my younger sister and brother. Without our parents, and unsure about when or even if they would return after that bad argument, we had to figure out how we would survive. I was scared, but I didn't feel alone. I saw an example of the love of Jesus through the lives of others who made the choice to move into an urban slum, because they were able to be there for us when we really needed someone.

I think my calling to serve God among the poor started during that difficult week when the missionaries took care of us. I reflected on the fact that they were not even our relatives, but they loved us and they took care of us. I knew in my heart that this kind of love only comes from Jesus. I too desired to be the love of Jesus for others, especially those who are in hopeless situations like I had experienced. Being poor is hard—but being poor without Jesus is unbearable. It is utterly hopeless. There were times that I wanted to die because of all the hardships I faced in life. Words cannot describe what it's like to always be hungry and not know when you will eat next, not to mention not having enough money to go to school. It is even worse if your parents are always quarreling. But because I had Jesus, I had hope. In the Old Testament, I saw how God had been faithful again and again to His people. Joseph's story was especially impactful in my life; through many hardships God was able to uphold Joseph. I regularly preach this hope to myself, that no matter how bleak the situation is, God is faithful to help me.

I wanted to share the hope God gives with other people. When I finished high school, I wanted to study in a Bible school and be a missionary. I didn't think I'd be able to go to college because we didn't have any money. But I remained hopeful, and I prayed and trusted God's leading in my life. It turned out that God had a different plan for me than I expected, and Bible school would have to wait. On the last day of enrollment for college, a person who had spent his week of vacation in the Philippines living in our community sent money back to the missionaries in our church—for me to attend college.

The Bible school was already closed for enrollment, so I enrolled in a private college and majored in computer science. I thought that with this major I would be able to get a job quickly and help my parents right after college. The desire to serve God was still there, so I remained active at church during my college years. The money that had been sent for me to attend college was enough for one year of studies. But during the first semester I was able to get a half scholarship, which meant that I only had to pay the miscellaneous fees, and the tuition fee was waved. I was also able to maintain high grades, so that one year's worth of money stretched for two years. But in the third year the subjects were more difficult, so my grades dropped, and I had to pay for my full tuition in the fourth and last year. The school had a policy that students could not take exams unless their tuition was fully paid, so I was anxious about whether I'd be able to finish. But somehow God was always on time; somehow God provided, and I was always able to pay all my tuition payments and finish college.

During my third year of college I met Aaron, who is now my husband. He lived in our community, and we got to know each other while we were working together in the church. Eventually, we fell in love. He asked me to marry him, and we began to prepare for a move to the

United States. Even though I didn't go to Bible college, I now got to spend my life with a man who had committed his life to serving God. God knew my deep desire to serve Him, which is really why I wanted to go to Bible school. Although differently than I had imagined, God fulfilled that desire by bringing Aaron and me together.

LIFE IN AMERICA

DURING AARON'S LAST semester studying in the Philippines, we started preparing to go to the United States. To get my visa, I had to commute over an hour for three consecutive days to the United States embassy's doctor to make sure I did not have tuberculosis (TB). We celebrated when my visa finally arrived. When the day came for me to leave, I felt nervous because it was going to be my first time to fly in an airplane, and I knew I would miss my family. But God gave me another family in Aaron's family.

The pastor who performed our wedding ceremony in the United States was Filipino, and he was married to an American and pastored a Filipino-American church. After we got married we joined his church. Our church was like a family: we had Bible study at people's houses and fellowship afterwards. We also went on different excursions together—to the mall, apple picking, and one time even to the Pentagon because one of the members of our church used to be a chef there. It was a good experience of church.

We lived in Aaron's parents' house during our time in the United States, along with Aaron's two sisters and two nephews. I felt at home right away. It felt like one large Filipino family staying together—even though all the children were married and had their own children. Aaron's parents are a big inspiration for me. They have loved and supported their children no matter what. I told myself that someday I wanted to be that kind of parent. Even though it felt like home, I was still homesick at times, missing my family and Filipino food.

My first experience of culture shock living in the United States was actually ordering a Subway sandwich. In the Philippines, the restaurants typically have a picture on the menu, and what you see is what you get. Not in America! I had to choose what kind of bread, what kind of cheese, what vegetables I wanted to put on it, whether to have the bread toasted or not, and what kind of dressing I wanted—on top of that, I was very hungry. It was almost too much for me. I was so overwhelmed with choices and questions, I almost cried.

Three months after I arrived in the United States, I looked for work, and my employment experience in the United States redeemed my painful job-hunting experiences in the Philippines. In the Philippines, the application requirements discriminate against short people. Most job requirements have age, height, and sometimes weight requirements. When I had graduated from college and applied to work at a drugstore, I was told that I was under the height requirement. A friend was also rejected for being underweight. It was hard to find a job in the Philippines. In the United States, I found a job quickly at a department store as a sales associate. Even though I had a tough time reaching the register, they still accepted me. One Saturday, when I was cashing my paycheck at a bank, the manager asked me if I wanted to work there. I filled out the application, and I started working that next Monday morning. I worked at that bank for more than a year and a half. When it was time for me to return to the Philippines, almost two years later, my manager said I could come back to work there anytime.

Life in America was great, but it was always in the back of our minds to go back to the Philippines to minister among the urban poor. I was ready to go back to Manila.

CALLED TO RETURN

DURING OUR TIME in the United States, we began looking for a mission agency that would send us back to the Philippines. We felt led to go back and live where I used to live and to share the hope and joy we had found in Jesus. We wanted to share with those who, like one billion others in the world, live in a slum or squatter area, but are often without vibrant churches to worship in, or the ability to learn about Jesus right there in the midst of their lives in a slum.

We interviewed with one mission agency, but they didn't want to send us back to the Philippines. We were told that they don't send anyone back to their home country because they have had problems in the past when family members found out how much money the mission staff made. I was shocked. This mission agency doesn't send workers who already know the language and culture because they make too much money? It seemed to me that all they had to do was lower their staff salaries.

Thankfully, God led us to Servant Partners. We set our salaries to what an ordinary public school teacher in the Philippines would normally make. It is not a lot, but we try to live simply. We were also able to get back to the Philippines more quickly because we didn't have to raise a whole lot of support for a big salary. We bonded well with others in Servant Partners because we all had similar values. After joining Servant Partners, we returned to Manila with the goal to bring hope in Jesus to the urban poor, and to host internships and new staff training for Servant Partners.

We decided to partner with my home church, Balic-Balic Christian Church. But returning to my old neighborhood was not easy. Within a month after arriving, Aaron contracted dengue fever and was miserably sick for several weeks. I also faced my own struggles. Most people in my community were puzzled when I returned. In their minds, I had an opportunity to have a good and comfortable life in America, so why on earth would I come back to a squatter community in the Philippines? But from my perspective, why would I not move back? I had found hope in Jesus, and I wanted those crushed by poverty and oppression to also have hope in Jesus.

It was hard for me because they seemed to think that I had not chosen well, that choosing to have a "good" life was better than serving God in the slums. But accepting Jesus means choosing a purposeful life rather than a comfortable life. Unfortunately, this truth is not taught with consistency in the Church, which is why moving back seemed so strange.

Another struggle was a feeling of inadequacy because my parents were separated, I felt that perhaps this disqualified me to serve. But God reminded me that His "power is made perfect in weakness" (2 Corinthians 12:9, NIV). After all, no family is perfect.

✳

Life in the slums is difficult. Aaron and I have always lived in a one-room squatter house, first in Balic-Balic and then in Botocan. We now are a family of four, and all of us sleep on the floor with mattresses together. Neighbors sometimes keep us up at night with loud karaoke machines, and another neighbor often comes home drunk at 2:00 a.m. He does not go to sleep but talks loudly to himself or looks for someone to fight. He constantly bangs his loud sheet metal door until sunrise, and sometimes he continues with his loud noises through the whole next day.

Some people around us are so poor they don't have an oven or stove, so they cook with wood or sometimes charcoal in a little stove made out of cement outside their own houses. And since the houses are close to each other, this kind of cooking regularly smokes us out of our house because it makes it so hard for us to breathe. One neighbor also turns his motorcycle on for five minutes, just down from our window, and all the exhaust comes into our house. There isn't much we can do about him and his motorcycle because he is one of the community officials that has the power to make life difficult for us and our church if we get on his bad side. He is easily angered and picks fights with everyone, as it is.

There is dog poop everywhere. It is an ongoing community complaint that those who live here talk about during the community's town meetings, but we haven't come to agreement on a solution yet. Our window faces our neighbor's roof, which has cat and bird poop on it. We try to ignore it, but I know it can't be good for our health.

The harsh environment, tight living quarters, and dirty air exposed all of us to TB. Aaron and I and both of our boys were treated for TB, my youngest when he was still an infant. The pollution combined with the intense TB medication left me with permanent lung damage. When my lungs are strained, they begin to bleed and I cough up phlegm with blood. The first time this happened I was very scared. I thought I was going to die because a woman from our community had started coughing up blood one day only to die that evening. I have had test after test to try to figure out what the problem is, but it is just damage from the environment and TB medication. It is not contagious, but it is a daily cross that I must bear because it is painful and gross, and there is no cure for it. The doctor explained that it heals by itself when I have enough rest.

SCATTERED SEED

ONE OF THE BURDENS of living in a squatter community can be a lack of stability because of the fact that no one owns the land they live on. One of the most deeply painful times that I felt this burden was when the government demolished all the shanty communities along the railroad tracks, including our old community, Balic-Balic. It is impossible to describe the sadness and powerlessness felt when your childhood home, church, and the homes of all your closest friends are destroyed because politicians think your homes are ugly. Development that only benefits the rich is not development at all.

The government said they had to demolish the community because they were going to upgrade the train system. Tens of thousands of homes were destroyed and the poor trucked to far away relocation sites, all in the name of development. A development that never actually happened. There were minimal changes to the train system. They just replaced the trains. So much pain and suffering happened for a project that never even got off the ground. Little by little, the displaced people are returning and building makeshift homes again in the same place. As long as they are left alone, a bustling community will once again develop along Manila's railway line.

At first our church tried to oppose the demolition by joining protest rallies and even attending a meeting with the Philippine vice president at that time. But at the meeting, the vice president told the poor residents they have been mooching off of the government for far too long. They needed to quit smoking and drinking and be thankful that they were being moved to a safe location outside the city. And of course, nothing is free—so they will have to pay for it if they choose to move to the government housing. It was at that point that our church realized that this was a national project and we would not be able to stop it, even if we organized well at the local level.

Our church began to view the demolition as the scattering of the members to different places for the spread of the gospel, like in Acts. There are various relocation sites, so the church members have had many opportunities to spread the gospel in many different areas. It was a painful time because we were all scattered and far away from each other—but at the same time it was good, because we were able to minister in the new places where each of us has ended up.

Before Balic-Balic was demolished, Aaron and I prayed for a community that we could move into. We looked for different communities, and we felt the Lord was leading us to Botocan. We began to partner with a middle-class church near there, and we set out to live in Botocan.

At first it was hard for me, even though in some ways it was very similar to my old community. There were suspicious people lurking around; one man kept on looking through our window several times not saying anything. People regularly warned us that we lived in the most violent section of the community. Our section of the community is called "Waray," which in the Philippines is a people group from Eastern Visayas. The Waray people are known for their fighting and violence. It is a stereotype, but there is one Waray man in particular who holds a long knife and swings it around when he is drunk.

Botocan also seemed somewhat secluded and hard to get to compared to where we had been living—the immensely crowded train community of Manila. The big market is farther away, and the transportation fee is more expensive than it was from Balic-Balic. Initially, Botocan felt so far away from everything. We didn't know anyone, and we didn't know where anything was. It took a little exploring to discover that it wasn't just a scary and isolated place. We discovered just how wonderfully located and accessible Botocan actually is. We found out that we live very close to the University of the Philippines, which means lots of trees, rice fields, and beautiful open spaces. That was a plus. In Balic-Balic, there were not many trees; it was train tracks and concrete everywhere with a dirty creek running through. We were so happy to find out that we were within walking distance to nature. In fact, it's even possible to go on a short walk from the massively crowded basketball court in Botocan—where you are surrounded by literally hundreds of people—and suddenly find yourself standing in the middle of a rice field, with not another person in sight.

✳

When we began meeting people in Botocan, life got better. Aaron and I went on prayer walks in the community. I often opened the door and made myself available for people to talk to and hang out. We moved to Botocan when my first born Zach was about six months old. Being chubby and cute, Zach was always a conversation starter, and neighbors would stop and talk to us because of him. Young children would come over almost every day to play with Zach. He was too young to play, but they still liked to come over. After a few months, I decided it was time to start a children's Sunday school. We already had a house full of kids, so Sunday school—which was not limited to Sundays—was a fun time to do Bible stories and crafts. The children loved to do art projects, and a few of them began following Jesus.

Over the years I have seen these children grow up. I think that's what is wonderful about staying in one place for a long time. You really get to see how people change their lives. Our current Sunday school teachers are teenagers now—they grew up attending Sunday school as young kids. It's so exciting to see God work in their lives. And you never really know how God will turn a life around. One of these teens used to be a bully at school, lazy about doing her schoolwork, and at her young age had already started drinking alcohol. I thought that she was not serious in her faith; I was losing hope and I prayed for her often. Today, she is very active and excited about how God is working in her life. She is even being discipled by one of the girls that I disciple. What a joy!

In Botocan we built relationships little by little, and after one year of living there we knew a lot of people—so we decided to start a church. The launching of Botocan Bible Christian Fellowship was an exciting time. We invited the local government officials to our first service, and the room was full. Many committed to the church, and I have poured myself into our young children's ministry and to discipling some of the mothers and teens who live nearby.

❄

Very few people who have found a way out of poverty go back to where they are from. In most poor communities, the goal is to get out as soon as possible. We are socially conditioned to desire the lifestyle of the upper class. In reality, who does not want to live in a very nice house? Most young professionals who have escaped the slums never look back. Especially when they have their own families, they do not want their children to experience the same things they experienced as children living in the slums. They want them to have a better life. Outside of the slums, there is less sickness, violence, and danger of fires and floods. Many do not even go back to visit friends and family. They want to forget all the difficulties of life in the slums.

This is understandable, and yet when no one goes back, everyone loses, both the poor and even the newly rich. Being rich does not mean you should abandon the poor people you once lived with and only socialize with people who are also rich. Those who once lived in poverty can actually give a particular kind of support to those who live in their community of origin because they are from the same background. They can better understand the deepest needs because they have a relationship with them, better than any outsider could. It might be that God helps someone overcome poverty so that they can in turn help others.

Recently, I've been thinking more about what I can do to help raise up more people who are like me, from a squatter community, to raise up those who can return, to live in the midst of poverty and then be a light, a giver of hope, and a transforming agent of Jesus in the community. I might be able to make a small difference, but if there are more Christians in our neighborhood—Christians with the same values as Jesus—then maybe we can make a big difference.

One day I realized how God had already begun to answer my prayers. I did not have to think of new ways to call people back to the slums; I was already doing that kind of work by living in the slums and discipling girls in my community. I meet with several girls one on one—that way it is more intimate and they can share with me issues they may not share in a group. We first do a Bible study followed by a sharing and prayer time. We also share life together, doing tasks they need to do, chores I need to do, or hobbies we both enjoy; in so doing we learn more about how to love God and each other in an informal way. Some of the girls I am discipling are now thinking about staying in the community and investing themselves in it.

HOW THE CHURCH GROWS: STORIES OF HOPE FROM BOTOCAN

FROM BEFORE THE CHURCH began until now, we have used many strategies to develop people in their faith and in their leadership potential, while together trying to serve and love our community. These strategies include individual discipleship, activities with the children, painting nails, camp for some of the older kids, teaching high school equivalency classes, and doing some social work and counseling with families in need. We have been busy praying, working, and watching as the church grows.

⁎

Sometimes, transformation happens through seemingly simple efforts of kindness. Most of the kids in our neighborhood have never received a birthday cake, so I began baking birthday cakes for the kids. Baking cakes is challenging in my small kitchen. All I have is a one burner electric stove and a toaster oven. But it's enough to bake small cakes that help the kids feel loved and special. Most kids cry because they've never had any birthday cakes or even celebrated their birthdays. It has had a greater impact than I could have realized when I began.

Baking cake in my house with a toaster oven often becomes a kind of training for the teenagers and moms who are curious. They learn how to bake and decorate cakes. One mom was really encouraged with this, and now she has a business at home baking cakes and goodies. It's also a fun bonding time for the kids and me. While baking we talk about their lives, and I ask them how they are doing and encourage them in whatever situation they are facing. Every time it's somebody's birthday, the kids get very excited. They all want to help bake a cake. One time I wasn't there for somebody's birthday, so the other girls took over the task and baked a cake without my help. Now that is what I call empowerment!

✳

God has also used my interest in arts and creativity to open doors for ministry. I paint the toenails of the teens I disciple with fancy designs. They love being pampered and looking beautiful. Their external beauty helps them to feel beautiful and confident.

They are interested in learning how to do nail art. We will sometimes have sessions painting each other's nails, and I will use that time to teach them how to do specific designs. One young woman was later employed as a nail artist in a salon. When we do nail art at our church, neighborhood people are often interested as they walk by us painting each other's nails. We end up meeting a lot of new people, and many end up visiting our church. Doing nail art together with the girls serves as a bonding time, a one-on-one time where we get to talk about our lives. The girls always look forward to the monthly treat when they get their nails painted, and they never run out of stories to tell. I realized how hungry these kids are for someone to listen to them and spend quality time with them.

I have also taught calligraphy to some of the young women I work with. I print out practice sheets to let them practice the letters. The kids are interested because they can use it for their school projects. I try to do something artsy after we do our Bible study, and the kids really like that. Doing arts and anything creative seems to helps us to look into beauty, which I think of as a gift from God. There is not a lot of beauty in the slums, but through art and creativity we can create, cultivate, and appreciate the beauty that is all around us. Using art in my discipleship has been empowering for myself and the women I work with. They are able to gain confidence as they learn artistic skills.

⁜

One of the women I discipled had lived in awful situations. Once she used to sleep on the streets with her grandmother. Another time, when she was living in Balic-Balic, she had been sexually harassed by her mom's boyfriend. Most of her immediate relatives were pickpockets, including her mom, sister, and cousins. But because Jesus had found her, her life had turned a different way. She was able to finish college and inspire her other relatives that there were other jobs besides stealing. It is a joy to see transformation in the people who have come to know Jesus.

⁜

Another young girl I've poured my life into is Amor. Amor is a bright young woman whom I have discipled for years. My discipleship with Amor has been holistic. Beyond the formal Bible study, I've tried to address the various needs in Amor's life towards holistic transformation. Amor comes from a difficult family situation. When we first met Amor, her family didn't have enough money to feed her. She came over regularly and ate most of her meals with us. At that time, her main struggle in school was not having enough money to pay for the materials for her projects. She would often go to school without lunch money and have to get through the whole day without eating. Since we had a relationship with her, we felt it was appropriate to provide her with snacks or even a small amount of cash to buy her school lunch. After persevering she finally graduated—the first person in her family to finish high school.

After graduating high school, Amor met some Servant Partners interns and new staff trainees. A Servant Partners staff member organized a fundraising effort to collect money to help Amor and another girl from our community go to college. And after persevering in school, Amor graduated from college. Even before she officially graduated, she was offered a job from The Philippines' Bureau of Fisheries and Aquatic Resources, which has an office near our community. Amor now has a much different future in front of her. The cycle of poverty has been broken.

Recently, Amor was sharing her testimony with two younger teens. Things could have gone very differently for Amor. At fifteen, her grandmother wanted her to take a job as a a maid for $50 a month. At that point it was a tempting offer, and she considered dropping out of high school. When she told me about it at the time, I encouraged her to trust God and finish high school. A few years later, before she started her sophomore year in college, somebody offered to pay for all of her schooling expenses in exchange for working for them during all of her free hours. She was specifically told that she would not be able to go to church. By this time Amor was maturing in her walk with God, so although it was an enticing offer, she did not take it. She chose to be active in church and trust God.

In addition to one-on-one time and Bible studies, the church was developing a vibrant youth group. Our youth membership was boosted when we were able to secure a grant to take the youth to the beach for a youth church camp, every summer for three years, through a partnership with a foundation. Although the Philippines is an island, the youth in Botocan are not able to go to the beach very often.

The camp had its very challenging moments, with youth sneaking out, robbing local vendors, and getting into fights. But all of those issues paled in comparison to the evening that one of the campers told me that someone had stolen a knife from the kitchen and was going to stab another camper that night. The knife thief wanted revenge against a guy who had put a mango seed into his mouth while he was sleeping. Though they were members of the same street gang in Botocan, there was tension because the gang had split between the younger members and the older members.

Reymon, one of the youth leaders in our church and the camp director at that time, called an emergency meeting of the leaders of the camp to determine how to handle the situation. Because I was taking counseling classes, all of the pressure to diffuse the situation fell on me. I had never handled a conflict situation between fighting gang members, but everyone looked to me to facilitate the negotiations.

I had them sit in a circle and I stood in the center. I laid the ground rules for the discussions. Only one person was allowed to talk at a time, and they could not talk until I gave them permission. Each person had to sit and listen to the others' concerns. At one point in the discussion, one of the guys stood up, took off his shirt, and said, "We're going to fight anyway so we might as well fight right now." He was over a foot taller than me and outweighed me by about one hundred pounds. I stood between them, put my arm out, and told him to sit down. By the grace of God, he listened to me. At that point, one of the older gang members stood up and lectured them about disrespecting me. He told them to start cooperating and work out their issues. They apologized to each other and agreed not to fight at the camp or back in Botocan. One of the guys who was involved would later become my student in the high school equivalency classes I now teach. He is no longer so hot-tempered.

Following the summer of that first camp, with the dramatic intervention, our youth ministry took off, and God opened the door for me to disciple several more teenagers. We followed up with most of the youth who had attended the camp. We prayed for them and asked them if they wanted to participate in one-on-one discipleship.

✳

One of the girls who showed interest was Pau. She had two younger brothers and in the process of her discipleship, they also became Christians. Pau first saw me as someone who could give her dating advice. She asked my opinion about a guy whom she initially said had been courting her for a long time. When I asked how long has he been courting her, she confessed that it had only been one week. In the Philippines, the tradition for dating relationship is that a young man courts a girl, meaning he gets to know the girl, visits her house, gets to know her family, and brings flowers or chocolates if possible. But the culture has changed and teens now court through text messages. She felt pressure to say "yes" to be this young man's girlfriend after text messaging for one week. I told her to really think about it and pray over it. She decided she wouldn't date until after she finished college. Instead, she started focusing on growing in her relationship with Christ and became a Sunday school teacher. She also started discipling another girl.

Pau really showed her faith during her last year of high school. That year she was the assistant camp director for the youth camp. The graduation practices fell on the same week we were having the camp. In the Philippines, graduation is extremely important. The graduates practice the ceremony for a whole week. One of her teachers told Pau that if she didn't attend the graduation practices, she would not graduate. It was important for Pau to attend the graduation ceremony because she was the eldest among three siblings, and her parents would be very disappointed if she didn't graduate. But Pau trusted God and decided to serve at the camp.

When she came home, one of her teachers gave her the graduation gown, and she was able to attend the last day of practice and go on stage on graduation day. The whole church witnessed God's goodness in her life. One of Pau's cousins was mad at her for making the decision to help at the camp instead of practicing for graduation, but through Pau, she also became a Christian.

SUFFERING AND JOY

I GREW UP in the slums, I have lived in middle-class America, and I went back to living in the slums again because of God's calling in my life. I have returned to the poverty of my childhood in order to proclaim the hope I have in Jesus because I know how it is to be poor and not have Jesus. And now my hope is to also encourage and inspire others to live in the slums and help the community transform by the love and hope of Jesus. This is done through building meaningful relationships with people, even though some of them are gaining the means to move out. That is essentially what Jesus did—he came down and dwelt among us.

Problems are plentiful in Bocotan, and we know we cannot address them all. But with God's help we can address some of the problems, little by little. The suffering has been great, but so is the joy. This joy—of seeing gang members stop fighting, of Amor graduating from college, now with a steady job and able to help her family with their daily needs, and of other lives transformed for the glory of God—encourages me to continue on this journey of ministry among the urban poor.

12

THE VOICES THAT SHAPE US
Mini Mathai Palmer

Mini served with Servant Partners in India for two years. Previous to her work with Servant Partners, she was a health educator in California with the San Bernardino County Department of Public Health in the HIV/STD Prevention Program. As part of her work she enjoyed getting to know people from all walks of life including residents of the county jails and juvenile hall, and sharing a lot of humorous and honest moments with them as they discussed how to protect their own health and that of their communities. Mini now lives in Long Beach, California where she engages in learning and writing about things that interest her, spiritual direction and formation, and other expressions of being herself. She is working on her first book, a collection of essays about hearing God. She has the pleasure of being married to her husband David, and being a mommy to her two lovely and loving daughters. She enjoys comedy in any form (stand-up, improv, romantic) as well as movies and reading. She finds deep joy in listening to God, herself, and others.

MAKING SPACE FOR GOD'S VOICE

WHAT IS THE MESSAGE?

MISSION. The word denotes a sense of purpose. But whose purpose? Is it ours, someone else's, or God's? When I went to the mission field, I assumed all Christian missionaries had the same purpose: to share the knowledge and love of Jesus with others. And maybe we all did have that in common. But I quickly observed—both in our team and in the context of other Christian missions groups—that ideas on how best to accomplish that purpose varied as much as the individuals in the group.

There were six of us who went to Mumbai, India together. Mumbai used to be known as Bombay. Bombay was the name given to the city by the British, and even Bombay was the Anglican version of the Portuguese name for the city, which was Bombaim. But the indigenous people referred to it as Mumbai, and in 1995 the city's official name was changed to reflect that truth. There is something inspiring about a people who decide they no longer want to accept what has been chosen for them and choose to identify themselves in their own voice.

Interestingly enough, that combination of English, Portuguese, and Indian voices that shaped Mumbai would come together again on our team. There were two White American men, two White American women, one Brazilian woman whose native language is Portuguese, and me, a woman born in India and raised in America. Our goals were to learn the language and culture and help train and equip local Indian men and women who were planting churches in urban poor neighborhoods. Like the British,

Portuguese, and Indians, we had different interpretations of how to meet those goals.

Some people felt it best to focus on building relationships with the local people and deprioritized building and maintaining healthy relationships within the team. But what does it teach the people we are reaching out to, when we talk about the importance of Christian community and building healthy relationships, and neglect to practice it ourselves? Others felt that we should start leading and serving in different ministries right away without taking the time to learn about the people and culture and what the local people wanted. Some Christians believe in focusing on evangelism first and then meeting people's practical needs. Some Christians believe the order should be reversed. The one thing that the people and missions who held all these differing views seemed to have in common was the idea that they knew the one best way to do things.

IS THERE MORE THAN ONE MESSAGE?

BUT IS THERE really one right way of ministering—or even living life? Rarely, if ever, during my foray into international missions, did I meet people who seemed open to and accepting of the validity of differing approaches to missions and ministry. However, when I think of Jesus during his time on earth, I am struck by the multitude of ways he responded to different people and situations. One of the beautiful qualities of his life and ministry was that He himself was not bound to one particular way. For example, He responds to the blind beggar, Bartimaeus, who is calling out on the side of the road, by immediately restoring his sight (Mark 10:46-52). But when his friends send a message that their brother Lazarus is sick, He waits two days before going to see them, and Lazarus dies (John 11:1-43).

In Jesus, we see the unlimited power of God work in unique ways, that enlarge our concepts of who He is and what He is capable of. In Bartimaeus's story, we see Jesus miraculously changing something in his life that is considered irreversible, the condition of blindness. In Lazarus's story, we see Jesus supernaturally change the ultimate irreversible condition, death, and bring Lazarus back to life. But we would not have observed His power to raise someone from the dead, had He not intentionally waited before responding to His friends. Miracles transpire precisely because Jesus does not stick to a limited playbook of what is and is not possible in the world.

On the other hand, when I hear leaders and other people talk about the way to do things without making space for the value of other methods, it puts an artificial limit on what is possible—not just for the people involved, both missionaries and local people, but also for God. This would be the saddest trade, to believe that conformity to God's will means conformity to each other. There is a reason that God created us uniquely. We each reflect a different part of who He is. To lose that difference or variety is to lose a vital part of our picture of God.

How then do we stay open to God and live out our personal calling from Him while working with others? We ask God to show us what He wants and then we make space to listen for His answer. I believe that God is able to reveal to us what He wants us to do in any situation. If people have different goals, then it may be better for them not to work together, as going in different directions can create distractions and a lack of focus. If people have similar goals and similar approaches, they have a situation conducive to working together. When people have similar goals and different approaches, the situation can still be conducive to working together if they are given freedom to pursue their own approaches. But this can only happen if we trust that God can speak to each individual in a way that he or she is able to understand. God is able to choose the mode of communication that best fits the way He made us. But if we say that God can only speak through burning bushes because that is how Moses heard Him, we limit His ability to communicate with us.

MAKING SPACE FOR GOD'S VOICE IN OTHERS

WHO GETS TO TALK?

THIS LEADS ME to another question. Do we trust God's voice in others, and do we trust His voice in ourselves? For missionaries, this is especially important, as many feel called to the field because of their belief in a core message that they have heard from God directly or from someone else. They often want to share this message with those they meet on the field. But it is also important to ask what the local people are hearing or feeling called to. If we do not make space for God's voice to be heard in them, we perpetuate the colonialist mentality that we are the only empowered messengers of God's will.

We also become engaged in a closed mindset. We stop listening to the people we are serving and deprive them of the opportunity to practice hearing from God themselves. They are not encouraged to discern what God is doing around them and practice using their authority to decide how they will respond to what they see and hear. We miss out on hearing about the longings and passions that God has put in their hearts, and we miss the chance to encourage them to pursue those passions in ways that bring life to them and others. Or, those we are serving may bury their own longings and adopt our agendas for them because we supposedly know better. The result is superficial relationships with people based on the limited point of view of one person or organization, instead of deeper relationships based on mutual openness and respect.

Sometimes I have heard people in ministry talk about their concern that the people they are serving are not able to hear from God or might hear incorrectly. But couldn't the same concern be true of these ministry leaders or us? Too often, Christians describe feeling disconnected from God, yet they continue to go to church and serve in ministry roles. Or they make choices that hurt themselves or others and attribute these decisions to "God's will." Yet God continues to give us the freedom to listen and respond to Him, or not, as we choose. If God himself gives us freedom, why do we then so quickly rush to take that freedom away from others?

I wonder if it is because we are afraid. In 1 John 4:18, it says that perfect love casts out fear. The only perfect love that has ever existed is that which God gives.

I believe He gives us the freedom to live and learn and make mistakes because He is not afraid of what might happen. He is God, and therefore fully capable of handling anything that happens because of the choices we make. Even when we are out of control, it does not impair His ability to remain in control. But perhaps when people take on a leadership or ministry role, they also take on a responsibility, consciously or unconsciously, to control what happens among those they are working with. Unlike God, as human beings we tend to feel threatened by a lack of control over others. And so, we do what we can to maintain control, including limiting others' freedom and input, so that we can have conditions conform to what makes us feel comfortable and safe. We choose to follow the siren call of protecting ourselves instead of the voice of love and truth, which invites us to trust in God's ability to bring about our good regardless of the circumstances.

WHO GETS TO BE HEARD?

HOW DO WE LEAD or minister in a way that brings freedom and empowerment? Jesus was the perfect example of making space for God's voice, choosing to obey whatever God called Him to moment by moment, offering to people what He received from God and giving them the freedom to choose how they would respond. He wanted relationship with people, but only if it was true. He wanted them to choose Him out of love and not coercion.

For example, in Mark 10:17-27, a rich young man runs up to Jesus and asks Him how he can inherit eternal life.

Jesus shares some of the ten commandments in response. The man states that he has obeyed them. Jesus looks at him with love, invites him to sell everything he has, and follow Him. When the young man hears he must give up all his stuff to be perfect, he is disappointed. The truth is that he wants his possessions more than he wants God. He has done as much as he can in his own power to get eternal life, by following the other commands. By giving up his wealth, he would have to rely on God's power to take care of him. He could no longer be god of his own life. Even though he chooses to walk away, Jesus still makes space for him to reveal his true longings and decide for himself what he values more: the choice either to put his whole life in God's hands or to stay with the safety he associated with his earthly treasure. Jesus does not force the young man to choose Him. He lets the young man decide for himself what he wants, even if it is not Jesus.

Like Jesus, with this young man, we can be a safe space for people to express and process their true desires if we do not impose our own expectations on them or try to force them to make choices they are not ready for. Jesus does not force things. He listens, offers, and invites. And then he lets us choose.

My first term in India lasted almost two years. As the end was approaching, I remember feeling a sort of pressure to see one of my close friends choose to accept Jesus before I left. Then I felt God speaking to me and reminding me that it is He who draws people to Himself, and that if He wanted my friend to put her faith in Him, He was capable of accomplishing that whether I was with her or not. It was actually a relief for me to receive this reminder and realize that I am not responsible for other people's relationships with God. He is. If He chooses to use me in other people's lives, that is an invitation He offers at His discretion to partner with Him. It in no way implies that I now have the authority or responsibility that is rightfully His to bring people to Him. This is the truth that sets me free.

Once I realized that it was not my responsibility to control how others respond to God, I was able to focus on enjoying being present with my friend for the last couple of months I was in India, giving her the freedom to be herself. I did not need to be God in her life, telling her what is best for her. I just needed to be who God made me to be and let her be who God made her to be.

MAKING SPACE FOR GOD'S VOICE IN ME

WHAT DO OTHERS SAY ABOUT ME?

THE IMPORTANCE OF BEING who God made us to be was one of the lessons God was teaching me during my mission trip in India, though I wasn't conscious of it at the time. When I went, I was in my mid-twenties and still letting other people define me. Not only was I the youngest person on our team, but I was also the only Indian person. The local people viewed me differently than the rest of my team, even my husband, who is a White American. All six people on our team wore Indian clothes, but when we were out in public, the local Indian people were excited to talk to the others. When I was with them, I was often not addressed at all, because I appeared to be just another Indian person. One time we were at a church event and the pastor, who was Indian, called out the names of the White people on our team to lead the small groups. Thankfully, our team leader mentioned it and the pastor apologized for overlooking my Brazilian teammate and me. My teammates would strike up conversations with strangers, who praised them for speaking a few Hindi phrases. When I tried to talk to strangers, they derided me for not knowing the language better. Since I looked like a local person, I was expected to know the cultural norms and act accordingly. Though I understood why I was mostly ignored, I still felt the hurt and isolation of it.

I couldn't turn to my fellow teammates for comfort, either. We had all received the same training in outreach and language and culture learning. However, most missions training is developed for people who are going to a country different from their ethnic origins. Some of my teammates criticized the way I interacted with the local people, not understanding that I faced very different expectations than they did.

I remember one of our first meetings as a team. Afterwards one of my White teammates angrily complained, to the point of cursing, that we looked lazy sitting around talking while the Indian woman we had hired to help with cleaning and cooking had been working around the house at the same time. I was surprised because I remember visiting my extended family in India when I was growing up, and they all had servants. My family members worked, but they also hosted people in their homes and had tea and conversation while the servants went about their work. My teammate communicated that we were being culturally insensitive, but her assumption about what our helper was thinking did not match my own experiences of having actually stayed in India before. During my visits to India, my understanding was that it was important that we paid the servants fairly and treated them well, not whether we appeared productive to them. But I felt too intimidated by this person's anger and confidence in her viewpoint to share my own thoughts.

Sometimes meetings with local Christian leaders were arranged, and the two White women on our team would be invited, but the Brazilian woman and I were not. Another time, one of my White teammates and I were initially assigned to the same language tutor. When we arrived for our first session, my teammate talked almost the entire time. I realized I would need to get my own tutor after that if I wanted the chance to talk.

What message does it send when you say you want to empower local people and women, yet you continually ignore the one person in your group who represents both of those populations? I felt hurt and angry, followed by guilt for being hurt and angry. I also assumed that the way others were treating me was somehow my fault. If only I was different, I reasoned, I would not be treated so badly. My response was to try to adjust my own behavior in order to please others and meet their expectations of me. Welcome to the emotional wasteland that results when you have been fed messages that your reason for being is to make other people happy, especially people in power, and that thinking about your own needs and desires is selfish. This is not just a message I picked up being raised in an Asian Indian immigrant family, it was also consistently reinforced by the Indian and American churches my family attended, and the world's general view of women.

My time on the field in India was when I lost all my moorings. Before I could find who God made me to be, I needed to face the truth that I was lost. The things that gave my life meaning and value before, that rooted me to others were gone. I went from being able to intelligently express myself whenever I chose, to struggling to form complete sentences in Hindi. I went from having a job as a health educator where I had felt competent and productive to being a missionary struggling to learn the local language and culture and build relationships and survive daily life in a slum. I left a strong, loving, supportive network of family and friends to be in a place where I felt unappreciated by both the locals and my fellow missionaries.

As I reflected on my experiences, God's response was, "I know that I have stripped you of everything that gave you value before and that you feel crushed. But I did it so that you would learn how to root your identity in me and find your value solely in what I say about you. That way, even if all these things were restored to you, and you were stripped of them again, at that time you would be able to stand and not be crushed because your identity is rooted in me." Seeing God's vision for me gave me the strength to accept what had happened and continue on because I deeply wanted to become the person He had shown me.

I realized that even though the things that previously gave my life value were not bad in and of themselves, they could become a hindrance for me if I attached my worth to them. Ultimately, our worth is not in what we do, or what others think of us, but how God sees us and what He says about us. Until that point, I had been giving others undue influence and power over me to define who I was. God wanted me to allow Him and only Him to have that kind of power over me. And I was so ready to surrender to that invitation from Him. But first I needed to shed the old fruit of letting others define me by learning how to forgive those who had hurt me, so that I could make room for the new fruit of an identity rooted in His unchanging love for me.

My first year in India passed with much pain and loneliness. I called my mother one night after a year of being there and asked her to pray for me, because I was not sure I could go on if things continued the way they had been. That night I spent the whole night crying and pouring my heart out to God. Once again, I felt Him teach me many things.

God spoke to me about forgiveness and told me He understood why I was hurt by the local people. He reminded me that He had brought me to India to reconcile me to my people and culture. The devil had wanted me to play the blame game to explain my hurt feelings. Whenever I had gotten hurt, I had either blamed myself or blamed others. God wanted me to know that it was not my fault that I was different from my teammates. He intentionally created me this way. He did not want me to blame the local people because they had no experience relating to an Indian American. The locals knew how to relate to each other and foreigners, of which I was neither. I looked like any other Indian person, but I had the language and mannerisms of an American. He wanted me to forgive them from my heart and learn how to love them regardless of whether they changed their behavior towards me or not.

God used a book I had been reading, *Failure: The Back Door to Success*, by Erwin W. Lutzer, to walk me through the practical steps of forgiveness. I had known that forgiveness was important, but I did not know how to go about accomplishing it. When someone hurt me, I would try to overlook the offense and continue on as if nothing had happened. That's what I thought forgiveness looked like: to continually sweep things under the rug and avoid confrontation in order to maintain a relationship. Another way to put it is that I bottled up my hurt feelings. The problem is that there is a limit to how much pain a person can hold, and eventually, the bottle bursts. In reading the book, I came to understand that in order to forgive someone, you have to first acknowledge that they did something hurtful. This was a revelation to me. Suddenly it made sense to me why my efforts to forgive certain people had felt hampered. I was trying to convince myself that the things they did were no big deal, and I should be able to forgive them and move on. But the truth was that it was a big deal to me, and I needed to be honest about the pain I was experiencing before I could move forward.

That night I practiced the steps towards forgiveness I had learned in the book. I asked God to bring to mind everyone I needed to forgive. Then, one by one, I prayed over each person's name and told the Lord and myself the specific things that they had done and the different feelings I experienced as a result of their actions. Then I told the Lord that I was making a conscious choice to forgive each person and releasing to Him whatever debts they owed me. I asked Him to heal my wounds and give me the grace to continue in my relationships with them without harboring any grudges. After two hours of prayer, I came to the end of the list of names God had given me. I felt like a weight had been lifted from my spirit and a deep sense of peace and rest had taken its place. I felt God lovingly exhort me to continue forgiving people like this as soon as I was hurt so that I would not have to carry the burden of pain with me for so long. God accomplished the work He called me to India for. From that moment, I felt the freedom to love my people and culture, as well as others, and forgive them regardless of how I was treated.

WHAT DO I SAY ABOUT MYSELF?

WALKING WITH GOD through the process of real for-giveness and letting go of my pain made space for me to recover. It also made space for more truth to flourish in my life. Learning to tell the truth about who or what hurt me also opened the door to telling the truth about what I really wanted and enjoyed. Instead of waiting to be told what to do by my team, I took the initiative to tell my team leader that I was not enjoying the roles I currently had. During my time in India, I heard about a non-profit cooperative that employed local women to create paper products from local materials. I asked if I could try working with this cooperative and see where it led. My leader listened to and accepted my request. I enjoyed working alongside the women, assembling journals and cards and giving input on design ideas. Working with them gave me a reason to talk with them, and it was much easier to build relationships because we had something in common.

I also thought I might enjoy learning a classical South Indian dance called Bharata Natyam, which is used to tell stories. I had seen people perform it in America and I was fascinated by the graceful, sculptural movements that communicate spiritual themes. I asked a local friend about it, and she referred me to a teacher who conveniently lived in our building. I signed up for private lessons and became good friends with my teacher Sarita.

My relationship with Sarita was a blessing and one of the most satisfying experiences of my time in India. She was someone who accepted and loved me for who I was. As I arrived at her door one day, she asked me how I was. I felt safe to share openly with her, so I told her about my loneliness and sadness because I had not made many friends since coming to India.

She listened graciously. "Mini, aren't you a follower of Jesus?" she asked.

I smiled and said "Yes."

"Didn't Jesus only have twelve friends?"

"Yes."

"If Jesus only had twelve friends and He was a supernatural being, how can you expect to have more friends when you are only a human being?"

I had to laugh and felt warmth immediately spread through me. Here was a Hindu woman with limited exposure to Christianity, and God was using her to speak truth in love to me in my time of need. I was so grateful to Him and my friend for this unexpected grace.

Again, I saw God empowering me and giving me life as I took the risk to tell the truth about my life, both what I wanted and what was hard for me. If I had not acknowledged my desire to express myself through dance and pursued that desire, I would not have discovered this precious friendship. If I had not been honest when my friend asked me how I was, and not shared my struggles, I would have missed the opportunity to see how God empowered her and gave her wisdom to encourage me.

Another time I was talking with Shakti, a lovely Indian woman who had grown up in a slum and became a leader in the local ministry our team partnered with. She asked me how I was doing, and I shared openly about some of my struggles. She listened well and then told me how surprised she was by my response. She said that she and other local people assumed that foreigners never had any problems, and it was only local people like her who had problems. She said no foreign missionaries had ever shared their struggles. It was my turn to be surprised.

I had always felt that I was never above anyone else. I truly believed that God had created us all equal. Did the world's systems support that truth? Absolutely not.

But that did not make it any less true. And now I was confronted with the fact that it was not just the world's systems undermining that truth, it was also the foreign missionaries who had come to the field to save the world, and asked the locals to be vulnerable, but did not have the courage or awareness to share their own vulnerability. Even Jesus, who really is the only one who can save the world, in His earthly existence shared honestly about His needs. When mourning the possibility of sacrificing His life, while in Gethsemane, He asked His disciples to keep Him company and pray for Him. The prophecies in Isaiah talk about how He was well acquainted with grief. It is precisely because He struggled on earth that we have a high priest who understands and empathizes with us in our trials. This is what makes it possible for us to have an authentic relationship with God. By expressing the truth about His experience on earth, He makes space for us to tell the truth about our own experiences. And suddenly we realize that God who seems so different from us is actually able to relate quite intimately with us. Like God's honesty with us, my honesty with Shakti had created a bridge between us, causing her to realize that we were more alike in our experiences than she might first have assumed.

WHAT DOES GOD SAY ABOUT ME?

THROUGH THESE INTERACTIONS and others, I began to see how God was giving me the experience of feeling blessed for being myself rather than feeling punished for who I was. For example, with the two women I mentioned above, my natural openness and vulnerability were welcomed and helped break down barriers, rather than being considered weaknesses. Now that I had released other people's false power over me by forgiving their hurtful definitions of me, God was reasserting His true power over me and in me by showing me how He defined me.

I had expected the physical conditions of poverty in India to be hard and they were. But the emotional conditions of poverty were what broke my spirit. Blending in with the local people allowed me to experience what it was like to be overlooked, ignored, and hidden in plain sight. God revealed to me that this is how the poor are often treated. They are robbed of their humanity and its accompanying value by people who would rather look past them than at them. If I had struggled after living with this experience for two years, what must it be like for people who had spent their whole lives in poverty? God showed me how being Indian in India allowed me to incarnate beyond a physical level to an emotional level with the poor. He also showed me how by doing so, I was following Jesus' example of connecting with people. Jesus not only lived among them physically, but He also shared their experiences of joy, grief, anger, and frustration. He too was ignored, overlooked, and hidden in plain sight until He manifested the miraculous powers God had given Him. This experience—of struggling with the loneliness and anonymity that the absence of perceived value can bring—was helping me to connect more deeply with Jesus as well as my neighbors.

Another way I felt connected with Jesus was through the shared experience of being rejected by my own people. Jesus knew what it was like to be underestimated by His townspeople and even members of His own family.

It opened my eyes and comforted me to see that even if people reject me, it does not change my value or what I have to offer. Jesus had so much to offer, although He was not always treated that way. In Matthew 13:58, when asked why He did not perform more miraculous works in His hometown, Jesus responded that the people there did not have faith in Him. This was the Son of God. Yet He still felt limited by the lack of faith people had in Him. As a result, He moved on and went to people and places that did make space for Him and His power to work.

WHICH VOICE DO I CHOOSE?

ONE OF THE WAYS I saw God manifest His power to work in me came towards the end of my time in India. I was sitting in a medical office, listening to a doctor tell me that I was probably in the process of losing my first pregnancy. I had experienced spotting, losing small amounts of blood during the first few weeks of my pregnancy. An ultrasound ordered earlier by the doctor did not show an embryo. Now the doctor wanted to admit me to the hospital and have a dilation and curettage procedure done to clean out my uterus and ensure that I didn't get an infection. As I listened to her explaining this to me and tried to absorb what seemed like a foregone conclusion in her mind, a question arose in my own mind. "Why don't you get another ultrasound, just so that you will know there is nothing there for sure before you get the procedure done? You don't want to always wonder what might have been afterwards."

I asked the doctor if I should get another ultrasound to make sure that there was no baby, and she said it would be a waste of time and money.

In India, it is disrespectful to question the doctor's orders. But the still small voice inside me kept convicting me to do the ultrasound anyway. While one part of me just wanted to accept the doctor's recommendation and not risk displeasing her, another part of me was asking for space. Space to confirm her story before acting accordingly. Space to explore the possibility that something else could be true. It was a clash between my normal modus operandi of letting someone else define what was happening for me and a new invitation to at least pause and reflect on whether I agreed with that definition before accepting it as truth. I chose to listen to the voice inside me rather than the doctor's voice of authority. I told the doctor we would come back after getting a second ultrasound.

Lying in another office, I waited for the ultrasound technician to tell me that there was no fetus. Instead, he turned on the speakers and told us that he could hear the baby's heartbeat. In that moment, I knew that it was God's voice in me that had saved our baby's life. By listening to His voice, I made space for Him to tell me a different story about what was happening inside of me. I went to the ultrasound office looking for proof of death. Instead, God offered me proof of life, communicated in the lovely sound of my daughter's heartbeat.

✳

337

WHAT DO I WANT?

I HAD INITIALLY GONE to India because I felt God inviting me to learn how to forgive and be reconciled to my own culture and people. And He did teach me how to do that. He also taught me to value the friends I made and consider it a gift when He allowed me to connect deeply with someone. He also gave me a whole new respect and empathy for my immigrant parents and anyone who has ever experienced being a stranger in a new land. But as we neared the end of our first term in India, I was faced with discerning whether I was called to return for a second term. Part of me felt a pull to say yes to returning to the field because it seemed like that is what our supporters and others expected of us. But I quickly realized that if I said yes to coming back to India, but did not have God's support or calling for me to do so, I would not be able to sustain living there in my own power. So I told God the truth.

I had tried different activities and roles during my time in India, but in many ways, I felt emotionally and spiritually starved. I still did not feel like I had a place there. But I trusted in God's wisdom. If He called me to stay, I would surrender and obey. I asked Him what He wanted me to do and listened for His answer. It came in a feeling of peace as I thought about leaving. He told me I had learned what He wanted me to in India and that I could go home now. I checked in with my husband about his process, as I wanted to be open if He felt called to return. After praying and sharing our perspectives with each other, we decided to go home and see what God would have for us next.

WHAT AM I CALLED TO?

SIX MONTHS AFTER returning from India, our missions agency asked my husband Dave to go to a conference on the topic of spiritual formation among urban ministry workers. Intrigued by the topic, I asked my husband if I could come along. This was the first time I had heard of spiritual formation, the process by which our souls or spirits are formed. This process includes not only our specifically religious practices, like going to church or participating in Bible study, but everything we experience and our response to it.

My passion for spiritual formation was both immediate and cumulative. Immediate, because I was drawn to this ministry from my first moments of exposure to it. Cumulative, because I had so many thoughts and experiences related to spiritual formation throughout my life, which until that conference I did not have the words to describe. I felt like a mute person who had suddenly been given the ability to express herself in a way other people could understand. I wanted to learn everything I could about spiritual formation. I was drawn to the practice of spiritual direction, in which one person sits with others and listens to what is happening in their lives, helping them reflect on if or how they are experiencing God and His invitations.

In January 2010, I started my first week of classes to become a spiritual director. In October 2011, I graduated. The first time I met with someone for direction, I felt like all of my different gifts were coming together and being expressed at the same time. Congruence is another word for it: when everything comes together into a complete whole and there is harmony between all of the different parts. But the harmony isn't just within you; it's occurring with God and His will too, so that you are more, so much more than the sum of your parts. And you can relax and let go because the moment you decide to accept and honor who He made you to be, you open the door for His power to flow through you and carry you home—home to Him and everything He offers. That is the place where miracles can happen, because with Him anything is possible. Yes, my friends, it truly is that spectacular!

As amazing as that sounds, God has continued to teach me that my true identity and value go beyond what I do or what role I am in. The true gift He wants me to experience is the ability to be all of who I am, wherever I am and whatever I am doing. While I enjoy seeing people for direction when He gives me the opportunity, He wants me to know that being a spiritual director or how many clients I have is not what defines me or gives me value. It is too small to build my whole world around. Similarly, I know that I am also not supposed to build my world around being a wife, mom, or writer. There is nothing inherently wrong with any of those things, but they are just parts of who I am in any given season. He sees and wants me to see the whole of who He has made me to be in all of life. And honestly, that feels so much better. Then I am not trying to fit into a box of preconceived notions about what each role means. On the contrary, there is no box for me. There is just limitless space to explore and grow with God. And that gives me the freedom to be anything He wants anytime He calls. Mercifully, God does not typecast us. Instead, He invites us to co-create our lives with Him, moment by moment.

How do we co-create our lives with Him? We do it by participating in the process of call and response. First, we listen and make space for God. Then we notice what He is saying or doing. Finally, we choose how we want to respond. If we identify ourselves as followers of Jesus, we might assume this process happens by default in our lives. But that is not true. We still live in a world that offers multiple stimuli to respond to, from a multitude of sources. Not all of those sources are from God. For example, you could go to church and have two people give you very different opinions, or go to work and have other people give you very different input, or watch television and hear even more advice. Obviously, we can't respond to all the stimuli present in our lives. So we have to choose what we listen or pay attention to, and how we respond to it. Some people choose based on which voices are the loudest or sound the most confident. Others may choose based on which ones have the most power over them or scare them the most. But we can also consciously choose to listen for the still, small voice of God—the voice that sounds like love and truth. If we do, then we can begin the journey of discovering how His voice interacting with our voice shapes the course of our lives. If we do not, then we are still co-creating our lives, but it is in response to someone or something other than God.

THE VOICE THAT LEADS TO LIFE

YOU SEE, the field is us, and our mission in this life is to decide who we are going to listen to and how we are going to respond. The more I have listened to the voice of God in my life, the more life He has given me. I enter relationships and roles now out of desire and calling, rather than obligations and expectations. I am present with people because of who they are and who I am, not because I wish them to be different or myself to be different. Now, my relationships feel authentic and life-giving rather than one-sided and life-draining. If change does happen on my part or someone else's part, it is because we feel called to transformation by God, and it matches the desires He has planted in our hearts. Those are the changes that last and bring healing and freedom to ourselves and our world.

13

BITTERSWEET GOSPEL
Grace Weng

Grace Weng grew up in Southern California, and her first exposure to urban poor ministry came through a summer missions trip in Los Angeles during her time as a UCLA student. In 2010, she returned to that same neighborhood in South Los Angeles as an intern with Servant Partners and began serving with a local youth ministry. In addition to finding her vocational calling during the internship, she also met her husband James, a fellow intern. They married three years later, and Grace joined Servant Partners staff to do full-time youth ministry. Currently, she serves as the young adult pastor for Church of the Redeemer, where she oversees the youth and young adult ministries. She enjoys developing young leaders, and enjoys seeing youth and young adults grow in their faith and authority. In addition to her work, Grace loves elephants, succulents, boba, crafting, and "The Office."

I AM A PETITE 5'2" Chinese-American woman in my thirties. But were you to meet me in person, you may guess differently about both my age and ethnicity.

Because of my darker skin tone and more ambiguous facial features, I am often mistaken for a whole range of ethnic backgrounds. Most commonly, people presume I am Filipino—so much so that when I was in the Philippines for a visit to a Servant Partners ministry site, people would speak to me in Tagalog! The wildest guess at my ethnic identity was by a man I happened to walk past one day on my street in South Los Angeles, who insisted, "You have to have some Black in you, and something Latin, too."

People also often view and treat me as being younger than my actual age. Perhaps the most ridiculous time this happened was when I was seated in an exit row on a plane—on my honeymoon, no less—and the stewardess approached me to tell me that I was too young to sit in the exit row. I may look young, but fifteen? In my first year of serving with our church's youth group, I mentored two high school students. One of them thought I was a student in the youth group when she first met me. I've been told by a woman I looked "cute" after I preached. Most recently, on a prayer walk around the community, I was asked if I was a student at the local university. Even on the verge of my thirties, I was still being mistaken for an undergraduate student.

In the same way someone may not be able to accurately identify my ethnicity or age just by looking at me, someone may also have difficulty guessing my present vocation and calling if he or she was to simply consider my upbringing and background. As the daughter of Chinese immigrants from an educated, suburban, middle-class background, my family and friends might not have guessed that I would be an inner-city minister. I myself would not have expected this calling—to serve cross-culturally and cross-class within an impoverished community in South Los Angeles. But I do. Whether you look at me passing by on the street or you study my demographic data on paper, easy assumptions only get you so far.

The same is true with characters we find in the Bible. At times, we streamline and simplify biblical stories for easy retelling, perhaps to introduce someone who isn't familiar with one story or another. But another reason I think we simplify and sanitize biblical characters, sometimes even to a caricature, is to avoid the discomfort of how human sin and human suffering threads through the lives of all the biblical stories and characters—and how both sin and suffering thread through our own lives as well. I could choose any part of Scripture, and within it find marks of sin and suffering. But one story that has stood out to me is that of the intertwined lives and stories of Abram, (later Abraham), Sarai (later Sarah), and Hagar (who does not receive a new name from God, but rather gives God a name, as "the one who sees her").

ABRAM, SARAI, AND HAGAR: SIN AND SUFFERING

ABRAM, SARAI, AND HAGAR'S story can be found in Genesis 12 through 25. Abram, who later became the first patriarch, was a man of God's great promise and blessing, indeed the man from whom every nation on earth would be blessed. But in nearly every retelling I can recall, their story has been changed to his—Abram's—story, and it has also been simplified and sanitized: the uncomfortable parts of the plot are cast aside, along with the other people within those narratives. Here is one simple telling we may hear: *After the death of his father, Abram leads his wife Sarai and relatives in search of a special land that was promised to him by God. Along the way, he rescues his nephew from the clutches of an enemy army, dines with powerful rulers, amasses great fortune, and births children who carry on his legacy as "the father of many nations."*

But note what has been left out. One significant and often untold part of the story is that Abram lied about Sarai being his wife, not once, but twice. Would we ever accept such behavior from any of our spouses or significant others? No, but for some reason we justify his actions. We say it was probably culturally acceptable. We say he must have been afraid for his life. We say he was just trying to problem-solve. Rarely, perhaps never, do we call it what it is—Abram gave away his wife because he feared for his own life, and he chose not to protect hers. Abram put his wife in the way of potential harm for the sake of his own personal safety.

Rather than overlooking this story as a minor stumble in Abram's life, we should see it for what it is. It is a pattern of self-reliant sin and doubting God, whereby Abram tries to make his own way rather than trusting God's great promises to him. The harm done to others aside, the depth of sin in this lie is made plain when we consider that God's covenant over Abram was promised protection that is affronted by Abram's self-reliance. "I will bless those who bless you, and him who dishonors you I will curse," the Lord promised to Abram before he was sent out from his father's land, "and in you all the families of the earth shall be blessed" (Genesis 12:3, ESV). God had Abram's back, and Abram ignored that.

Abram's fearful response is a sin so deeply rooted in his life and family that he repeats it twice in his life and also manages to pass the behavior on to his son Isaac, who similarly lies about his wife Rebekah. If we simplify Abram into a perfect forefather of faith who did no wrong, he becomes only a mirage, with no true substance. But when we see Abram for who he actually was, a sinful man with real struggles and doubts, we encounter a man who is relatable to us and relevant as a fellow brother, trying to follow God even in his imperfection. And we are able to engage with the powerful truth that God did not abandon Abram after his failures. Abram continued to be blessed as a conduit of blessing for future generations. When we see Abram for who he is, we can also more fully encounter the God who covenants with Abram—the God who is powerful to work in spite of Abram's doubt and disobedience. This same God is similarly with us, making covenant with us in our imperfection, not giving up on us, and working powerfully through us, in spite of our many—and often significant—shortcomings and failures.

The other loss we suffer when we amplify and center on only one biblical "hero" in any given story is that we lose the opportunity to learn from all the other characters' viewpoints and experiences, especially when, for whatever reason, we've recast things as simpler than they actually were. Perhaps we do that because we wrestle with the complexity within our own hearts and lives. Perhaps it's hard to hold the absolute and continual goodness of God, together with the fact that God is somehow still able to shine through our world, as undeniably broken and ugly and sinful as it is. Perhaps it's just easier to love a simpler story. It's easy to love the hero who has no flaw, to hate a villain who has been stripped of any remaining image of God's imprint, and it's easy not to give much thought to the supporting characters.

In our singular focus on Abram, for example, we forget peripheral characters like Sarai and Hagar, women whose lives hold crucial lessons. Looking again at "Abram's" story, let's consider what was going on for Sarai. She and Abram had made many journeys in their life together. Leaving her husband's homeland for a divine, if somewhat unclear calling outward, they resettled in a place that was soon overcome by famine. Heading for Egypt, and traveling in a foreign land, Sarai was separated from her husband. In Abram and Sarai's culture, the husband was supposed to protect and provide for his wife, but instead Abram asks Sarai to lie and pretend to be his sister rather than his wife. Sarai is then sent to live—alone—in the house of foreigners. Likely unable to understand their language, and knowing full well that she was there because of her physical beauty, she would understand, as any woman might, the implications of what that abandonment could mean for her and her body. But while Abram failed in his obligation to protect her, we see God's faithfulness to deliver Sarai from situations of extreme vulnerability. When she is in the house of Pharaoh, God extends plagues over Pharaoh's house until Sarai is returned to Abram. Later, in the house of Abimelech, God speaks to Abimelech in a dream, urging him to return Sarai to Abram lest he face punishment.

When we see Abram clearly for who he is, and not as the single flawless character in the story, it opens up the heart space to learn from the other characters. Then we don't miss seeing who God is and how He was at work in the midst of that complex story. We can then more easily see how God could be at work in the midst of our own complex world and this present time—the present time almost always being more complex than the already-lived past or the yet-to-be-lived future. We can more clearly see our God who is near to this woman, Sarai, whose beauty and body could be exploited for the benefit of another. We can more clearly see the God—our God—who stands up for a woman in a place of great vulnerability and power-lessness. Our God who will bring her and her husband to a new land, and many years later, give her a son.

But just like Abram, Sarai is also deeply flawed. In her impatience for the child that God has promised, she commands Abram to sleep with a concubine named Hagar. Hagar, as a character and a person, could also easily be missed in the story. Hagar is a young Egyptian slave girl caught up in Abram and Sarai's failure to trust God for a son. Sarai was getting old and hadn't conceived, and she felt it was time to take matters into her own hands. Hagar's is a story of serving as a slave to foreign masters, forced to sleep with her master's husband, then mistreated and abused when she succeeds—as they'd intended—and con-ceives and bears a child by him. In Hagar's story, Abram is at best a bystander. Rather than provide protection or care for the slave girl he impregnated, who is still living in his house and serving his wife, he acquiesces to Sarai's cruel requests. And not long after being forced to sleep with Abraham, Hagar runs away from her master's house because Sarai was treating her harshly.

There is a Chinese idiom called *chi ku*, which translates into English as "eating bitterness." It is an idiom that describes the quality of enduring unpleasantness. *Chi ku* can describe the more toxic eating of bitterness that can break a person down, or it can represent the more intended hopeful characteristic of eating bitterness good-naturedly, with a hope for something better. This quality of "eating bitterness" can cover a wide range of actions or qualities. It can be used to describe the methodical way in which a guitar student practices the same song over and over in spite of painful finger calluses; it can also describe enduring the antagonisms of an unfair boss or an unpleasant neighbor. "Eating bitterness" can even be applied to situations where we must put our head down and press forward through the bitterness, even if the source of bitterness comes from systems of oppression or injustice.

Hagar lived with bitterness, perhaps her whole life, specifically eating the bitterness that resulted from her unfortunate status as handmaiden to an unhappy, dysfunctional couple. But God was not far from Hagar in her bitterness, and God is not far from us when we eat bitterness. There are times when we may find ourselves in a bitter place, perhaps one we cannot escape. The good news is that if we, like Hagar, unfairly receive insult and injury—if our mouths, like hers, are full of bitter words we may not even be able to speak—God will still hear us, and

God will still see us. We see this in Hagar's story. When she flees the house of Sarai and Abram, God pursues her:

> The angel of the Lord found her by a spring of water in the wilderness, the spring on the way to Shur...And the angel of the Lord said to her, "Behold, you are pregnant and shall bear a son. You shall call his name Ishmael, because the Lord has listened to your affliction." (Genesis 16:8 and 11, ESV)

God saw Hagar's affliction, her misery and bitterness. She was not alone, even though her circumstance would seem otherwise. And as Hagar realizes this, her response is to acknowledge God as El Roi, the God who sees. She says "You are a God of seeing...truly here I have seen him who looks after me" (Genesis 16:13, ESV). We should note that in calling God El Roi, Hagar is the first character in the Bible to give God a new name. How significant that this is done not by the great patriarch Abraham, but instead, by a Gentile woman from a pagan nation, an outcast slave, who sees and acknowledges God in great worship and faith. Hagar has experienced God as one who is lovingly watching over her, in protection and provision, in the midst of her loneliness and rejection. It is with this revelation and truth that Hagar is able to return to her master's house, no doubt continuing to endure bitterness in an unhappy household, until things fall apart again fourteen years later.

When Isaac is finally born to Sarai, she begins to look with contempt on Hagar's son, unaccepting of a rival heir. So Hagar is cast out of the household, sent away with only bread and water, to wander the wilderness of Beersheba.

Eventually Hagar runs out of water. Anticipating the death of her only son, Hagar cries aloud and weeps in anguish. In this place of bitterness, she is found again by God:

> And God heard the voice of the boy, and the angel of God called to Hagar from heaven and said to her, "What troubles you, Hagar? Fear not, for God has heard the voice of the boy where he is. Up! Lift up the boy, and hold him fast with your hand, for I will make him into a great nation." (Genesis 21:17-18, ESV)

Hagar is met by a God who listens to her affliction and who hears her cries once again. In both stories, God pronounces a promise to Hagar, first that her offspring would be multiplied such that they cannot be counted (Genesis 16:10) and later that her son Ishmael would be made into a great nation (Genesis 20:18). Interestingly, these promises parallel God's covenant to Abraham. As much as God is the God of Abraham, the covenanted father of faith, He is also the God of Hagar and Ishmael, the exiled living in bitterness. Through God, Hagar receives water in the wilderness in place of her bitterness. In the first account, the Lord "found her by a spring of water" (Genesis 16:7), and in the second instance, God found them and opened her eyes so that she "saw a well of water" (Genesis 21:19).

EATING BITTERNESS: GOD SEES US

HAGAR'S STORY REMINDS us that God sees us when we eat bitterness. Even when we are used and abused, in distress, alone, and in need of help, we are found by God. He seeks us out and provides for our needs, even promising a good future to us when all we see around us is the bitter desert. But eating bitterness is not on its own an inherent virtue or promise of blessing. Hagar had an openness to God in the face of her bitterness, but this may not always be the state of our hearts toward our bitterness. Within Chinese culture, eating bitterness often has an element of hiddenness in the face of suffering or hardship. That is, it is inappropriate to complain or draw attention to oneself. Instead the proper thing to do is to suck up—to eat—your bitterness and move on.

Eating bitterness has been a foundational part of the Chinese-American narrative within the United States. Chinese immigrants endured decades of intense racism in the form of harsh immigration laws, anti-miscegenation, and unfair labor laws. Yet there was an understanding that the harshness of this country was still preferable to the poverty and corruption of the lives they had left behind. The bitter sacrifice would be worth the eventual ability to make a better life in America, and to give one's children a better future.

The problem, however, is that this quality of eating bitterness can be inwardly focused and divorced from faith. As a form of self-silencing, it encourages anyone who has been trained in eating bitterness to be voiceless in the face of systemic oppression. Stories of racial pain and communal suffering are swept under the rug instead of acknowledged. Rather than confronting the systems that perpetuate this racial pain, we push them aside and press on. Our silence has even made us complicit in the creation of a model-minority myth where Asians and Asian-Americans have become stereotyped as a false model of hard-working and high-achieving success stories pitted against other people of color. This myth is an excuse for both degrading other races and stifling our own stories, needs, and voices. Our silence oppresses us even as it oppresses others, especially anyone who might not fit the model-minority mold.

In such a place of silence, there is no communal space to voice any sort of pain or to acknowledge racial pain specifically. It's how we've come to sweep aside national injustices as big as the Chinese exclusion act. Whole generations of immigrants have carried shame in silence rather than speak up against the systems that caused their oppression. There has been no appropriate outlet to process suffering and pain, to be reconciled to those who chose to oppress and caused this pain, or to heal from the wounds caused by the oppression. Neither has there been time and space to stand up against the sources of any oppression and pain and demand a response, apology, or change to current oppression. This silence then becomes a way to numb one's own pain, and it extends into a self-protective ignoring of others' racial pain. It's why Asian communities often seem to have a tough time engaging with movements like #BlackLivesMatter or for immigration reform. To a people used to eating bitterness, outspoken movements against injustice are counter-cultural and thus often misunderstood. The rhetoric is that if we as a people group can suck it up and press on through our bitterness, then so should others.

While this coping mechanism has lasted for generations, we must understand that it is not a biblical way to approach pain or injustice. For those of us who are followers of God, eating bitterness is an act that can be damaging if we do not bring our bitterness to God. Attempting to keep our pain and bitterness from God can cause our faith lives to be divorced from the significant biblical narrative of our God who hears the cries of the needy and responds. God is not distanced from us when we encounter bitterness or suffering. He does not leave us to endure and eat bitterness alone. Rather, He is a God who hears our cries as He heard Hagar's. He is the God of the psalmist who sings out:

> The eyes of the Lord are toward the righteous and his ears toward their cry. The face of the Lord is against those who do evil, to cut off the memory of them from the earth. When the righteous cry for help, the Lord hears and delivers them out of all their troubles. The Lord is near to the brokenhearted and saves the crushed in spirit. (Psalm 34:15-18, ESV)

Our God is more than a big abstract ear who hears our cries. God not only receives our cries for help, but He cuts off those who work evil, and He saves the righteous. If our practice of eating bitterness keeps us from engaging with God as one who hears our cries, then we will also be unable to understand God as one who cuts off evil, who upsets systems of oppression, and who enacts righteousness on behalf of the needy and marginalized.

HANNAH: UNDERSTANDING THE FULLNESS OF GOD

THE STORY OF HANNAH provides a positive example of a woman who understands the fullness of our God who hears, responds, and sets right. While Hagar was surely met by God in her bitterness, Hannah knows God as one who responds with righteous restoration to both our personal bitterness as well as our communal bitterness. Though Hannah had a loving husband, she faced the depression and desperation of being unable to give birth, for the Lord had closed her womb (1 Samuel 1:5). Year after year, Hannah endured the taunting and irritation of her husband's second wife, who had many sons and daughters. In 1 Samuel 1:9-11, Hannah enters the temple with great bitterness of soul and she approaches God in grief, weeping bitterly as she prays to the Lord. In this place of deep bitterness, Hannah makes a vow and plea to the Lord, that if God would give her a son, then she would give that same son back in service to the Lord.

Not long after, Hannah conceives. She gives birth to Samuel, who becomes a great priest, judge, teacher, and prophet for the people of God, even anointing their first king. After bringing her son Samuel back to the temple to fulfill her promise, Hannah bursts into worship of God in 1 Samuel 2. It is a song of thanksgiving that begins with personal thanksgiving to God for hearing her prayers and granting her a son, but it moves to exalting God as one who humbles the proud and uplifts the lowly. Her song is full of role reversals: those who are in places of power will be brought down, while those who, like herself, were in places of bitterness, powerlessness, and helplessness will be lifted up:

> He will guard the feet of his faithful ones, but the wicked shall be cut off in darkness, for not by might shall a man prevail. The adversaries of

the Lord shall be broken to pieces; against them he will thunder in heaven. The Lord will judge the ends of the earth; he will give strength to his king and exalt the horn of his anointed. (1 Samuel 2:9-10, ESV)

Hannah understands that the same God who heard her prayers and responded to her bitter cries is the God who breaks the bows of the mighty and arms the humble with strength—a God who will reverse the roles of the rich and the poor, the full and the hungry, the beggar and the prince.

When one's natural inclination is to only eat bitterness, it's difficult to allow oneself to be angry, or to call out another's sin that has caused so much pain. But when we are able to bring our anger, pain, and bitterness before God, we are met by a God who is with us in our places of utter desperation and bitter weeping—the same God who will judge the earth, pursue His enemies, and cut off the wicked, the same God who invites us to join Him in seeking justice, reconciliation, and righteousness, personally and with others for our world.

LEARNING TO DEMAND JUSTICE

THE FIRST TIME that I can recall moving past only eating bitterness to a kind of righteous anger was when I stood up for myself during a group project in high school. In this particular case, I had been assigned to one group for my entire sophomore school year to work on ongoing projects. There was one classmate in this group who never did his work, which meant it fell on someone else to do. Several times that year, I was the one all the work fell on. I had to pick up the slack for this classmate, and I hated the fact that he got the same grade as everyone else while doing no work. Toward the end of the year, we were in a group meeting, and I exploded in anger at him. I don't recall what I said, but I remember expressing my frustrations that he was taking advantage of everyone else in the group and that he needed to get his act together and contribute. Though he never fully contributed his fair share, he did step up his game for the remainder of the year. And though this was only a slight injustice in the grand scheme of things, I learned to stand up for myself and not just ignore or needlessly endure something that was unfair.

As an undergraduate, my journey of learning to pursue God's justice expanded from self-defense against group-project bullies to compassionate service for those I began to meet who shared experiences of pain and oppression, and who experienced deep bitterness from a number of systemic injustices in our society. Through Scripture study, I became captivated by a God who defends the cause of the weak and powerless, and who calls His people to the margins of society to enact His compassion and justice on behalf of the most vulnerable. I also began to learn the importance of applying and living out my faith beyond intellectual study or discussion.

I began taking trips to serve the homeless; those trips led to another trip over spring break to learn about injustices happening at the United States-Mexico border. Later I went on a summer missions trip to work with students from low-income communities. In my senior year at UCLA,

I was invited to replant a Bible study for African-American students on campus, who were underrepresented in the student body. This was a big leap of faith for me because I had grown up in Cerritos, California, a predominantly White and Asian city, attended a predominantly Chinese-American church, and had spent the first three years of college in Bible studies that were also largely White and Asian.

Before you get excited about what an "ideal" Christian I was, learning about justice and applying it in radical ways, which is what I did truly want to do, let me fill out the full story, including the part where God convicts me of my sin and leads me from there. I'd joined InterVarsity Christian Fellowship because of its multi-ethnic focus and make-up of students, but I had still chosen largely to surround myself with close friends who were very much like myself.

My junior year, my InterVarsity staff leader asked me to mentor another young woman who was White. That was still cross-cultural for me, even given the city where I'd grown up and my last three years in college. So I chose to mentor a Chinese-American woman instead, because I thought it'd be more comfortable and easy. But that mentoring relationship ended up not being a very fruitful relationship for the gospel, while the White woman I'd been encouraged to invest in ended up being committed, involved, and bearing much fruit for Jesus. God convicted me later that school year about the hypocrisy between my stated desire for multi-ethnic community and my actions. That conviction coincided with another call, one that I would follow this time—to help replant a Black student Bible study for our fellowship.

As I led cross-culturally through that Bible study, I was privileged to be welcomed into friendship with African-American students both within our Bible study and through our participation in the Afrikan Student Union. I was honored to be entrusted with stories of racial pain and struggle, and I was also humbled that they would hear and affirm my own stories of racial pain.

That year happened to be a year of great racial tension throughout the UC system: fraternities were throwing parties that caricatured African-American culture, a noose was found in a library at UCSD, and budget cuts disproportionately affected the ethnic studies departments at UCLA. Part way through the year, the Afrikan Student Union at UCLA organized a sit-in at the chancellor's office. For months, I had attended meetings of the Afrikan Student Union as a way to be more in touch with what was happening among African-American students on campus. Much of my involvement had been through the posture of a learner and a listener. But this was a clear invitation into action, where my voice and body would stand in solidarity with my brothers and sisters whose bitterness needed to be heard and responded to by campus administration.

The day before the sit-in, the Afrikan Student Union held a training where we learned about the list of demands that would be presented to the chancellor. This language of "demands" is very counter-cultural to those of us who are accustomed to eating bitterness. As a Chinese-American woman who'd been conditioned to put my head down and endure bitterness, my natural inclination in the face of injustice was to bear with it and move on. Participating in this sit-in meant that I would be pushing past these inclinations to join in a collective and communal demand for justice in the face of bitterness.

Rather than enduring injustice or suffering, demands require being not only seen and heard, but they further require insisting—to someone who may not want to hear—that the injustice be set right. This element in particular is sometimes a major point of disconnect in being able to understand the present #BlackLivesMatter and racial justice movements. Especially within a shame-based culture that eats bitterness, there isn't a natural ability to understand or identify with this element of demanding that a wrong be set right. This disconnect can exist for anyone conditioned to toughing it out, swallowing abuse, or eating bitterness, not only Chinese Americans or other Asian immigrants.

The day of the sit-in, we gathered in one of the quads on campus and received instructions for a series of chants ("Real Pain! Real Change!") that would be used during the march to the chancellor's office. Even something so small as yelling out a chant was an unfamiliar and intimidating action for me. Outside standing up to that high school group-project bully, I had rarely been vocal about a wrong that needed to be righted. I remember that as the chants first began, I only had enough courage to mouth them. A short time later I could say them out loud, but in my normal speaking voice. But by the time we reached the chancellor's office, I had finally joined in the chorus of shouts. I shouted! About a hundred students were gathered that afternoon, and we waited in the hallways while a key group of student leaders met with the chancellor to discuss demands for diversity needs on campus, as well as an appropriate official response to the hateful and disturbing acts of racism on campus.

Though this sit-in was a significant and foundational part of my journey toward seeking justice with God, it was only a small blip in the movement for racial justice at UCLA. The sit-in had opened a conversation with the dean that continued throughout the year. It was also one of the first more unified actions that had taken place this school year, and it led to future conversations and collaborations. Yet there were few tangible results from that action. The naive and inexperienced part of me had hoped for much more. In hindsight, I understand that the journey of seeking God's justice is one marked by long-suffering perseverance, more so than it is by the type of quick fixes I might have hoped for in the moment.

After the sit-in disbanded, I went back to my job with what felt like a secret badge of honor. I felt like a different person; this Chinese woman had actually shouted. I also felt a new kind of kinship with my Black brothers and sisters. Partaking in this action with them felt like I was invited into a place of intimacy and vulnerability with them through an event that was simultaneously an act of power and resistance. That afternoon, something in me had been unlocked. I had been given a new sense with which to navigate the world.

Up until this point, I had only been able to engage in the pain of the world by eating bitterness. That had been the only tool I had to navigate oppression or injustice. But

I was given a new tool at the sit-in, one of passive resistance and civil disobedience. It has continued to serve me as I choose to walk alongside brothers and sisters in our South Los Angeles neighborhood who daily face injustices brought about by brokenness in our criminal justice, immigration, and educational systems. The kinship I felt with my Black brothers and sisters in college also unlocked a deeper kinship with Jesus himself, whose works of justice and restoration were so many times at odds with the institutions and norms of the day: healing on the sabbath, conversing with a woman at a well, eating with sinners and tax collectors, and clearing out money-men in the temple.

This is not to say that the choice to eat bitterness is something to be completely left behind and avoided. Rather, it should be just one of the many ways we can respond to systems of injustice. The people of God endured oppressive rulers for generations. In our own day and age, we continue to live in a world that is not yet fully redeemed for God's purposes. As much as we are called to speak up and cry out for justice, we are also called to endurance, and sometimes we are called to patience. What's more, suffering is presumed for every follower of God. To follow and honor God, to care about the things that God cares about, will bring suffering. It's not just a possibility, it's a guarantee.[42]

THE PATH OF JOY

FROM MY VERY first summer in South Los Angeles, I have continually encountered a deep richness of faith present among my neighbors who intimately know a life of suffering and of eating bitterness. Through them, I have been introduced to new levels of spirituality, to faith that has been shaped by the duality of both having to suffer and eat bitterness and of experiencing God in this suffering and bitterness.

James 2:5 (ESV) says, "Listen, my dear brothers and sisters: Has not God chosen those who are poor in the eyes of the world to be rich in faith and to inherit the kingdom he promised those who love him?" Though many of my neighbors live in material and financial poverty, they are rich in faith and have taught me much about what it means to love and serve God. Fueled by their faith and power in God, they are living out the gospel message, shining as light in dark places, hope in desperation, and joy in suffering. They follow God, not for blessing or riches, but because they have encountered a God like the God of Hagar, one who finds them, sees them, and is with them. They also know the God of Hannah, who can set right even the deepest situations of brokenness that cause suffering. They know the God of Abraham, who, even though he was a sinful man, continued to relate with God and follow Him, with more and more humility, until he would at the end of his life become known as a friend of God.

I see many of my neighbors praise God regardless of their physical circumstances, many of them have hope in God in ways that seem unfathomable to me, they regularly give beyond their means, and they serve with all that they have. I have witnessed families who extend hospitality when they are struggling to provide for their own families; I have known neighbors who worshiped and praised

God in the face of death, and time and again they declare that "God is good" even when facing the bitterness of lost jobs, health crises, or uncertain immigration status.

When we have community action days, many of my neighbors participate with hopeful hearts, loud voices, and confident hope in God's ability to set right what is wrong. This richness of faith has not been gained through education, work, or financial stability, and it was not found through a simplistic or easy story. Instead, it was born of God's love within the complexity of receiving His love in the midst of human sin, and within trials and suffering. This richness of faith was deepened in the face of regular oppression, and trying to forge a way forward in faith through that oppression. It was refined through desperation and even times of defeat that might be spiritual, or emotional, or physical, just like we all encounter at various points in our lives.

I've been blessed to more clearly see a less simplistic version of faith than I knew or might have expected during my early and more comfortable first few years in college. I've been able to see the faith and resilience born out of deep reliance upon Him through times of suffering—faith in a God who sees us and hears us, strengthened by testimonies big and small of how God dwells with us in the complexity, in our places of pain, and carrying our bitterness.

For those who understand *chi ku*, there is also an ability to endure suffering and swallow bitterness for the sake of someone else. Within the immigrant narrative, it's understood that eating bitterness in one lifetime is done for the sake of the next generation. The premise is that if one generation is able to endure and eat bitterness, then the next generation will have a life of sweetness. When eating bitterness is redeemed within the kingdom, we understand it to be a powerful act of sacrifice and humility for others, but also for ourselves. Bitterness is endured in the present for the sake of sweetness in the future. This future is the eternal rest, comfort, and inheritance promised within God's coming kingdom.

The archetypal biblical example of eating bitterness for the sake of shared future sweetness is Jesus' death on the cross. We know that Jesus endured bitterness. He was rejected by His hometown, He lived without a home, and He faced ridicule and suffering throughout His ministry. On the cross, He tasted the most bitter death. Matthew tells of His anguish:

> Then Jesus went with them to a place called Gethsemane, and he said to his disciples, "Sit here, while I go over there and pray." And taking with him Peter and the two sons of Zebedee, he began to be sorrowful and troubled. Then he said to them, "My soul is very sorrowful, even to death; remain here, and watch with me." And going a little farther he fell on his face and prayed, saying, "My Father, if it be possible, let this cup pass from me; nevertheless, not as I will, but as you will." (Matthew 26:36-39, ESV)

Though He knows what is to come, Jesus wrestles with God in this place of bitterness, all the while in full submission to God's will. As the author of Hebrews writes, Jesus endured the cross "for the joy that was set before him" (Hebrews 12:2, ESV). Though Jesus' death on the cross was surely bitter, there is great joy and sweetness found in His victorious resurrection—and in the promise of resurrection that exists for those who follow Him. Such is our invitation as the people of God. No matter how deep or long lasting the bitterness, we have confidence in a future sweetness with God. We are promised an eternity with God in a restored and redeemed creation, if only we will wrestle with Him and not turn away from Him in our pain.

Yet not only is our sweetness assured in the future, but it is also assured to us in the present. Jesus' death and resurrection inaugurated a new reality. Though we will not experience the fullness of God's coming kingdom until Jesus returns to fully establish His reign of light over the bitterness and death of the present world, God's Kingdom is already coming now, in the present. Even in the face of tremendous bitterness, we can with certainty know the sweetness of God in our present lives. As Paul writes in Philippians 3:8 (ESV), "I count everything as loss because of the surpassing worth of knowing Christ Jesus my Lord." The joy and sweetness of knowing God surpasses not only all the treasures of the world, but it also surpasses any and all bitterness that we taste and experience.

Jesus' incarnation led Him straight from heaven into a life with no small amount of bitterness. Jesus took on the sin of others and received their condemnation for the sake of their redemption. When we choose to eat bitterness for the sake of others, we demonstrate that no bitterness compares with the eternal hope we have for our future. When we share in each other's bitterness, we bring God's Kingdom here on earth as it is in heaven. We suffer with each other and with Jesus so that together we can create transformed communities that ameliorate suffering for all of God's children, especially those who are marginalized, voiceless, and oppressed. When we choose to let Jesus redeem our bitterness and suffering, we become the light of God in dark places. We become those who can say they are forgiven and empowered by a God who has and will continue to overcome the bitterness of this world.

[42] See Luke 9:23, 2 Timothy 3:12, Philippians 1:29, 1 John 3:13, 1 Peter 4:12-13.

14

BLACK GIRLS DO

Shabrae Jackson Krieg

Shabrae Jackson Krieg is a social worker with more than 18 years of experience working in the United States and internationally. She is passionate about empowering, equipping, and co-creating with others to bring about personal and communal change. As a facilitator and practitioner, she enjoys creating community-based tools and shaping spaces for creativity through processes such as experiential learning, the expressive arts, sports, and movement-based methodologies - exploring the spaces where play and transformation can meet.

Along with their son, Shabrae and her husband Jean-Luc have lived on the outskirts of Mexico City for the past twelve years. They started Urban Mosaic, an NGO that works in partnership with local people and movements to develop models for transformation and holistic development in urban poor communities. Shabrae is currently the Director of Learning and Collaboration with Servant Partners, a Coordinator with First Aid Arts, and has a Masters in Expressive Arts for Conflict Transformation & Peace-building.

IN 2004, I was sitting in an airplane at LAX aboard a double-decker plane, asking myself if I was crazy or if maybe God was crazy. "Lord, you know I don't do flying. Tell me again: why am I here?" The thing is, I knew why I was there. I was just still in disbelief that I was actually doing it. Also, I hated flying. What I really wanted to say to God and what I was definitely thinking to myself was, "You know black girls don't do things like this!"

I was headed to Bangkok, Thailand and Manila, the Philippines for training through the missions organization with which I would be serving in Mexico together with a man—a White man—who would become my husband ten days after returning home to Philadelphia. Not a single one of those things, I felt, was something Black women, like me, were supposed to do. But there I was, preparing to do all of them and having a moment of reckoning inside myself while the other passengers buckled their seatbelts and perused the in-flight movie options.

✳

This was not the first difficult crossing between cultures—which sometimes felt like different worlds—that I had made in my life. My life and calling, and maybe all lives and callings, have been shaped by the moves and movements I have made. And for me, all these movements, which have sent me across and between cultures, have shared in common the feeling of being unable to communicate about them. Not being able to find the words, in any language, to explain myself in a way that seems to land with others.

No one tells you that you can lose your language. When you cross between worlds, you can forget your tongue. Each time I gained the tools to navigate the new world I had entered, I also lost part of myself. Each time was a struggle to understand and be understood, and mostly to believe there was nothing wrong with me.

Even writing this story, the one you hold in your hands right now, has been a fight. A fight to believe I can make sense of my story in a way that can make sense to others, that I can translate the things in my head and heart, filtered through all the cultures I have lived in, into something understandable. To take off the masks that one must use to exist outside of the places one calls home, and speak to you. To choose the right parts of this story to tell you, knowing I can't tell you everything in this space, knowing that some will feel certain aspects of this story will have been given too little or too much attention. To trust that if this is a story you need to be blessed by, that God will take the words which may or may not otherwise be enough, and give you understanding.

❄

I did get through my panic on the airplane. I went to South East Asia, I returned home and married that man, and together we did move to Mexico City where we have lived for the past twelve years. But that is only part of the story.

BEAUTIFUL FEET

While visiting family in the South recently, I went to see a cousin who runs a small day care program in a local church. I noticed a nice display towards the entrance. As I drew closer, I saw the map of the world displayed on a wall with a banner that read, "Beautiful are the feet of those who bring good news." I agreed with the sentiment. Surrounding the map were pictures of all the missionaries that the church supported. All the photos were of white couples and families. There were neither photos of single missionaries nor people of color.

I wondered what message this might unintentionally communicate to anyone who visited this church, about what a missionary looks like. Later as I shared my visit with my mom, we discussed the possible narrative that this could create. She responded honestly, "Well, I didn't know a black missionary until you!" We laughed, but I also felt the impact of her statement, recognizing that I was representing a role that even my own mother didn't believe was possible or existed before me. To see a person with whom we identify, who is doing things beyond any static paradigm, helps us to see all the possibilities before us.

Like the display I saw at the church, I did grow up hearing stories in church about international missionaries, but none of those stories were about Black international missionaries. I just assumed that there weren't any, until I spent a year working with Mt. Carmel Baptist Church in Philadelphia. They celebrated Blacks in mission every year during missions month. Here I learned about our deep cultural roots and history in mission and of the many who had gone before me. I heard names like Lott Carey, who served in Sierra Leone and Liberia; Betsy Stockton, who is recognized as the first single missionary to serve in modern missions; and John Stewart in 1818, just to name a few.[43]

At Mt. Carmel, I realized there were people who looked like me doing "mission work" around the world. Without this exposure, I'm not sure I could have open-heartedly considered moving to Mexico. There is importance in seeing people who look like you doing a variety of professions, being in leadership, and providing an array of examples in how to navigate life. When a young black boy named Jacob was able to visit the first African-American president in the White House in 2013, he asked to know if the president's hair was like his. President Obama encouraged him to touch his hair and see for himself. And as Jacob touched his hair, he exclaimed, "Yes, it does feel the same!" We all need to be able to connect to others who can relate to our experience. When I am in a place where I am the "only" one of me, I almost always look around for others who look like me. The Reverend Tega Swann says it well, "Representation matters. People need to look up and see others like them at the table. People who can understand and relate to them."[44] Being an "only" in any group can come with a high level of expectation at times. In some groups, leadership can point to the "only" and claim that they have progressed and are now a diverse organization. In other contexts, it could mean that others are depending on the "only" to open the door of opportunity for them as well.

LEAP OF FAITH

MY MOVE TOWARD missions, Mexico, and marriage began as I was living and working in Philadelphia with an organization called Mission Year. One day, my co-worker Dave told me a story of how the police had wrongfully broken into the home he shared with a roommate, looking for a person who was apparently the tenant some years back. Dave's roommate and one of his best friends, Jean-Luc, from the Ivory Coast, didn't have any issues telling off the police. I was intrigued by this character in Dave's story, this bold West African telling off the police. When I finally met this Jean-Luc in person at another friend's birthday party, I found myself face-to-face with a White boy with blonde hair and blue eyes. Turned out, Jean-Luc was a Swiss missionary kid born and raised in Ivory Coast.

Nonetheless, we became friends and found that we had other friends in common as well. Jean-Luc was planning to move to Mexico and, in his words, decided that "it would be great to have an African-American on the team with urban work experience," and he began to recruit me. Whether it was a dating tactic or a new recruiting tool, Jean-Luc would talk with me for hours about the need for more African-Americans in international development and global missions. He often cited the wealth of experience in the Black Church and community and how this was needed in many places.

Our relationship moved from friendship to dating, and we had to be very honest and direct with each other on our thoughts about the future. Since the age of eighteen, Jean-Luc had felt a calling to work with the urban poor in Mexico City. He explained early on that he would only date me if I was willing to move to Mexico. I explained, in turn, that not only was I unsure if I was ready to date a

White man, but that I didn't follow men to other cities or countries—I would also need to be called. Through some pushing and pulling, we found some common ground about our diverse backgrounds and calling. Jean-Luc accepted that I was willing to go wherever God led me (even Mexico City), and I was willing to accept that he was not your typical White boy, as he was from and deeply connected to Ivory Coast.

Our dating became more serious and I found myself faced with several significant questions. First, the common question, "Is this the man for me?" Second, "What will it mean for me to marry a person outside of my race and culture?" And third, "Am I being called to work in Mexico City?" As I navigated these three major questions, issues around identity flared up. As might be expected, the second two questions were the hardest.

I wasn't sure about marrying cross-culturally, not to mention marrying a White boy, regardless of the fact that he grew up in Africa. During this season of questioning, I was challenged by one of my mentors when he asked me, "Shabrae, do you want a man who looks good in the family photo, or do you want someone who understands your bi-cultural experience?" This question struck me deeply. But I wanted both: I wanted a Black man who would look right in the family photo *and* someone who understood my diverse lived experience. But my mentor's question was a turning point, and not just because of the question itself. It helped me think through the real reason why I wasn't yet saying yes: I knew that it would change everything.

I had been moved outside of my cultural comfort zone as a child and, to be honest, I did not want to step out of my culture again. I was comfortable where I was. I loved Philly, I loved what I did, and I loved who I worked with. What would it cost me to walk through this door with Jean-Luc? Was I willing to pay it? And yet I felt like my calling and the calling of Jean-Luc seemed to fit together, and that was unusual. We shared a common call to work in the margins of society—as I had been doing in Philadelphia at Mission Year. I just wasn't sure about the international margins Jean-Luc was called to—whether I wanted to go, and whether I was called to go.

I started having anxiety attacks as I tried to wrestle, emotionally, with all of the questions and decisions before me. My heart would actually race and my knees would literally shake. I knew that it felt right to marry him, and I was beginning to feel that Mexico held something new for me, but I didn't know how to move through my fear because of the costs I would pay in following my heart. I was terrified to give up so much to gain him.

After much prayer and discernment, and no little amount of continued trembling for what this decision meant, I felt a "yes" in my heart. Yes to all of it—to the leap of faith. Leaping, to be clear, means jumping. And there was no guarantee I would land on my feet. But in 2005, instead of staying in a place of fear, I jumped into marriage and into a move to Mexico, knowing that I would have to learn new ways to be and move in that new place, where I had never lived. I was unsure what life held for me there. And I had no idea what it was going to feel like to be me, in my skin, there, nor what it would take for me to learn Spanish.

LOSING AND FINDING MY VOICE

DURING MY FIRST two years in Mexico I needed to learn Spanish. I formed part of a team of four and everyone else was already fluent in the language. I struggled to learn and understand the grammatical concepts, stumbling over words and pronunciations. It became an emotional struggle. There were obvious reasons for this. I felt inadequate in my speech. I felt like a child in certain situations in which I could not participate with my own voice, I could not speak without a translator. This created difficulties between Jean-Luc and me, as he would make decisions for me since I did not always understand what was happening due to lack of language. I felt stripped from my tongue. I felt silenced.

There were also some less obvious, deeper reasons why the pace of learning Spanish was so difficult, which went all the way back to my childhood. It would take me awhile to uncover those. In the meantime, I started to believe that I was not capable of learning the language and that I myself was inadequate. I struggled to recover myself—to find words and the will to learn as I compared myself to my teammates who seemed to have learned the language in lightning speed. But I could not. What took some only six months seemed to be taking me two years. Weariness set in; I was tired of not being heard and understood.

During a team retreat about a year into my language study, I decided to share about what was going on. I don't like to share about my vulnerability, but I broke my own confidentiality rule and shared with the group about my difficulty learning Spanish. It helped that my teammates were not American. Although they had learned Spanish quickly (before I got to Mexico), they had all lived in several countries and cultures, so they too shared my story of feeling silenced and misunderstood. During the retreat we prayed for my voice and for the courage to keep trying to learn how to bring it forth. As we did, I recalled my childhood and how I had always felt misunderstood. This, I then realized, was part of why feeling incapable of communicating was so very hard. It was so deep.

❊

My parents gave me the name of Lanette Shabrae Jackson, after the famous singer, dancer, and actress, Nanette Fabray, and my mother's name, which is Annette. My family, however, has always called me by my second name: Shabrae. It was the name that my mother spoke to me while I was in her womb and the name that my neighborhood friends called when it was time to play. But then something happened, and my name was lost for a long time.

❊

After growing up in the South and graduating from college in the sixties, my parents sought to move North. They hoped they might find new opportunities and less outright racism and discrimination. My parents settled in Grand Rapids, Michigan—because my mom already had some family there—worlds away from Louisiana. They would start a new life there. They found new jobs, started a family, and joined a vibrant Black Baptist church in the community where they lived.

Eight years later my father had what he would describe as a "new conversion" experience. As a result, we left our vibrant Baptist church and joined a large 4,000-member Pentecostal church in the city. That church was a shock to me at five years old, as it was predominantly White. There may have been a few hundred people of color, but among the thousands of members, you couldn't tell. Then my parents decided that my brother and I needed a "Christian education," and they enrolled us in the school that was connected to the church. In a matter of months, we shifted from an all-Black existence (neighborhood, church, and school) to a world in which we were in the minority. On the margin.[45]

At school, we were one of five other families of color. I was the only Black girl in my class. We continued to live in the same neighborhood, so each day we would take a thirty-minute car ride, moving between our "Black world" and this new "White world." My whole life I'd been centered in my own community. We now commuted into the center of another community six days a week, the railroad tracks and highway acting as reminders of my daily borders. I felt on the edges of the new world, but not fully part of it. It was clear that my new classmates had no understanding or experience with my reality, nor I with theirs. I was already learning day by day how to manage my body in both places.

It was here that I lost my name. My records showed my legal first name to be Lanette, so that is what the teachers called me. I was five, and I had no idea I could correct them. As a young girl who was trying to navigate an all-White world for the first time, I never spoke up and asked them to call me Shabrae.

The loss of my name in this alternate world began a pattern in my life, a dance between two worlds. Being Lanette at school meant acting and behaving one way, while being Shabrae, with my family and in the neighborhood, meant another. Being Shabrae meant I was safe; it meant I was home. Being Lanette meant adjusting how I spoke, changing how I walked, and being ready to explain my hair and way of life. This is known as code-switching. And at age five, I had already picked up the survival tactic.

At that young age, I found myself without words, not knowing how to act in order to avoid looks, public grammatical corrections, and being viewed as an outsider. I had to learn this new "language," in order to make friends, learn, and understand what I was supposed to do. If I wanted to fit in and not be in the margin of either group, then I needed to be observant, and learn how to talk and act to be accepted and safe. I became an expert at studying people's facial expressions and nonverbal stances so that I could defend myself if need be. I quieted my tongue, willfully choosing to filter my voice. To be quieter, smaller. Little did I know that this complicated survival mechanism would haunt me for decades. My emotional survival depended on my ability to adjust my behavior within each environment. Perhaps it was fitting that I had another name in this other place; it punctuated how different it felt to be me, how uncomfortable I was, how uncomfortable my classmates may have been with me.

There were so many ways this was evident, but one sticks with me the most. I can clearly recall moments—multiple—in class when another child would read a text with the word "black," such as "the family had a black dog," and I would become visibly uncomfortable. As the word was read, even though the context wasn't racial, it suddenly felt like there were twenty pairs of eyes on me. I was very aware that living in my skin marked me as "different," as "other." In time, I would even learn that living in this body would sometimes mark me as a "threat." One of my earliest memories is when I was playing with my brother in our front yard and a school bus stopped to drop off some kids nearby. I remember two kids sitting towards the back of the bus pointing their finger and looking at us with anger, loudly shouting "N——." I recall moving towards my brother out of fear. Although I was in my own yard and space, it felt like they could reach through the window and harm us.

As my brother and I engaged on a daily basis with our new reality and spent more time there, I started to feel out of step within my own Black culture and community. At school, I felt like I stuck out and could not blend in. And in my home community, I presented myself with the corrected and edited speech and behavior from the White context I spent so much time in, which didn't land with people. I was on the fringe in my own Black community, as I could not accurately give words for my experience nor explain all the changes going on within me. I didn't like it; I wanted to feel whole. As I moved into high school and planned for university, the desire to reconcile my two worlds only grew. I wanted to feel normal somewhere.

The dance of differing identities became a habit. During my time in university, for some reason I kept using both names. Perhaps I had become accustomed to the separation of my identities and the lack of integration. It didn't feel good to be two people, but it felt normal.

The stress and complication of moving between two names came to a point of reckoning when I started working with a group of youth after I returned to my hometown of Grand Rapids, Michigan. I was working as a social worker, and one of my childhood friends invited me to volunteer with her in a ministry called Urban Young Life. Initially I didn't think that I had the time nor capacity to volunteer in the ministry due to my stressful job, but she kept calling, so I finally accepted her invitation to visit the group. As I prepared for my visit, I realized that some of my initial hesitation to consider her request was due to my fear of how I would be seen by the group of youth. Would I be rejected? Would my experiences outside our Black culture—with White folks—be an obstacle in being able to relate to youth from my own culture? Would my words—which were grammar-policed as a child—now be seen as too proper?

With some fear and nervousness, I went to one of the gatherings which had about fifty youth. It was an hour filled with high energy, fun, community building, and life-on-life talk. I loved it. And as I started to engage relationally with the youth, I found that I was warmly accepted. It turned out that my own internal fears had been holding me back from the integration I craved. The youth weren't looking at external characteristics, my mannerisms, or my social circles; rather, they respected real and authentic people and were thus generous in their acceptance, embrace, and welcome. Their way of being ended up giving me a safe space to bring my whole self and all of my experiences into my relationship with them. In this surprising place, filled with laughter, tears, and community, I began to integrate the pieces of my life and one of the markers of my internal division: my name.

Since it was a childhood friend from my neighborhood who had invited me into the Urban Young Life gathering, she introduced me to the youth as Shabrae. As I started to work with them more, interacting with the youth as well as the regional and national leaders, more people came to know me as Shabrae. This started to cause some confusion for anyone who had known me as Lanette, and my worlds often collided.

A moment came when I decided I could no longer live divided. As Lanette, I had been trained in how to navigate a new world through my speech and polished behavior, making me more acceptable at school, and yet I lost pieces of myself in the process. The work with youth from my own culture had connected me to a deeply personal yearning to be whole. I had begun to feel even more at home in my own skin and the full diversity of my lived experience. I no longer felt there was any need to hide any part of myself. Instead, I could hold both of the previously divided parts: what I had learned from growing up within my own culture, and what I had learned from being outside of it.

This embrace of my own identity was a coming home to myself. And I wanted my name to feel like home to me too. So, from the moment of this realization, in the midst of this work with the youth, I then always introduced myself as Shabrae: I reclaimed my name and my identity. But integrating my lived experience in this way also prepared me for something else, something I could never have expected or foreseen. It opened me up to a calling that would come in the years ahead, way out of my known territory and my comfort zone.

⌗

As I prayed with my teammates in Mexico about my struggle to learn Spanish, all these old memories emerged—these feelings from my past of being misunderstood, unheard, silenced, and divided. It brought some healing to a story that I had been carrying with me for a long time. It highlighted and reminded me of how hard it was to live as anything less than my whole self. I made a decision that day that I would learn Spanish—but I would do it in my own time and in my way. I would no longer continue the unhealthy comparison to my teammates and push myself to be something that I was not. I could no longer live in fear of the many mistakes that are necessary to truly learn a language. I could no longer sit silently instead of trying to speak or speak quietly for fear of being misunderstood. Instead I learned to embrace my strong voice, even as it was marked with imperfection, poor pronunciation, and at times, a lack of the precise words I wanted. Because it was mine.

MOVEMENTS AND MOVEMENT IN
AFRICAN AMERICAN HISTORY

I recognize the importance of physical movement in my own life as well as the rich cultural history of movement and movements I am part of as a Black American. We are not known for being missionaries (there are a lot of reasons for that, including that the "work for God's kingdom" traditionally done in Black communities isn't called "missions"), and we may not be known as thrill-seekers or world travelers. Our movements have been about survival. But make no mistake: there has been a lot of movement.

Through slavery, our ancestors were forcibly put into motion across the Atlantic for many years. Before emancipation, the Underground Railroad[46] provided a passage for others to find a better life. Later, what's known as the Great Migration between 1915 and 1970 shifted more than six million African Americans from the South to cities in the North. Many had come from places and spaces in which their "movements" had been restricted for so long. The Black body had been restricted by lynchings, rape, abuse, segregation, unjust laws, and more. Yet God designed all of our bodies to move. The Great Migration was an attempt to loose the shackles that kept us bound, that restricted our movements and beings. It was a radical act of faith for so many to courageously embrace the unknown and move, hoping the North would be better.

My own parents migrated from Louisiana to the North in 1973 on the heels of the Great Migration and its promises. They dreamed of something different, but they also needed something different. Dad grew up on a plantation. He left the plantation for the first time when he went to college. His own father, my grandfather, was a sharecropper on a cotton field. The nature of sharecropping was unfair; the wages were poverty. My dad remembers how "Christmas was a nervous time around our house because you would meet with the boss man and he would do the accounts for the entire year. We supposedly got some profit from one of the fields, but it would always be adjusted based on the loans that we took during the year because there hadn't been enough money; you were always waiting anxiously to see if you came out on the plus side."

No one ever did. As was every sharecropper, my grandfather was continuously in debt to the boss man, Mr. Wilson. My grandpa told my dad he needed to find a way to leave because, he said, "If something happens to me, the boss man will try and keep you in debt, and keep you here."

My parents longed for a new life, a new place where they might live out the promised American dream. They were recent and proud graduates of a Historically Black College, Grambling State University, but they still felt limited: the Deep South in the fifties and sixties was marked by outright racism and discrimination. They hoped that they might find new opportunities in the Great North. Yet it was a risk; Black bodies in motion are never safe. But neither was staying where they were.

I grew up learning at a young age that being in my own body could bring me harm. And this knowledge was a scary thing to deal with. Being Black in America, thinking about where I live and around whom, has always been at the forefront of my mind. Will I be safe? How will people receive me? Will people accept me? How will they look at me? Will I be taken seriously? Will my voice be heard? Do I have space to grow here? These same questions followed me to Mexico. I wondered how this Black body—that causes so much conversation in the States—would be received in Mexico. Is there space for me here? It had been hard to find a safe space in my own country, and at times even within my own Black culture. And now I was moving to a different one? These were all the very important, yet unanswered questions.

I can imagine that during the Great Migration, my own parents and other families grappled with similar questions. How did they summon the courage to leave and push beyond the many forces against them? How did they have faith in the face of a country that had historically rejected them? I had never lived outside the United States, yet I was carrying my American experience with me, fearful that Mexico might be the same. My parents could rely on stories that they heard from family members and friends who had gone before them when they moved North. However, as I looked out at the international mission scene, I saw few people who looked like me. Why were there so few African Americans involved in international global missions? Who would tell me stories of their journeys? Who would prepare the way for my own international migration?

⁕

For my ancestors, bodily movement was a way to exhibit our freedom, to speak out against the oppressive boundaries set by race, class, and gender. From the early days of the Black American Church, dance and movement has been a part of the experience. This is no accident, but by design. This was one space where we could be free, where we could move. The simple act of being able to safely move and express oneself can bring healing and restoration. I'm not sure if our ancestors knew this as they danced during church or out in the fields. But perhaps their own bodies knew what they needed, what was required to shake off their bondage. To endure. To resist. By finding space to move freely they could imagine another life and be reminded that they were not just slaves in the master's fields. They were human beings made in the image of God; created to breathe and have movement and dignity.

Growing up in an African American home, we were encouraged to move at an early age. If not to Michael Jackson in the living room, then at church. While at church, different members would always get the Holy Spirit and start dancing right there in the aisle. I would study them, watching their focused faces scrunching up with a sort of concentration that looked almost painful. They showed passion as they cut a rug for the Lord, and I remember hoping that I too would be ready to dance the next time the Holy Spirit fell.

During a supervisory meeting at one of my first jobs out of college, my boss noticed that I was always moving, rocking, and asked me why. I don't think I had been aware of my constant movement until then, and I walked away from that meeting feeling embarrassed and self-conscious. But through the years I have come to embrace this movement as a gift from my mother. As a baby, my parents did not own a rocking chair, but my mom would sit on the couch and rock me in her arms. She gave me a way for my body to self-soothe, find balance, and shake off what it doesn't need.

In thinking of the way my body has been in motion, dancing through this unknown choreography, I think of my mother and how she moved. She moved, kneeling by the sofa in prayer and submission. And she moved in the living room, dancing to Michael Jackson, swaying her hips, playfully inviting us to join her. I can see the joy on her face as she danced.

ALTERNATIVE NARRATIVES IN MEXICO

I HAVE CONTINUED to move. I worked to build a new home in Mexico. Jean-Luc and I settled into one of the poorest communities on the outskirts of the Mexico City, where our initial work was focused on building relationships with our neighbors in order to identify community needs and work together towards change. I quickly saw that I had as much to learn as I was hoping to give. I attended an official language school for only eight weeks, and then continued the bulk of my learning with my neighbors. As I have mentioned, learning Spanish did not come easily to me. In the long run, I am glad I learned Spanish the way I did: in the community, among our new friends. Some ladies who lived nearby also taught me how to navigate the local market and life in Mexico. It was these same ladies—friends now—who helped me when I was pregnant with my son and on bed rest. Along with team members, they cooked meals and cleaned my home. And after giving birth to my son six weeks early, these neighbors snuck into my home and decorated it in preparation for our arrival. I could fill a whole book with stories about the help of my neighbors and the mutual learning and work that has passed between us through the years.

Along with learning Spanish and building friendships, I had to grapple with just how different I was as a Black woman in Mexico. People often stared and gazed openly at me. Yet I quickly noticed that many of the gazes seemed to come from curiosity and not hostility. As we started our work in a community in which the majority of our neighbors came from an indigenous background, I found myself amongst people who would say things like, "I always wanted skin like yours!" to "I used to pray that God would give me color like yours." I had never heard anything like this from another race or culture in my own country. And these positive comments about my skin color have not only come from my neighbors in Mexico, but I heard them also in the Philippines, South Africa, the Middle East, and various other places.

As I anticipated, I was on the margin in Mexico, different, with not a lot of people who understood my specific experiences. Most people in Mexico assume that I am from Africa, Cuba, the Caribbean, or Haiti. I must specifically tell them that I am American, and it is often met with surprise. Once I was accepted as an American, this meant I was seen as coming from a dominant group, based upon Mexico's relationship to the United States. Usually when my Mexican neighbors find out that I'm American, some will often start talking about struggles that they have heard from their family abroad or the latest American slight against Mexico. In Mexico there is a common saying taken from a past Mexican President, General Porfirio Diaz, "Pobre México, tan lejos de Dios y tan cerca de los Estados Unidos." The literal translation is, "Poor Mexico, so far from God and so close to the United States."

Initially, as someone who has lived on the margin within my own country, I was tempted to distance myself from these aspects of America, whether policy or culture. I didn't share those views; I didn't support them. But my friends weren't looking for arguments. They didn't want me to prove anything. They just wanted me to hear their stories. And there were many of them. I had only known their side of this tension, the feeling of being on the margin. It was new to be on the other side, representing a place that was a center of power which had impacted them harmfully. Even in this Black body, often so misunderstood or rejected in America, as an American in Mexico, I represented the oppressor, with the long history of injustice between the United States and Mexico. This I did not see coming.

As an African American who had experience on the margin, how could I challenge myself to not become comfortable as the "American," even in a setting that accorded me power and voice as a foreigner? How could I use who I was and what I had learned on the margin in such a way as to give space to those I served in a country that my own country had marginalized? And if I am finally able to sit "at the table" within this country and context, then how do I make space for all others at the table? How together could we shift the dynamics at the table?

When we sit down with others, whether those we are seeking to serve, or those we are serving with, there is often some previous paradigm or way of looking at the situation. There's a narrative that has been passed down. And unless we can listen to all the ideas, that narrative can be singular,[47] And it can be harmful.

For example, if there is the singular idea that a "poor" community can only receive from the outside, and it needs those of us who are "knowledgeable" to lead the way and change their environment, then that becomes the narrative, trapping a community in unnecessary cycles of dependency. This assumption—that help, change, and transformation can only come from the outside, from those with money and resources and often from those who do not look like those who are receiving the help—is a single narrative that has often been told and re-told within and outside of "poor" communities. But one point of view, one narrative, especially when that narrative originates from outside of a community, doesn't bring real movement. Such a narrative is more likely to trap people in choreographies that those in power have written for their own benefit.

One of the ways I've found to make space as a person coming from a place of power is through a community organizing approach. What I appreciate about organizing is that it leads with processes of listening before acting, identifying local leaders before finding stand-alone solutions that may or may not involve the community. The process alone challenges any single story of the "poor" being unable to effect change without the help of a political party. The single narrative in Mexico is that you cannot change things. Even though the Mexican constitution says otherwise, many believe that you are not able to bring about change if you are not connected politically.

In one of the first community projects we attempted, we asked neighbors what they cared about, or thought needed change. Neighbors identified a large empty field to be cleared due to safety concerns. Some months before, a young woman's body had been found in the field, and it was a zone known for robbery, as thieves could hide behind the tall grass when people walked by. At this time, we were a small group of about twenty neighbors working for change. In faith, we started to gather each Saturday to pull weeds and clean out the field which had become the neighborhood dumping spot. Weeding is dirty work, as is cleaning up all the trash caught in the knee-high or stubby weeds. But with gloved hands and rakes we gathered, among other things, food wrappers, used diapers, old torn clothing and shoes, a doll with no eyes, a dead dog.

As we cleaned, sometimes other neighbors would pass by and inquire about what we were doing. As we shared our project and vision with them, many would look at us strangely. We shared our idea of how we planned to gather all of the trash into piles and that we would then request the municipal government to come and pick up the trash. They would often laugh and say, "Santa Claus will come before the municipality comes to gather the garbage in this community!" What we were trying to do was seen as impossible. Many neighbors thought that you could only get the government to do something for you if you promised those in power something in return. After a year's worth of Saturday cleanups in the field and numerous letters and visits to our government office, they finally brought the trucks. It took seventy garbage trucks to remove all the trash and debris that we had gathered.

This project challenged the single narrative that many in our community had come to believe—that based on their economic status, they could not effect change. Encouraged by this community win, our group of neighbors began to take on other projects within the community and step out as leaders. By stepping out in new roles, they were enhancing their own image of not just being an at-home mom, a welder, a child, or a youth in the community. Now their narrative included that they were agents of change who were also mothers, welders, children, and youth.

These kinds of limiting narratives can be changed, but it often takes the courage to move against fear, earlier paradigms, and simple convenience. It was not convenient for some of the local political leaders to see our neighbors in the community step out of the single story that had been laid upon them. These political leaders tried to raise their voices by recounting the single story of dependency through intimidation tactics, disruption, and violence. The political leaders attempted to coerce and take over our projects, hoping that our neighbors would return to the choreography assigned to them, to the narrative others had written for them. But our neighbors had grown beyond it.

EMBRACING THE INVITATION

DURING MY CHILDHOOD, I had developed some unfortunate ideas about what Black girls do and do not do. First, don't marry a White boy. Second, don't travel too far; stay close to home. Third, if you have the opportunity, graduate, be successful, and move to a "better" neighborhood. None of these messages were spoken to me directly by any family members or other African Americans. I formed some of these messages based on what I saw and did not see around me. At the age of twenty-seven, I found myself taking on the entire "Black girls don't" list at once: White boy, move to Mexico, and my "better" neighborhood turned out to be a squatter-poor neighborhood with no running water, electricity, or basic services.

If you would have asked me twenty years ago if I would be working in Mexico, traveling around the world, and married to a White man, I would have laughed and likely shared some strongly worded sentiments. In embracing my integrated self, I found myself leaving the familiar to move beyond more boundaries, embracing new radical possibilities. Since my early days of college, I felt a call to serve the poor and marginalized in any city I lived in. I would even move to Philadelphia from my home of Grand Rapids, Michigan to do so. But what Black girl moves to Mexico? As it turns out, this Black girl. This Black woman. I come from a longer legacy of big movements and Black missionary work than was first apparent. I come from bold people who know how to survive and push beyond the stories other people have written for their lives. And I've realized that I too have a story to tell. A story that holds all of my pieces and experiences. A story that requires that I bring my voice forward. A story to be shared with others.

I have now been in Mexico for over twelve years. My work has shifted and changed as I have grown, from learning Spanish and culture to community organizing and youth work, to training other practitioners, and there have been many endings and new beginnings. Part of my own journey in the movement between worlds was in many ways an embrace of my multi-layered self. Bringing all of what I was into life and ministry meant that I was inviting others to see beyond their own single narratives of me, themselves, and the world. I am a Black American woman with roots in the South, who grew up bi-culturally in the North, married cross-culturally, lives in a foreign country, speaks Spanish, has a Mexican-born son, and so much more.

Over the years, God continues to invite me into new movements, dances, that are marked by wholeness, vulnerability, suffering, courage, failure, and the beautiful unknown. This requires me to step out of spaces that have become comfortable and embrace what I do not know. This requires walking in the darkness at times, stumbling and wrestling with my own doubt or maybe with the fact that I'm simply lost. I will not paint a picture of a journey that is not filled with moments of hopelessness and fear. These too form part of the story. To risk and to lean into the invitation, to jump in and embrace the journey, requires an experience with all the elements that may be encountered.

⌗

Whether it is being called to missions, to teach, to be a community leader, to serve your own children in a new way, or to move from one place to another, all of these movements are needed because the world needs each diverse story of strength and struggle. So move. And then keep moving. Take a step. Then take another. Keep responding to what is before you. Keep seeking God's voice and then leap. Jump. Embrace the journey that you are being invited into, a place of radical possibility. And when you are ready, tell us all about it. The community of faith is waiting for your story. I am waiting for your story.

[43] The Traveling Team, "African American Missions," *http://bit.ly/2JFz8QF* (accessed June 2, 2018).

[44] Rev. Tega Swann "A Face like Mine," September 12, 2017, *http://bit.ly/2uDghRH* (accessed June 2, 2018).

[45] The term "margin" is used in connection with marginalization referring to (but not only) contexts in which individuals or groups experience inequality, injustice, and exploitation in their lives. In addition, I am referring to concepts used in some anti-oppression work, in which every group is seen as having a mainstream and a margin. Mainstream refers to qualities, behaviors, and values supported by the group in which some of these qualities and behaviors are at the center and others are on the edges, the margin. The relationship between the two is not static but instead shifts. (Mindell 1992, 1997).

[46] The Underground Railroad was a secret network organized by people who helped men, women, and children escape from slavery to freedom. It operated before the Civil War (1861-1865) ended slavery in the United States. The Underground Railroad provided hiding places, food, and often transportation for the people who were trying to escape slavery. The people who helped slaves escape were called "conductors" or "engineers." The places along the escape route were called "stations."

[47] One can move into what Nigerian writer Chimamanda Ngozi Adichie calls in her now famous TED talk, "The Danger of a Single Story." This refers to what happens when we apply a single narrative to a complex situation. She argues that each person contains a multitude of stories (personas), and by reducing a person to just one, you are taking away that person's humanity. Chimamanda states, "The single story creates stereotypes, and the problem with stereotypes is not that they are untrue, but that they are incomplete. They make one story become the only story."

ACKNOWLEDGEMENTS

ROBYN G. BARRON

I would like to thank my family and friends who gave me the courage to share this story. In particular, I would like to thank my longtime friend Amber who was instrumental in helping me share my story. In addition, I would like to say thank you to the many mentors, family (spiritual and biological), and friends God has brought into my life who have walked with me on this journey.

JENNIFER CHOU BLUE

I would like to thank my parents for always telling me how much they loved me growing up, and my dear friends Alex and Susan Van Riesen who invested in my spiritual development in an important season in my life. I am so grateful to my husband, Kevin, for all of your love and support, and all the editors who so faithfully kept pushing this project forward. Last but not least, I want to thank my dear friends and community at Church of the Redeemer. It is my honor to be part of God's work together with all of you.

TERESA KU-BORDEN

I would like to thank my husband, Ryan, for encouraging me to use my voice in leadership, and especially for sacrificing sleep to calm the babies during those late nights of writing. To my children, thank you for helping me discover new depths of love I never knew I had. And finally, thank you to Felipe, Taily, Giselle, Jenny, and Jess, whose love and friendship, honesty and willingness to be present, not only helped me survive the last three years, but also moved me to write this chapter.

RACHEL CHRISTINE BRAITHWAITE DAVIES

I would like to thank my parents who planted the seeds to understanding my worth. Thanks to my girls, Keira, Jordan and Ashlyn, for teaching me that when I am healthy, you are healthy and for keeping me humble and human by not being that impressed that I am a part of this book.

Thank you to Asifa Dean, Clint Fong, Kim Porter, Sabrina Sommer, Beth Jaurez, and Cathy Passmore, for being a part of my journey in understanding who I am as a black woman and encouraging me in the knowledge that I am made in God's image.

And lastly thank you to my husband Trevor, who has stood back and given me space to grow into my own words and identity, listened to the countless number of stories of racism and prejudice, and looked for ways to stand and lead, teach and encourage on behalf of those without privilege.

SHABRAE JACKSON KRIEG

I would like to thank my husband Jean-Luc and our son for their ongoing support throughout this project. I am also thankful for the stories of my mother and father and the wisdom received from my family who have gone before me and provided courage for the journey. Finally, I am grateful for the many women in my life who have used their voice to encourage others to bring their stories forward. May this book join its voice with other fellow women around the world.

JENNIFER CHI LEE

I am grateful to all of the other voices of people dwelling in tension in the margins. Thank you for graciously honoring me with both truth and mercy in our journey toward liberation. And to God, who holds me firmly in gentleness, thank you for loving me.

ANNABEL MENDOZA LEYVA

I thank God for having patience with me and for choosing my family, friends and community. I am truly blessed. Natanael, Emily, Nathanael, Mom and Dad, what a joy to serve our community together. Servant Partners, Janet and Andy thanks for the opportunity to learn and serve using my gifts for my community.

MICHELLE KAO NAKPHONG

I would like to thank my family and friends for all the support and love in the pursuit of unconventional goals. I would also like to thank all the communities that have so graciously welcomed and invested in me, especially the Samaki Pattana community in Bangkok. Lastly, I would like to acknowledge God for His generous presence and lovingkindness.

BEAUTY GUNDA NDORO

I would like to thank my husband Phillip for all his support through this project. I am so thankful to my children, Tadiwa-nashe and Tinodaishe, for their understanding and support. A huge thank you to God for His grace and faithfulness. I would also like to acknowledge the Servant Partners Press team for all their work.

MINI MATHAI PALMER

I would like to thank God for giving me a voice and the courage to stay true to it and the space for it to be heard. I am also grateful for my friends and family who have encouraged me and loved me through the process of creation. Thank you especially to my parents, Mathews and Moni, who were my first teachers in knowing what love and a relationship with God feels like. Finally, I am deeply grateful for the gracious and generously supportive and understanding editorial team who believed in my voice.

CLAUDIA SALAZAR

I want to thank the person in my life who has been a constant support and reason why I am able to write this chapter, and that is my mother Nora. She has shown me how to be dedicated, work hard, and persevere. I also want to thank my church family and friends for supporting my growth and encouraging me to take on new challenges and opportunities.

JANET BALASIRI SINGLETERRY

I would like to thank my mom for her support even in times of uncertainty and fear in the journey. I would also like to thank my husband, Andy, for his loving patience during this writing process and always. Shalom Iglesia del Pacto and The River Church community in San Jose, as well as Faith Church in Indianapolis, are foundational in my walk with Jesus. Finally, I am grateful to Nayeli for the inspiration and beauty of her faith in the midst of struggle.

EMMA SILVA SMITH

I would like to thank Jesus for the joy and privilege of sharing my story. Thank you to the wonderful editing team at Servant Partners Press. Thank you to my friends in Balic-Balic and Botocan for journeying with me. I would also like to thank my loving and supportive husband Aaron, and my two boys, Zach and Ezra.

GRACE WENG

I would like to thank my family and friends, who have supported me and helped me become the woman I am today. I especially want to thank my husband James, who helped provide the time, space, and encouragement I needed to complete this project. Most of all, I want to give glory and thanks to God for being my good and loving shepherd!

SERVANT PARTNERS PRESS
Proclaiming God's Presence among the Urban Poor

Servant Partners Press is dedicated to supporting the growing movement of people who are called to live and work alongside the urban poor. We publish theological reflections, narratives, and training materials that speak to God's transforming power in the inner cities and slums of our world.

To learn more about Servant Partners Press or to purchase books, visit us at *ServantPartnersPress.org*.

CPSIA information can be obtained
at www.ICGtesting.com
Printed in the USA
BVHW080939131022
649271BV00004B/451

9 780998 366548